REEXPLORING THE BOOK OF MORMON

Copublications of Deseret Book Company and the Foundation for Ancient Research and Mormon Studies

An Ancient American Setting for the Book of Mormon,
by John L. Sorenson

By Study and Also by Faith: Essays in Honor of Hugh W. Nibley, 2 volumes
edited by John M. Lundquist and Stephen D. Ricks

The Sermon at the Temple and the Sermon on the Mount,
by John W. Welch

Warfare in the Book of Mormon,
edited by Stephen D. Ricks and William J. Hamblin

Rediscovering the Book of Mormon,
edited by John L. Sorenson and Melvin J. Thorne

Reexploring the Book of Mormon,
edited by John W. Welch

The Collected Works of Hugh Nibley

Old Testament and Related Studies
Enoch the Prophet
The World and the Prophets
Mormonism and Early Christianity
Lehi in the Desert/The World of the Jaredites/There Were Jaredites
An Approach to the Book of Mormon
Since Cumorah
The Prophetic Book of Mormon
Approaching Zion
The Ancient State
Tinkling Cymbals and Sounding Brass
Temple and Cosmos

Audiocassettes

Time Vindicates the Prophets
(seven cassettes),
by Hugh Nibley

Lectures on the Book of Mormon
3 volumes (twelve cassettes each),
by Hugh Nibley

REEXPLORING THE BOOK OF MORMON

The F.A.R.M.S. Updates

Edited by John W. Welch

Deseret Book Company
Salt Lake City, Utah
and
Foundation for Ancient Research and Mormon Studies
Provo, Utah

To Lisa, Bobby, Matt, Adam, Serena, and David, the children of Robert J. and Linda Grow, with the hope that this research concerning the Book of Mormon will strengthen the faith and expand the vision of their generation.

Library of Congress Cataloging-in-Publication Data

Reexploring the Book of Mormon / edited by John W. Welch.
p. cm.
Includes bibliographical references and indexes.
ISBN 0-87579-600-1
1. Book of Mormon—Criticism, interpretation, etc. I. Welch, John W. (John Woodland)
BX8627.R398 1992
289.3'22—dc20 91-47719
CIP

Printed in the United States of America 8006-4593

10 9 8 7 6 5 4

CONTENTS

INTRODUCTION

In December 1984, the Foundation for Ancient Research and Mormon Studies (F.A.R.M.S.), based in Provo, Utah, issued its first monthly Update. That one-page bulletin announced the discovery of domesticated barley in the Americas before Columbus. That finding was significant since Alma 13 says that barley was a Nephite crop. Before that discovery, however, no evidence existed of cultivated barley in ancient America.

Since that first Update, researchers have written and circulated a steady stream of innovative findings and insights. This book collects all those Updates, together with similar studies from the F.A.R.M.S. newsletter. Encapsulated here is a decade of exciting and fruitful exploration about the Book of Mormon.

The Updates are brief, readable reports of new research on the Book of Mormon, aimed at a general audience. They set forth the essence of a research topic and new discoveries that bear on it. They represent ongoing studies from a variety of fields. They report intriguing ideas and developments that emerged while reexploring the Book of Mormon from many perspectives.

Most Updates shed new light on a particular passage or concept in the Book of Mormon. This book arranges these short studies in the order that those key passages or concepts appear in the Book of Mormon. In addition, new illustrations and charts have been included.

These Updates were written by many people but were originally published as unsigned articles because they emerged from collaborative research efforts. No Update has been released without close scrutiny by several scholars. Notes have now been added at the end of each chapter to identify the principal researchers and to refer the reader to other more recent, related material. In many cases, the Updates were the leading edge of new discoveries that were subsequently developed, expanded, debated further, and published in scholarly articles or books.

At first, F.A.R.M.S. wanted to communicate the developments to a small audience of donors and researchers. However, the Updates proved so popular that they were soon distributed in annual packets. Eventually the demand became so great that they became a regular feature of the F.A.R.M.S. newsletter.[1]

The eighty-five chapters in this book chronicle some of the ongoing Book of Mormon research of the 1980s and early 1990s. Not all Book of Mormon research projects lend themselves to short Update treatment, but in many cases a topic can be opened up to the public by such a report. Often they remain the most useful, concise statements available on the topic or issue.

In many ways the Updates have changed the face of Book of Mormon research. No longer are new scholarly insights into the Book of Mormon held in remote corners of cluttered file cabinets. Approaches taken and discoveries made by Hugh Nibley and others a generation ago[2] have expanded in type and number. Respect for the Book of Mormon has grown.

These Updates will interest all people who want to know what's new in Book of Mormon research. They will be informative to inquisitive minds—old and young—who want to know the questions that many scholars are asking, researching, and answering. They will appeal to minds that enjoy thinking about novel approaches and prospecting for new information. They will appeal to all who enjoy learning more about the Book of Mormon—its messages, language, and setting; its astonishing details, miraculous existence, and incomparable mission.

Believers of the Book of Mormon as ancient scripture, however, realize that human ingenuity will never be enough to answer all questions about its origins and contents. But people can separate the questions that cannot be answered (either in whole or part) from those that can. Then they can work on the viable ones, gather relevant information, and propose and evaluate possible answers as far as current knowledge will allow.

Thinking this way about Book of Mormon issues has been a part of Latter-day Saint intellectual history since the days of Joseph Smith. After reading an extract from Stephen's *Incidents of Travel in Central America,* the Prophet commented: "We can not but think the Lord has a hand in bringing to pass his strange act, and proving the Book of Mormon true in the eyes of all the people. . . . The world will prove Joseph Smith a true prophet by circumstantial evidence, in experiments, as they did Moses and Elijah."[3] Thus, to probe and ponder the circumstantial evidences of the scripture's truthfulness is one of the purposes of Book of Mormon research.

Circumstantial evidence, however, is not the primary source of knowledge that the Book of Mormon is true. Perhaps the clearest statement to this effect was published by B. H. Roberts in 1909. His classic comments embrace both the primary evidence that comes from the Holy Ghost and all other forms of evidence, which, although secondary, may still be of first-rate importance:

> It is frequently the case that a proper setting forth of a subject makes its truth self-evident; and all other evidence becomes merely collateral, and all argument becomes of secondary importance. Especially is this the case when setting forth the Book of Mormon for the world's acceptance; in which matter we have the right to expect, and the assurance in the book itself that we shall receive, the co-operation of divine agencies to confirm to the souls of men the truth of the Nephite record; that as that record was written in the first instance by divine commandment, by the spirit of prophecy and of revelation; and, as it was preserved by angelic guardian-ship, and at last brought forth by revelation, and translated by what men regard as miraculous means, so it is provided in God's providences . . . that its truth shall be attested to individuals by the operations of the Holy Spirit upon the human mind. . . .
>
> This must ever be the chief source of evidence for the truth of the Book of Mormon. All other evidence is secondary to this, the primary and infallible. No arrangement of evidence,

> however skilfully ordered; no argument, however adroitly made, can ever take its place; for this witness of the Holy Spirit to the soul of man for the truth of the Nephite volume of scripture, is God's evidence to the truth. . . .
>
> To be known, the truth must be stated and the clearer and more complete the statement is, the better opportunity will the Holy Spirit have for testifying to the souls of men that the work is true. . . . [However,] I would not have it thought that the evidence and argument presented in [here] are unimportant, much less unnecessary. Secondary evidences in support of truth, like secondary causes in natural phenomena, may be of firstrate importance, and mighty factors in the achievement of God's purposes.[4]

All who have given their time and talents to the task of researching and writing these Updates echo these convictions and perspectives of Elder Roberts.

In addition to thanking those who have contributed their research over the years to these Updates, my colleagues and I gratefully acknowledge the many people who have helped produce and circulate them, especially Janet Twigg, Brenda Miles, Shirley Ricks, and Melvin Thorne, and, for her work on this book, Carolyn Cannon. The preparation of this volume for publication, especially the addition of the illustrations, was made possible by a gift from Mr. and Mrs. Robert Grow, in honor of their children. All royalties from the sale of this book are dedicated to the ongoing work of Book of Mormon research.

John W. Welch

Notes

1. Anyone interested in receiving the newsletter, now issued six times a year, is invited to contact F.A.R.M.S. at P.O. Box 7113, University Station, Provo, UT 84602.

2. See especially volumes 5–8 on the Book of Mormon in *The Collected Works of Hugh Nibley* (Salt Lake City: Deseret Book Company and F.A.R.M.S., 1987–88).

3. Joseph Fielding Smith, ed. and comp., *Teachings of the Prophet Joseph Smith* (Salt Lake City: Deseret Book, 1976), 267.

4. B. H. Roberts, *New Witnesses for God,* 3 vols. (Salt Lake City: Deseret Book, 1909), 2:vi–viii.

Chapter 1

HOW LONG DID IT TAKE TO TRANSLATE THE BOOK OF MORMON?

Title Page "Translated by Joseph Smith"

Long ago the Lord declared: "I will proceed to do a marvelous work among this people, yea, a marvelous work and a wonder" (2 Nephi 27:26; see Isaiah 29:14). In Hebrew, this emphatic text repeats the word *miracle* three times: "a miraculous miracle and a miracle." In this context, Isaiah prophesies of a book that will come forth in an extraordinary manner. That book is the Book of Mormon.

The Title Page of the Book of Mormon declares that the book is a translation of an ancient set of records, "sealed up, and hid up unto the Lord . . . —To come forth by the gift and power of God." On many counts, it is no ordinary book. The mere existence of the Book of Mormon is one of the greatest miracles in history.

Among the many amazing facts about the Book of Mormon is how little time it took for Joseph Smith to translate it. Recent research has shown more clearly than ever before that the Book of Mormon as we now have it was translated in a stunningly short amount of time. There was no time for outside research, rewriting, or polishing. Many contemporaneous historical documents sustain and validate the accuracy of Joseph Smith's account of the coming forth of the Book of Mormon.

The following historical details are well worth noting:

1. In the two months from April 12 to June 14, 1828, Martin Harris assisted Joseph Smith in the translation of what is referred

to in the 1830 preface to the Book of Mormon as "The Book of Lehi."[1] During that time, 116 pages of manuscript translation were written. But when those 116 pages, which Martin had borrowed to show members of his family, were lost, the "interpreters" were taken away from Joseph Smith and translation temporarily ceased (July 1828; see D&C 3).

2. Following the return of the "interpreters" on September 22, 1828,[2] the translation was resumed and proceeded sporadically, with Emma acting as Joseph's scribe. In Doctrine and Covenants 5:30, which was given in March 1829, Joseph was commanded to translate "a few more pages" and then to "stop for a season." An examination of the fragmentary original manuscript shows no evidence of Emma's handwriting, which indicates that very little translation work was actually accomplished during this time.

3. The process of translating the Book of Mormon as we know it began in full earnest with the arrival of Oliver Cowdery on April 5, 1829.[3] Two days later, Joseph and Oliver began translating and continued the process "uninterrupted" and "with little cessation" during the rest of April and May of that year.[4] By May 15 (see D&C 13), they must have reached 3 Nephi 11 since, according to Oliver's own account, "after writing the account given of the Savior's ministry to the remnant of the seed of Jacob, upon this continent, it was easily to be seen . . . that . . . none had authority from God to administer the ordinances of the Gospel."[5] It was this awareness that led to the restoration of the Aaronic Priesthood on May 15, 1829.

If their work began with 1 Nephi, this would mean that 430 pages (of the current edition) would have been written in thirty-eight days, or an amazing average of not less than eleven-and-a-half pages per day! If, on the other hand, Joseph's and Oliver's work together began with Mosiah 1, this would still represent 285 pages, an average of seven-and-a-half pages per day!

4. By about the middle of June, the Three Witnesses were shown the plates. According to the manuscripts of the *History of the Church,* a scripture found on page 110 (2 Nephi 27) of the

original edition of the Book of Mormon may have sparked this experience. Although this recently noticed detail in the manuscript of the *History of the Church* was not supplied until after 1852 (the 1842 publication of the *History of the Church* in the *Times and Seasons* left out the reference to page 110), it may well reflect an oral recollection concerning the immediate scriptural cause of the experience of the Three Witnesses.

This would mean that only 2 Nephi 28 to Words of Mormon remained, or about thirty-eight pages of text, to translate in late June. The manuscripts of the *History of the Church* confirm that the translation continued following that manifestation[6] and that the work was completed before the end of June. Another possibility is that the scripture in Ether 5 sparked the experience of the Three Witnesses, as later editions of the *History of the Church* indicate. If that were the case, there likewise remained thirty-seven pages to the end of Moroni to complete in late June.

5. If Oliver began transcribing in April with Mosiah 1, then 212 pages would have been translated from the time of the restoration of the Aaronic Priesthood on May 15 (3 Nephi 11) until the manifestation to the Three Witnesses in late June (2 Nephi 27). This is a period of approximately thirty days (including the four days spent in transit from Harmony to the Whitmer farm in Fayette), or an average of about ten pages per working day.

If Joseph and Oliver began their work in April at 1 Nephi, which assumes that Ether 5 sparked the experience of the Three Witnesses, there would have been only sixty-five pages (3 Nephi 11 to Ether 5) translated during the same thirty-day period of time, or an average of about two pages per day.

In our view, the "Mosiah First" theory seems more likely.[7] This supposition is strengthened by the fact that the Title Page, which stood at the end of the Plates of Mormon, was already translated before June 11, 1829. That is the date Joseph Smith applied for the copyright on the Book of Mormon and used the Title Page as the book's description on the application.

6. Under either theory, a span of no more than sixty-five to seventy-five total days was likely involved in translating the Book

of Mormon as we now have it, for an overall average of about seven to eight pages per day, conservatively estimated. At such a pace, only about a week could have been taken to translate all of 1 Nephi; a day and half for King Benjamin's speech.

Moreover, Joseph and Oliver could not spend all of that time concentrating on the translation. They also took time to eat, to sleep, to seek employment (once, to work for money when supplies ran out), to receive the Aaronic and Melchizedek priesthoods, to make at least one (and possibly two) trips to Colesville thirty miles away, to convert and baptize Hyrum and Samuel Smith (who came to Harmony at that time), to receive and record thirteen revelations that are now sections of the Doctrine and Covenants, to move on buckboard from Harmony to Fayette, to acquire the Book of Mormon copyright, to preach a few days and baptize several people near Fayette, to experience manifestations with the Three and Eight Witnesses, and to begin making arrangements for the Book of Mormon's publication.

As Oliver Cowdery a few years afterward testified, "These were days never to be forgotten—to sit under the sound of a voice dictated by the *inspiration* of heaven, awakened the utmost gratitude of this bosom! Day after day I continued, uninterrupted, to write from his mouth, as he translated . . . the record called 'The Book of Mormon.' "[8] Considering the Book of Mormon's theological depth, historical complexity, consistency, clarity, artistry, accuracy, and profundity, the Prophet Joseph's translation is a phenomenal achievement—even a miraculous feat.

Based on research by John W. Welch and Tim Rathbone, February 1986. This Update was followed by the publication of an extensive day-by-day chronological study: John W. Welch and Tim Rathbone, "The Translation of the Book of Mormon: Basic Historical Information" (Provo: F.A.R.M.S., 1986). A concise statement of that research appeared in the Church magazines: John W. Welch, "How long did it take Joseph Smith to translate the Book of Mormon?" Ensign *18 (January 1988): 46–47.*

Notes

1. *History of the Church,* 1:20–21.

2. Lucy Mack Smith, *History of Joseph Smith by His Mother* (Salt Lake City: Bookcraft, 1958), 134–35; compare D&C 10:1–3.

3. *History of the Church,* 1:32–33.

4. *History of the Church,* 1:35; Oliver Cowdery, "Letter 1," *Messenger and Advocate* 1 (October 1834): 14.

5. Cowdery, "Letter 1," 15.

6. *History of the Church,* 1:26.

7. See Stan Larson, "A Most Sacred Possession," *Ensign* 7 (September 1977): 87.

8. Joseph Smith—History 1:71 note; italics added. See Cowdery, "Letter 1."

Events Surrounding the Translation of the Book of Mormon

Date		Events
1827	Sep	Joseph obtains the plates from the angel Moroni
	Oct	
	Nov	
	Dec	Joseph and Emma move to Harmony, Pennsylvania
1828	Jan	Joseph translates some of the characters
	Feb	Martin Harris visits Professor Charles Anthon in New York City
	Mar	
	Apr 12 ↓ June 14	Book of Lehi is translated
	June 15	Joseph and Emma's first child is born and dies
		Martin Harris loses 116 pages
	July	Joseph travels to Manchester, New York
	Aug	
	Sep 22	Interpreters and plates reobtained
	Oct	
	Nov	
	Dec	David Whitmer makes a business trip to Palmyra, where he meets Oliver Cowdery

HOW LONG DID IT TAKE TO TRANSLATE?

1829	Jan	
	Feb	Joseph's parents come from New York to Harmony
		Joseph receives Doctrine and Covenants 4
		Lord appears to Oliver Cowdery
	Mar	A few pages translated
		Martin Harris visits Joseph from Palmyra
	Apr 5	Oliver Cowdery arrives in Harmony
	Apr 7 ↓	Book of Mormon translated
	Late June	
	July	E. B. Grandin and T. Weed decline to print
	Aug	E. B. Grandin agrees to print
		Martin Harris mortgages his farm
		Typesetting commences
	Sep	
	Oct	
	Nov	Oliver Cowdery's preparation of the Printer's Manuscript reaches Alma 36
	Dec	
1830	Jan	
	Feb	
	Mar 26	Printing finished

HOW LONG DID IT TAKE TO TRANSLATE?

The Translation of the Book of Mormon, April to June 1829

Date	Events	Where they were in the translation if they began with Mosiah 1		Where they were in the translation if they began with 1 Nephi 1
Apr 5	Oliver Cowdery arrives in Harmony, Pennsylvania			
7	Joseph and Oliver begin work	Mosiah 1	◊	1 Nephi
	Doctrine and Covenants 6, 7, 8, and 9 received			
May 10	Joseph and Oliver go to Colesville, New York		38 days	
	Aaronic Priesthood restored			
15	Doctrine and Covenants 10 received	3 Nephi 11	◊	3 Nephi 11
	About this time Joseph and Oliver may have gone again to Colesville		16 days	
25	Samuel Smith baptized			
	Doctrine and Covenants 11 received			
June 1	Joseph and Oliver move from Harmony, Pennsylvania, to Fayette, New York	Moroni 1 Nephi	◊	
11	Copyright application filed			
	Doctrine and Covenants 14, 15, 16, and 18 received		20 days	
15	Hyrum Smith, David Whitmer, and Peter Whitmer, Jr., are baptized around this date			
20	Three Witnesses see the plates around this date	2 Nephi 27	◊	Ether 5
25	Eight Witnesses handle the plates around this date		10 days	
30	Translation finished by this date	Words of Mormon	◊	Moroni

Chapter 2

THE ORIGINAL BOOK OF MORMON TRANSCRIPT

Title Page "If there be fault it be the mistake of men; wherefore condemn not the things of God."

The last of the plates of Mormon was the Title Page. It asks readers to understand that "if there be fault [in the Book of Mormon] it be the mistake of men." So read the Title Page in the June 1829 copyright application, the Printer's Manuscript, and the 1830 edition of the Book of Mormon. Although studies have verified, again and again, the precision and accuracy of the Book of Mormon, Moroni's statement allowed for the possibility of error in the human aspects of writing, abridging, inscribing, translating, transcribing, and publishing.

Typical of the minor changes made in the Book of Mormon through its various printings, Joseph Smith in the 1837 edition changed this statement to read, "If there are faults they are the mistakes of men; wherefore, condemn not the things of God." And it has been printed this way ever since.

From 1984 to 1987, F.A.R.M.S. published a three-volume text of the Book of Mormon showing the numerous but mostly inconsequential changes in the various editions. Recently Royal Skousen has been directing much further work on the Original Manuscript of the Book of Mormon, with the assistance of F.A.R.M.S.

Since the Original Manuscript was written under difficult circumstances, it was not always neat. A second copy was also needed to protect against loss. Accordingly, after the translation was finished, Oliver Cowdery copied the entire Book of Mormon onto a second manuscript, known today as the Printer's Manuscript. From the Printer's Manuscript, the 1830 edition of the Book of Mormon was typeset. All but one line of the Printer's Manuscript has survived (it is in the archives of the RLDS Church in Independence, Missouri). However, only about twenty-five percent of the Original Manuscript still exists (most of it in the LDS Church archives in Salt Lake City). The remainder of the Original Manuscript was either destroyed as it lay in the Nauvoo House cornerstone or was lost during the nineteenth century after being taken from the cornerstone.

However, with computers to tabulate exact comparisons, and with access to more legible copies of the Original Manuscript fragments and the Printer's Manuscript, a more thorough comparison of these manuscripts and the key editions of the Book of Mormon can be made. The study so far is yielding a deeper appreciation of the Original Manuscript.

When Joseph Smith translated the Book of Mormon in the spring of 1829, he dictated the text line by line. An examination of the Original Manuscript reveals that Joseph Smith, as he translated, apparently never went back to cross out, revise, or modify. The manuscript pages contain the words written by Joseph's scribes (primarily Oliver Cowdery) as the Prophet spoke the translation.

Several dozen differences between the Original Manuscript and the Printer's Manuscript, never before noted, have been detected. For example, Zenock is spelled "Zenoch" in the Original Manuscript (this spelling compares with that of Enoch). In Alma 51:15, the Original Manuscript reports that Moroni sent a petition to the governor "desiring that he should *heed* it." The 1830 edition typeset this phrase as "desiring that he should *read* it." In Alma 54:17, the Original Manuscript asserted that the Lamanites claimed that the government "*rightfully* belonged unto them." In the Printer's Manuscript, this word became "*rightly*." In other instances, "pressing their way" became "feeling their way" (1 Nephi 8:31), a "were" became a "was" (1 Nephi 13:12), and a "shall" became a "should" (1 Nephi 17:50). "Heard and seen" became "seen and heard" (1 Nephi 20:6), and the "poorer class of the people" became the "poor class of people" (Alma 32:2).

Analyzing the changes yields some important observations about the manuscripts:

1. The differences between the Original Manuscript and the Printer's Manuscript are few. Only about one difference per manuscript page exists—far fewer than one might have expected.

2. The differences between the Printer's Manuscript and the Original Manuscript are minor, and most of the errors are natural transcription errors. The Printer's Manuscript shows no sign of any conscious editing on Oliver Cowdery's part. These manuscripts show that he was careful to reproduce exactly what had been hurriedly written in the Original Manuscript.

3. As good as the Printer's Manuscript is, the Original Manuscript is even better. Of the thirty-seven differences in transcription noted so far, seventeen show that the reading in the Printer's Manuscript became more awkward or grammatically improper or unusual. In only seven cases was the Original Manuscript harder to understand, due for example to atypical spellings or awkward grammar (like Hebraisms).

4. Surprisingly, the copying errors in the Printer's Manuscript tend to make the text shorter rather than longer. Of the thirty-seven differences, only two changed a shorter word to a longer one, while in seven cases a longer word was contracted to a shorter one. This is intriguing because people working with biblical manuscripts generally assume that texts tend to grow as scribal transmission changes them. The experience of Oliver Cowdery manifests the opposite tendency.

Above all, close examination of these manuscripts yields solid evidence that Oliver Cowdery was true to his calling as a scribe. Though much of the Original Manuscript has not survived, we can reasonably estimate that Oliver copied the entire Book of Mormon onto the Printer's Manuscript with only about 140 differences—all of them apparently simple slips of the hand or eye. Considering the task of writing with a quill pen and the magnitude of the labor, the accuracy of Oliver's transcription seems almost phenomenal.

Based on research by Royal Skousen, December 1988. Work on the Book of Mormon manuscripts continues. For the latest detailed report, see Royal Skousen, "Towards a Critical Edition of the Book of Mormon," BYU Studies *30 (Winter 1990): 41–69. For information about the more recent discovery of several fragments of the Original Manuscript, see the F.A.R.M.S. newsletter,* Insights *(January 1991).*

Chapter 3

COLOPHONS IN THE BOOK OF MORMON

1 Nephi 1:1 "I, Nephi"

From the day the Book of Mormon was published in 1830, some readers have been struck by its distinctive modes of expression. Many of the oddities thought at first to be signs of ignorance or awkwardness turn out on closer inspection to be traces of ancient authenticity. "Colophons" in the Book of Mormon illustrate this.

Several of the books in the Book of Mormon begin or end with a statement by the author certifying that he is the author of his work. Often he tells what is to come in the following pages or explains or marks the end of what has just been said. For example, the book of Enos begins, "*I, Enos,* . . . will tell you of the wrestle which I had before God" (Enos 1:1–2); and the book of Mormon begins, "*I, Mormon,* make a record of the things which I have both seen and heard" (Mormon 1:1). Similarly, the book of Jacob ends, "*I, Jacob,* . . . make an end of my writing" (Jacob 7:27). Dozens of editorial entries like these are found in the Book of Mormon. What purposes do they serve?

Statements like these are known in ancient documents as colophons, and as Hugh Nibley pointed out several years ago, they appear in several Egyptian documents.[1] For example, the Bremer-Rhind papyrus opens with a colophon that gives the date, the titles of the author, genealogical information about his parents, and a curse upon anyone who might tamper with the document (in other words, an avowal that the record is true). These textual elements functioned in antiquity somewhat like a copyright or seal of approval.

In addition to the points made by Nibley, research has further examined what these colophons tell us about how the Book of Mormon was assembled. The fact that these colophons have been handled differently in modern printings has obscured their original nature.

Nephi, of course, set the pattern for the Book of Mormon. All we have from him in the books of 1 Nephi and 2 Nephi was written near the same time, some thirty years after he left Jerusalem (see 2 Nephi 5:28–33). He might have kept some sort of journal through the years and during his travels, but his words as he carefully phrased them on his plates form a single, planned work, through which he felt the need to guide the reader's steps.

And how does he guide the reader?

At the start of 1 Nephi, a heading that is not marked with verse numbers begins, "An account of Lehi and his wife Sariah, and his four sons," and ends, "I, Nephi, wrote this record."

In 1 Nephi 1:1–3, Nephi affirms that he has made the record and that it is true. "I, Nephi, . . . make a record of my proceedings in my days. . . . And I know that the record which I make is true; and I make it with mine own hand; and I make it according to my knowledge."

Then in 1 Nephi 9, Nephi gives a discussion (the entire chapter) about what chapters 1–8 have been about, plus a statement of what will follow next. The *amen* at the end of this chapter signals that he has finished his editorial aside.

In 1 Nephi 14 he again summarizes and again concludes with *amen:* "I bear record that I saw the things which my father saw, and the angel of the Lord did make them known unto me. And now I make an end of speaking concerning the things which I saw while I was carried away in the spirit. . . . And thus it is. Amen" (1 Nephi 14:29–30).

Many other similar editorial comments by Nephi could be mentioned (for example, 1 Nephi 15:36). They serve as markers and natural divisions in the text. In a way, they take the place of paragraphs, punctuation, and other modern writing devices not used in antiquity.

Readers of the Book of Mormon will find these natural markers throughout the book. Many Book of Mormon writers, including Mormon, followed Nephi's lead. Mormon provided prefaces for each of the books he abridged (except Mosiah, for which the Words of Mormon is an expanded prologue). In addition, he wrote introductions to chunks of original material that he incorporated unchanged into his ongoing abridgment of the plates of Nephi. Among the most obvious such spots are his comments preceding the record of the Zeniff colony (before Mosiah 9) and before Alma's account, which starts with Mosiah 23. Finally, Mormon lets the reader know, at Mosiah 29:47, that the book of Mosiah is done and that the orientation of the record is shifting.

The book of Alma begins with a sixty-eight-word preface and ends with a summary in the last verse. In between are other guides provided by Mormon. At the beginning of Alma 5, a preface starts, "The words which Alma . . . delivered," and concludes at Alma 6:8 with an editorial guideline complete with *amen*. A preface before Alma 17 starts the mission record of the sons of Mosiah (extending through chapter 26). Bracketing statements for the record of Shiblon are in Alma 63:1 and 11.

We can discern that, in some cases, sections of ancient documents in Mormon's possession were entered verbatim. Zeniff, for example, wrote in the first person, and Mormon incorporated his record intact. Helaman 7–12 has a formal title: "The prophecy of Nephi, the son of Helaman." At least a part of Helaman 13–15, headed "The prophecy of Samuel, the Lamanite, to the Nephites," is quoted from a document rather than paraphrased by Mormon. Meanwhile, the colophon at the beginning of 3 Nephi, which introduces what follows as the "Book of Nephi," provides genealogical information given nowhere else.

These colophons are not consistently presented or clearly identified in modern printed editions of the Book of Mormon, but readers can watch for them and see how they act as guides through this compilation of records that have been drawn together from many authors and from various plates and records.

This feature of the text shows not only the remarkable complexity of the Book of Mormon, but also the great efforts made by its writers and editors to make the record as clear as possible.

This July 1990 Update was based on research by John A. Tvedtnes. The topic is discussed at greater length in John A. Tvedtnes, "Colophons in the Book of Mormon," in John Sorenson and Melvin Thorne, eds., Rediscovering the Book of Mormon *(Salt Lake City, Utah: Deseret Book and F.A.R.M.S., 1991), 32–37.*

Note

1. *Lehi in the Desert,* in *The Collected Works of Hugh Nibley* (Salt Lake City, Utah: Deseret Book and F.A.R.M.S., 1988), 5:17–19.

Sources, plates, records, and manuscripts of the Book of Mormon.

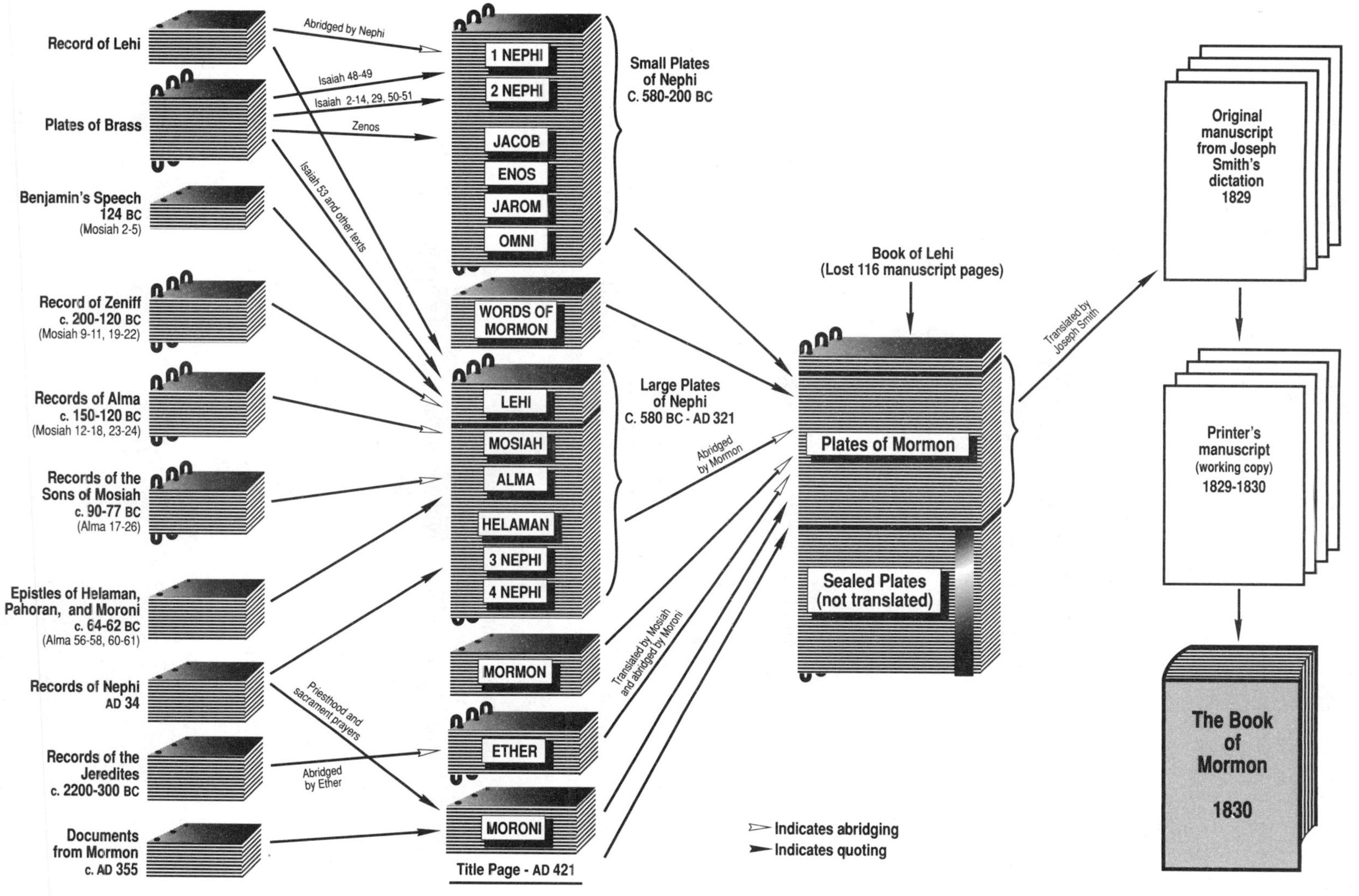
Record of Lehi
Plates of Brass
Benjamin's Speech
124 BC
(Mosiah 2-5)
Record of Zeniff
c. 200-120 BC
(Mosiah 9-11, 19-22)
Records of Alma
c. 150-120 BC
(Mosiah 12-18, 23-24)
Records of the
Sons of Mosiah
c. 90-77 BC
(Alma 17-26)
Epistles of Helaman,
Pahoran, and Moroni
c. 64-62 BC
(Alma 56-58, 60-61)
Records of Nephi
AD 34
Records of the
Jeredites
c. 2200-300 BC
Documents
from Mormon
c. AD 355
Abridged by Nephi
Isaiah 48-49
Isaiah 2-14, 29, 50-51
Zenos
Isaiah 53 and other texts
Priesthood and
sacrament prayers
Abridged
by Ether
1 NEPHI
2 NEPHI
JACOB
ENOS
JAROM
OMNI
Small Plates
of Nephi
C. 580-200 BC
WORDS OF
MORMON
LEHI
MOSIAH
ALMA
HELAMAN
3 NEPHI
4 NEPHI
Large Plates
of Nephi
C. 580 BC - AD 321
Abridged
by Mormon
MORMON
ETHER
MORONI
Title Page - AD 421
Translated by Mosiah
and abridged by Moroni
Book of Lehi
(Lost 116 manuscript pages)
Plates of Mormon
Sealed Plates
(not translated)
Translated by
Joseph Smith
Original
manuscript
from Joseph
Smith's
dictation
1829
Printer's
manuscript
(working copy)
1829-1830
The Book
of
Mormon
1830
Indicates abridging
Indicates quoting

Chapter 4

TWO FIGURINES FROM THE BELLEZA AND SANCHEZ COLLECTION

1 Nephi 1:2 "and the language of the Egyptians"

In light of the fact that Lehi and Nephi knew Egyptian and probably had traveled to the land of the Nile, what would you think if archaeologists found ancient Egyptian figurines in Central America? At least it would show that ancient ocean crossings, like Lehi's, were possible.

About twenty-five years ago, Gareth W. Lowe, Director of the BYU–New World Archaeological Foundation, photographed two figurines located in a display case in the Museo Nacional "David J. Guzman" in San Salvador, El Salvador, and he sent copies to John Sorenson.[1] According to the display caption, the figurines were excavated from three meters in depth from the eastern beaches of Acajutla, Sonsonate, El Salvador, on the Pacific coast near the Guatemala–El Salvador border.

Both figurines clearly belong to a class of ancient Egyptian funerary statuettes known as *ushabti.* Both are incised with hieroglyphic Egyptian texts: (A) a male holding in his hands portions of the Book of the Dead that refer to the Netherworld and its obstacles, and (B) Osiris, the crowned and bearded god of death and resurrection, with a royal cartouche and then his name in a vertical column. All Egyptians sought in death to identify with Osiris so that they too might be resurrected as he had been. More text may be inscribed on the backs, but detailed photos are necessary for closer study.

Ushabtiu figurines were popular for much of Egyptian history, including the time of Lehi and Nephi (the Saitic Dynasty). Why these two examples should have shown up in El Salvador, though, is a matter for speculation. We cannot be certain where they first surfaced, since they were not examined in place by archaeologists. At least we know that such figurines, made of wood, glazed faience, stone, or metal were deposited in Egypt with the deceased in their tombs in order to perform menial labor on their behalf in the "Eleusian" Netherworld. As with the two figurines, they normally contained the names of the deceased for whom they were made. While premature enthusiasm ought to be avoided, these figurines may be very important indeed.

This report, first issued in January 1984 and based on research by John L. Sorenson and Robert F. Smith, still calls for further information. Anyone who has relevant photographs or who is anxious to pursue this matter is invited to contact F.A.R.M.S., P. O. Box 7113, University Station, Provo, UT 84602.

Note

1. See also *Revista del Departamento de Historia* [San Salvador, El Salvador] 1, no. 3 (March 1930): 15.

Two Egyptian figurines, of unknown origin, discovered near the Pacific Ocean in El Salvador in the 1920s. Courtesy John L. Sorenson.

Translation –
J.S. " 2 sep. passages
which are separately
00's of pgs & wks of dictation

Chapter 5

TEXTUAL CONSISTENCY

1 Nephi 1:8 "He saw God sitting upon his throne, surrounded with numberless concourses of angels in the attitude of singing and praising their God."

The general mode of translation used by Joseph Smith in bringing forth the Book of Mormon is well known. He dictated the text to a scribe as he translated the record, going through the text only a single time. People do not often stop to think, however, about the implications and challenges of this unusual and formidible manner of writing.

For one thing, dictating a final copy of a letter, let alone a book, the first time through is extremely difficult. Yet the Original Manuscript of the Book of Mormon is remarkably clean. There are few strikeovers, and only minor changes were made as the book went to publication. The vast majority of those changes involved spelling, capitalization, punctuation, and grammar.

Even more remarkable are the extensive, intricate consistencies within the Book of Mormon. Passages tie together precisely and accurately though separated from each other by hundreds of pages of text and dictated weeks apart. Here are four striking examples:

1. In Alma 36, Alma recounts the story of his conversion. In describing the joy he experienced and the desire that his soul then felt to be with God, Alma thought of Lehi's experience: "Yea, methought I saw, even as our father Lehi *saw, God sitting upon his throne, surrounded with numberless concourses of angels, in the attitude of singing and praising their God*" (Alma 36:22). These words in Alma 36 are not merely a loose recollection of the

scriptural record of Lehi's vision. There are twenty-one words here that are quoted verbatim from 1 Nephi 1, which states that Lehi "thought he *saw God sitting upon his throne, surrounded with numberless concourses of angels in the attitude of singing and praising their God*" (1 Nephi 1:8). Obviously, Alma is directly quoting from the record of Lehi's vision in which he learned of the impending destruction of Jerusalem. It makes sense that Alma would have known these words, since he had charge of the Small Plates of Nephi (see Alma 37:2), which contained this sentence.

The impressive thing about these two passages (separated by hundreds of pages) is that they were translated independently by Joseph Smith. It is highly unlikely that Joseph Smith asked Oliver Cowdery to read back to him what he had translated earlier so that he could get the quote exactly the same. If that had happened, Oliver Cowdery would undoubtedly have questioned him and lost faith in the translation.

2. Another example comes from Helaman 14:12. There Samuel the Lamanite spoke of the coming of Christ, so that the people in the city of Zarahemla "might know of the coming of *Jesus Christ, the Son of God, the Father of heaven and of earth, the Creator of all things from the beginning*." The twenty-one words in italic appear to be standard Nephite religious terminology derived from the words given to Benjamin by an angel from God: "He shall be called *Jesus Christ, the Son of God, the Father of heaven and earth, the Creator of all things from the beginning*" (Mosiah 3:8).

These sacred words identifying the Savior evidently became important in Nephite worship after they were revealed through Benjamin. Samuel the Lamanite would have had the opportunity to learn these words through the ministry of Nephi and Lehi among the Lamanites (see Helaman 5:50), for the words of Benjamin were especially important to Lehi and Nephi. Their father, Helaman, had charged them in particular to "remember, remember, my sons, the words which King Benjamin spake unto his people" (Helaman 5:9). Nephi and Lehi likely used the precise words of King Benjamin in their preaching, just as their father had quoted to them some of the words of Benjamin: "Remember that there is no other way nor means whereby man can be saved, only through the atoning blood of Jesus Christ" (Helaman 5:9; compare Mosiah 3:18; 4:8).

3. Another example is found in the account of the destructions in 3 Nephi 8:6–23, fulfilling the prophecy of Zenos preserved in 1 Nephi 19:11–12. The ancient prophet foretold that there would be thunderings and lightnings, tempests, fire and smoke, a vapor of darkness, the earth opening, mountains being carried up, rocks rending, and the earth groaning. The fulfillment of his prophecy is recorded hundreds of years (and pages) later. Third Nephi 8 expressly speaks of the same list: tempests, thunderings and lightnings, fire, earth being carried up to become a mountain, whirlwinds, the earth quaking and breaking up, rocks being rent, a vapor of darkness, and the people groaning. Apparently, one of the reasons that Mormon gave such a full account was to document the complete fulfillment of that prophecy of Zenos.

4. Early in Book of Mormon history, King Benjamin set forth a five-part legal series prohibiting (1) murder, (2) plunder, (3) theft, (4) adultery, and (5) any manner of wickedness. This five-part list, which first appears in Mosiah 2:13, uniformly reappears seven other times in the Book of Mormon (see Mosiah 29:36; Alma 23:3; 30:10; Helaman 3:14; 6:23; 7:21; and Ether 8:16). Apparently the Nephites viewed Benjamin's set of laws as setting a formulaic precedent.

Other cases and kinds of extensive internal textual consistency occur within the Book of Mormon. In these and in many other ways, the Book of Mormon manifests a high degree of precision—both as to its underlying ancient texts and in Joseph Smith's translation. Given the fact that Joseph dictated as he went, the record's consistency points to an inspired source for the translation's accuracy. After all, can you quote the twenty-one words of Lehi or the twenty words of Benjamin without looking?

Based on research by John W. Welch, October 1987.

Chapter 6

LEHI'S COUNCIL VISION AND THE MYSTERIES OF GOD

1 Nephi 1:8 "surrounded with numberless concourses of angels"

When Lehi saw God seated on his throne among the council of his heavenly hosts, he was entrusted to deliver the decree of woe and judgment to be issued upon Jerusalem (see 1 Nephi 1:8–13). His vision was fully consistent with the spiritual experiences of other Israelite prophets of his day. Several other prophets, like Lehi, expressed their visions in terms of participating in an assembly in heaven and receiving the judgments of that council concerning God's will about the destiny of man and the world (see, for example, 1 Kings 22:19–22; Isaiah 6:1–10; 40:1–8; Job 1:6–12; 2:1–6; Zechariah 1:8–13; 3:1–7; 6:1–8; Jeremiah 23:18). This theme has been discussed at length by Theodore Mullen,[1] and his work is a valuable tool for placing Lehi's words more specifically in their preexilic Israelite context.

Interestingly, the Hebrew word for the "council" is *sod*. By association, it has also come to mean "a decree of the council." Because the council and its actions were not open to the general public but were private and intimate, these decrees were secrets, known only to the prophets. Accordingly, Raymond E. Brown has concluded that the Semitic background of the concept of the "mysteries" of God resides in the idea of prophets (like Lehi) being "introduced into the heavenly assembly and gaining a knowledge of its secret decrees"[2] (see also Amos 3:7).

Thus, it is remarkable yet understandable that when Nephi

described his desire to receive a personal confirmation of the truth of his father's words, he said that he wanted to "know of the mysteries of God." Those "mysteries" (*sod*) were apparently synonymous, in Nephi's inquiring mind, with the decrees and knowledge that Lehi had received in the council (also *sod*).

Based on research by John W. Welch. This study first appeared in the Fall 1986 F.A.R.M.S. newsletter. This topic was then developed further in John W. Welch, "The Calling of a Prophet," in Monte Nyman and Charles Tate, eds., First Nephi, The Doctrinal Foundation *(Provo, Utah: Religious Studies Center, 1988), 35–54.*

Notes

1. See *The Divine Council in Canaanite and Early Hebrew Literature* (Chico, California: Scholars Press, 1980).

2. "The Pre-Christian Semitic Concept of 'Mystery,' " *Catholic Biblical Quarterly* 20 (1958): 417–43, esp. 421.

Chapter 7

THE BOOK OF MORMON AND THE HEAVENLY BOOK MOTIF

1 Nephi 1:9–11 "He saw One descending out of the midst of heaven, . . . and stood before my father, and gave unto him a book, and bade him that he should read."

The Book of Mormon was once dismissed with the assertion "you don't get books from angels; . . . it is just that simple." However, evidence from the ancient world indicates that angels or other heavenly beings have delivered many sacred works to men. Indeed, according to Orientalist Geo Widengren, "Few religious ideas in the Ancient East have played a more important role than the notion of the Heavenly Tablets or the Heavenly Books," which are "handed over [to a mortal] in an interview with a heavenly being."[1]

The books of Exodus, Jeremiah, Ezekiel, and Revelation contain elements of the Heavenly Book motif, as well as more than a dozen books of pseudepigraphic literature (nonbiblical writings dating c. 200 B.C. to A.D. 200) and early Christian literature. Elements of this motif, also evident in Lehi's vision (see 1 Nephi 1:11) and in the story of the coming forth of the Book of Mormon, include these elements: (1) A divine being gives a book to a mortal; (2) the mortal is commanded to read the book; (3) he is then told to copy the book; and (4) he is commanded to preach the book's message to other mortals. In what follows, we shall consider the elements of this motif as they relate to the Bible, the Book of Mormon, the pseudepigraphic book of 1 Enoch, and the early Christian Vision of Hermas.

In Exodus 31, Moses went to the top of Mount Sinai to commune with the Lord. He received many instructions orally, which he then relayed to the children of Israel below. At the conclusion of his meeting, the Lord gave Moses "two tables of testimony . . . written with the finger of God" (Exodus 31:18; compare Ezekiel 2:9–10; Revelation 10:8).

In the books of Ezekiel and Revelation, the prophets were commanded to eat the scroll (see Ezekiel 2:8; Revelation 10:9–10), symbolically suggesting that they have internalized its message. Further, John was commanded that he "must prophesy again before many peoples, and nations, and tongues, and kings" (Revelation 10:11).

In the book of 1 Enoch, an angel commanded Enoch to "look at the tablets of heaven [and] read what is written upon them." Enoch did as commanded: "I looked at the tablets of heaven, read all the writing [on them], and came to understand" (1 Enoch 81:1–2). Then he was commanded to make a copy for his posterity: "Write it down for them and give all of them a warning" (1 Enoch 81:6). Thereafter, Enoch preached from the copy.

Another example is found in the early Christian book Vision of Hermas. During a vision, Hermas saw a "woman, arrayed in a splendid robe, and with a book in her hand; and she sat down alone, and saluted [him]." After a short conversation, she asked, "Do you wish to hear me read?" Hermas replied that he did. In response to her reading, Hermas said, "Then I heard from her, magnificently and admirably, things which my memory could not retain. For all the words were terrible, such as man could not endure. The last words, however, I did remember; for they were useful to us, and gentle" (Visions 1:1, 2–3). After reading to him, she asked him, "Can you carry a report of these things to the elect of God?" He replied, "Woman, so much I cannot retain in my memory, but give me the book and I shall transcribe it." "Take it," she said, "and you will give it back to me." Hermas then transcribed "the whole of it letter by letter." However, no sooner did he finish transcribing the book, than, as he reported, "all of a sudden it was snatched from my hands; but who the person was that snatched, I saw not" (Visions 1:2, 1).

Deeply rooted in this Judeo-Christian prophetic mode, Lehi similarly reported that he saw a divine being come down from heaven, who gave him a book and asked him to read it. From that book Lehi learned not only the judgments of God upon Jerusalem, but also God's plan of mercy, and he was commanded to declare those things publicly.

Similarly, the angel Moroni told Joseph Smith that "there was a book deposited, written upon gold plates, giving an account of the former inhabitants of this continent." Joseph Smith recorded, "While he was conversing with me about the plates, the vision was opened to my mind that I could see the place where the plates were deposited, and that so clearly and distinctly that I knew the place again when I visited it" (Joseph Smith–History 1:34–42). Later, "the same heavenly messenger delivered them up to me" (Joseph Smith–History 1:59).

Through "the gift and power of God" (Title Page, Book of Mormon), Joseph Smith was able to read and translate a portion of the plates that the angel Moroni gave him, which Joseph Smith's scribe recorded. The original (as in the case of Hermas) was returned to Moroni by Joseph Smith, but the translation has become a prime source of preaching, warning, and the basis of much missionary work since that time.

The theme of the Heavenly Book, which has been developed by several scholars over the years in relation to early Christian and Jewish texts, has been examined broadly and carefully by Brent E. McNeely in his paper, "The Angelic Delivery of the Book of Mormon: An Ancient Near Eastern Motif," from which this November 1990 Update was drawn.

Note

1. *Ascension of the Apostle and the Heavenly Book* (Leipzig: Harrassowitz, 1950), 7.

Chapter 8

OLD WORLD LANGUAGES IN THE NEW WORLD

1 Nephi 3:19 "Preserve unto our children the language of our fathers."

The Book of Mormon testifies that the Nephites were diligent in preserving and teaching Old World languages in the New World, although changes occurred over the years in their spoken and written languages (see 1 Nephi 3:19; Mosiah 1:2; Mormon 9:32–33). Most anthropologists, however, have long held that, except for inconsequential examples, the languages of the Old World never crossed the ocean barriers to the New. Those who have thought otherwise, like the Mormons, have been considered naïve. Recent developments in historical and comparative linguistics, though, suggest that the conventional orthodox view has itself been simpleminded, thus holding back serious study of the issue.

Professor Otto Sadovszky of the Department of Anthropology, California State University, Fullerton, has made a revolutionary proposal that two groups of languages separated by over five thousand miles are closely related. The first group is called Penutian, a group of Indian languages of central California that include Miwok and Wintun. The second group is called Ob-Ugrian and includes related languages like Samoyed. These are used around the Ob River of northwest Siberia.

The ten thousand cognate terms and the linguistic quality of the comparisons appear so impressive to Finno-Ugric specialists that they are now more widely accepting historical linkage. A few examples of cognates are Ostyak *āj–ko* "child" =

Miwokan *'aj–ko* "children"; Ostyak *łant-* "to get blisters from rubbing" = Miwokan *łanti* "to blister from rubbing."

Moreover, traditions, physical anthropology, archaeology, and cultural practices (i.e., obsession with the bear in ritual and ideology) of the two areas also confirm a relationship. Sadovszky concludes that these western Siberians moved along the Arctic coast to the Bering Strait, then expanded southward by boat along the salmon fishing grounds of North America (but no further south). On cultural and linguistic grounds, Sadovszky dates the earliest arrivals of Ugrian speakers in central California to around 500 B.C., which is within the archaeological "Middle Horizon" for that area.

He reports evidence that other Indian languages, which were apparently pushed into the California mountains by the newcomers, are related to still earlier Altaic tongues of western Siberia. Thus a whole series of movements, not just one small migration, may well have taken place.[1]

Interestingly, Sadovszky stumbled onto his study by coincidence. A native Hungarian, he came to Berkeley over twenty-five years ago to study linguistics. Most of the studies of Penutian had been done there, in the area where those Indian languages existed (most of them now extinct). Since Hungarian is an Ob-Ugrian language, he immediately noted connections other investigators had not seen. The lesson is clear: linguistic connections cannot be made until someone capable seriously looks for them.

Meanwhile, a study by Dr. Mary Ritchie Key of the University of California at Irvine addresses another interhemispheric linguistic "no-no."[2] She writes, "The languages of Polynesia contain elements found in North and South American Indian languages that suggest distant historical connections," then presents some of the evidence. Key has received a flood of new materials from colleagues stimulated by her publication.[3]

Obviously, if more long-distance linguistic comparisons of any kind were attempted, more such connections in general would be demonstrated and evaluated. Researchers should not be hindered by supposing that the conventional answers are adequate.

This January 1986 Update was based on notes and research by John L. Sorenson, Gordon C. Thomasson, and Robert F. Smith. It is augmented by the considerable research of Brian Stubbs, "Elements of Hebrew in Uto-Aztecan: A Summary of the Data" (Provo: F.A.R.M.S., 1988), demonstrating numerous Hebrew roots and features in the Uto-Aztecan family of Native American languages (see also chapter 82 in this book, "Hebrew and Uto-Aztecan: Possible Linguistic Connections," pp. 279–81).

Notes

1. See Otto Sadovszky, "Data Sheet for Sadovszky's 'Cal-Ugrian Theory'," University of California at Los Angeles, 1985; "The Discovery of California: Breaking the Silence of the Siberian-to-America Migrator," *The Californians* 2, no. 6 (November-December 1984): 9–20; "Siberia's Frozen Mummy and the Genesis of the California Indian Culture," *The Californians* 3, no. 6 (November-December 1985): 9–20; "The New Genetic Relationship and the Paleo-Linguistics of the Central California Indian Ceremonial Houses," *Tenth LACUS Forum,* 1983, Quebec City, Quebec (Columbia, South Carolina, 1984). For annotations on his work, see John L. Sorenson and Martin H. Raish, *Pre-Columbian Contact with the Americas across the Oceans: An Annotated Bibliography* (Provo, Utah: Research Press, 1990), 2:S008–17. Publications by Finnish, Estonian, and Russian scholars on a theory called "Nostratics," which links Indo-European, Afro-Asiatic, and Uralic protolanguages, seem to include initial evidence of the Penutian connection. Tiit-Rain Viitso, for example, published such an article in 1971.

2. Mary Ritchie Key, *Polynesian and American Linguistic Connections* (Lake Bluff, Illinois: Jupiter Press, 1984); see also John Sorenson and Martin Raish, *Pre-Columbian Contact,* 1:K062–73.

3. See also John L. Sorenson, "Evidences of Culture Contacts between Polynesia and the Americas in Precolumbian Times," M.A. thesis, BYU, 1952; and David H. Kelley, "Linguistics and Problems in Trans-Pacific Contacts," *Actas y Memorias, 35th Congreso Internacional de Americanistas* (Mexico City, 1964), 1:17–18. Kelley showed the presence of what appear to be specific groups of Uto-Aztecan and early Polynesian cognates clustered around ritual and sacred beliefs.

Chapter 9

COLUMBUS: BY FAITH OR REASON?

1 Nephi 13:12 "I looked and beheld a man among the Gentiles, . . . and he went forth upon the many waters."

First Nephi 13:12 tells how the Spirit of God was to come down upon a man who would go "forth upon the many waters" to discover the posterity of Lehi in the promised land. This verse has long been understood as referring to Columbus. In particular, Orson Pratt's references in the 1879 edition of the Book of Mormon made this identification explicit. Dominant historical opinion, on the other hand, has seen Columbus led by science, reason, restlessness, and conquest. Recently, historian Pauline Watts has taken a new look at this issue and argues persuasively that Columbus was in fact deeply influenced by prophecy and revelation.[1]

Some of Joseph Smith's contemporaries probably would not have disagreed with Nephi's description of Columbus. Clues to the spiritual side of Columbus were already found in a few English sources, though these references were vague and few.[2] Materials about the life and actions of Columbus by his son D. Ferdinand Columbus were republished several times in England during the eighteenth century, but the availability of sources and Joseph Smith's actual use of them are two entirely different questions.

But if the Book of Mormon's "Spirit of God" that "wrought upon the man" was not especially shocking to some Americans in 1830, it did stand firmly against the intellectual trend of the times, which focused on Columbus's rational, scientific nature and acknowledged the spiritual roots of his quest only grudgingly, if at all. In 1792, for example, Jeremy Belknap gave a commemorative discourse in Boston filled with scriptural references, but he nevertheless chose to emphasize Columbus's logical reasoning. He carefully reconstructed his motivations for sailing based on (1) natural reason, (2) the authority of ancient writers, and (3) the testimony of sailors (following the account of Columbus's son, Ferdinand Columbus). He does mention in passing that Columbus was "guided by th' Almighty hand," but even here all the emphasis is on "Reason's golden ray."[3]

Washington Irving's 1828 biography of Columbus is the closest in time and place to the publication of the Book of Mormon, and though he duly notes Columbus's "deep religious sentiment," he discounts it as "a tinge of superstition, but . . . of a sublime and lofty kind."[4] He attributes Columbus's discovery to the "strong workings of his vigorous mind."[5] Modern attitudes about Columbus and his motivations have been even more heavily influenced by the research of Alexander von Humboldt in the 1830s, who firmly established the image of the scientific Columbus.

Against all of this, the Book of Mormon boldly asserts that whatever else may have been involved, Columbus's *primary* reasons for sailing were *spiritual*. Thus it may be of interest to Latter-day Saints that much recent scholarship has come to agree with the Book of Mormon's original assessment of Columbus.[6]

In her article, Watts investigates the spiritual origins of Columbus's voyages. She discusses the influences of scripture, theology, astrology, apocalypticism, and medieval prophecy. She particularly focuses on a book that Columbus himself was writing but never completed, called *Book of Prophecies* (the fragments were first edited by Cesare De Lollis in 1894). In this book Columbus set forth views on himself as the fulfiller of biblical prophecies! Columbus saw himself as fulfilling the "islands of the sea" passages from Isaiah and another group of verses concerning the conversion of the heathen. Watts reports that Columbus was preoccupied with "the final conversion of all races on the eve of the end of the world," paying particular attention to John 10:16: "And other sheep I have, which are not of this fold" (see also 3 Nephi 16:3). He took his mission of spreading the gospel of Christ seriously. "God made me the messenger of the new heaven and the new earth. . . . He showed me the spot where to find it," Columbus wrote in 1500.[7]

Watts summarizes her argument by stating that "in the final years of his life, . . . Columbus came increasingly to see himself as a divinely inspired fulfiller of prophecy, the one who inaugurated the age of the *unum ovile et unus pastor*" ("one fold and one shepherd").[8] "He came to believe that he was predestined to fulfill a number of prophecies in preparation for the coming of the Anti-Christ and the end of the world"[9] (which also happens to be the context of Nephi's prophecies in 1 Nephi 13–14).

Here we have a picture of Columbus as a man who very strongly felt the Spirit of God directing his life and who sought to understand that influence using the best knowledge and resources available to him. Such is not far removed from Nephi's portrait. Columbus was fulfilling inspired words more precisely than even he imagined.[10]

The importance of Pauline Watts's research for the Book of Mormon was first detected by Grant Hardy, whose report on this topic was the basis of this March 1986 Update.

Notes

1. Pauline Watts, "Prophecy and Discovery: On the Spiritual Origins of Christopher Columbus's 'Enterprise of the Indies,' " *American Historical Review* (February 1985): 73–102.

2. See D. Gio. B. Spotorno, *Memorials of Columbus* (London: Treuttel and Wurtz, 1823), 224; A. & J. Churchhill, comp., *A Collection of Voyages and Travels* (London, 1704), 2:563.

3. Jeremy Belknap, *A Discourse Intended to Commemorate the Discovery of America by Christopher Columbus* (Boston: Apollo, 1792), 56–57.

4. Washington Irving, *A History of the Life and Voyages of Christopher Columbus* (New York: G. & C. Carvill, 1828), 1:38.

5. Ibid., 1:32; see 32–42. See also *The Life of Christopher Columbus* (Philadelphia, 1838; copyright 1832), 19–21.

6. See also initial notes in this regard by Hugh Nibley, "Columbus and Revelation," *Instructor* 88 (October 1953): 319–20; reprinted in *The Collected Works of Hugh Nibley* (Salt Lake City: Deseret Book and F.A.R.M.S., 1989), 8:49–53.

7. Watts, "Prophecy and Discovery," 73.

8. Ibid., 99.

9. Ibid., 74.

10. See also Helen Hinckley, *Columbus: Explorer for Christ* (Independence: Herald Publishing House, 1977).

The name "Christopher" literally means "Christ-bearer." Christopher Columbus saw himself as carrying Christ to the isles of the sea that there might be one fold and one shepherd.

Chapter 10

THE PLAIN AND PRECIOUS PARTS

1 Nephi 13:26 "They have taken away from the gospel of the Lamb many parts which are plain and most precious."

What does the Book of Mormon say about the Bible? Most people generally familiar with Nephi's prophecy understand that the Bible, as it "proceeded forth from the mouth of a Jew [the Lord]," originally came forth in purity (1 Nephi 13:24–25). Yet as it was handed down, important parts were lost, removed, or obscured. A more detailed and more informative picture than this, however, can be gleaned from the words of 1 Nephi 13:24–32, given by an angel to Nephi. Close reading shows that Nephi saw other, more fundamental factors first at work.

These words of the angel seem to identify *three* stages in this process—not just one. First, the Gentiles would take "away *from the gospel* of the Lamb many parts which are plain and most precious" (1 Nephi 13:26). This stage possibly could have occurred more by altering the meaning or understanding of the things taught by the Lord than by changing the words themselves. This changing of understanding was a fundamental problem seen by Nephi. What would cause many to stumble were those things "taken away *out of the gospel*" (1 Nephi 13:29, 32).

Second, the Gentiles would take away "many *covenants* of the Lord" (1 Nephi 13:26). This step, too, could be taken without deleting any words from the Bible as such. The knowledge and benefit of the covenants of God could become lost simply by neglecting the performance of ordinances, or priesthood functions, or individual covenants as the Lord had taught.

Third, Nephi beheld that there were "many plain and precious things taken away *from the book*" (1 Nephi 13:28). This step was apparently a consequence of the first two, since 13:28 begins with the word "wherefore." Thus, the eventual physical loss of things from the Bible was perhaps less a cause than a result of the fact that, first, the gospel, and second, the covenants had been lost or taken away.

Understanding this process helps us to see how the Book of Mormon corrects this situation. First, it contains the fulness of the gospel (see D&C 20:9). Its correct explanations of the divinity, the mission, and the atonement of Christ, along with the principles of faith, repentance, and the other plain and precious parts of the gospel, are taught with unmistakable clarity. By reading the texts of the Bible in light of the knowledge afforded by the Book of Mormon, many plain and precious parts of the gospel can be clearly understood; that is, "they are all plain to him that understandeth" (Proverbs 8:9; compare John 16:25, 29). Without that understanding, many biblical passages (although perhaps even textually sound) remain a source of stumbling for many.

Next, the Book of Mormon restores many covenants of the Lord. It provides us with the words of the baptismal prayer, along with instructions concerning the meaning and proper mode of baptism (Mosiah 18; 3 Nephi 11; Moroni 6) and of confirmation (Moroni 2). It preserves from ancient times the very words of the sacrament prayers (Moroni 4–5) and makes the Lord's covenants to the House of Israel understood. It also teaches the necessity of priesthood authority and the manner of ordination (see, e.g., Moroni 3).

Finally, while corroborating several biblical texts, the Book of Mormon also contains many additional words that the Lord spoke on earth. It also affirms that the Lord has spoken unto all men "in the east and in the west, and in the north, and in the south," and that they have been commanded to write (2 Nephi 29:11).

Recent scholarly developments may help us understand further these three stages seen by Nephi. A volume of Gnostic writings from early Christianity, newly translated by Bentley Layton, was published in 1987 by Doubleday. It gives many texts analyzed several years ago by Hugh Nibley in *The World and the Prophets* and *Since Cumorah,* showing ways in which early Christian doctrines changed under the influences of Hellenistic philosophy and mystic religion.[1] Today there is considerable evidence that secret and sacred covenants of early Christianity were lost early. Baptism for the dead, the use of prayer circles, and the sacrament itself underwent transformation, if not elimination. Similarly, asceticism and celibacy entered Christianity at an early stage to distort the meaning of the covenant of marriage and many passages in the Bible.

Likewise, one can now see that there were significant losses of text, and even of whole books, from the Bible.[2] A significant stir of criticism is now afoot in Christian theology, asking why certain books were excluded from the Bible and wondering what makes a text scriptural. Thomas Hoffman writes of the theoretical possibility "that a lost epistle of an apostle could still be accepted into the canon." He remarks that the reasons why "such books as the Shepherd of Hermas, the First Epistle of Clement, or the Epistle of Barnabas . . . were eventually dropped from the canon are not that clear."[3] Robert Detweiler sees it as "entirely conceivable" that if the Latter-day Saints become more influential, people will "come to view the Book of Mormon with something of the same regard [as Christians now] give to the Pentateuch."[4] The old cry, "A Bible! A Bible! We have got a Bible, and there cannot be any more Bible" (2 Nephi 29:3), is giving way in some circles like scarcely before.

These developments bear out Nephi's prophetic words. The Book of Mormon was written "for the intent that [we] may believe [the Bible]" (Mormon 7:9). This is indeed achieved by restoring our understanding of the gospel and its covenants and by making people respectfully receptive to the knowledge that all the Lord's words are not found in the Bible.

Written by John W. Welch in January 1987. Further information on the general topic of this Update can be found in Stephen E. Robinson, "Early Christianity and 1 Nephi 13–14," in Monte Nyman and Charles Tate, eds., First Nephi, The Doctrinal Foundation *(Provo: Religious Studies Center, Brigham Young University, 1988), 177–91; W. D. Davies, "Reflections on the Mormon 'Canon',"* Harvard Theological Review *79 (1986): 44–66; and John W. Welch and David J. Whittaker, "Mormonism's Open Canon: Some Historical Perspectives on Its Religious Limits and Potentials," presented at meetings of the Society of Biblical Literature and American Academy of Religion, Atlanta, 1986, available from F.A.R.M.S.*

Notes

1. Reprinted as vols. 3 and 7 of *The Collected Works of Hugh Nibley* (Salt Lake City: Deseret Book and F.A.R.M.S., 1987 and 1988).

2. See Hugh W. Nibley, *Since Cumorah* (Salt Lake City: Deseret Book and F.A.R.M.S., 1988), 26; Frank Moore Cross, "New Directions in Dead Sea Scroll Research II: Original Biblical Texts Reconstructed from Newly Found Fragments," *Bible Review* (Summer and Fall 1985): 12–35.

3. Thomas Hoffman, "Inspiration, Normativeness, Canonicity, and the Unique Sacred Character of the Bible," *Catholic Biblical Quarterly* 44 (1982): 463.

4. Robert Detweiler, "What Is a Sacred Text?" *Semeia* 31 (1985): 218.

Chapter 11

NEPHI'S BOWS AND ARROWS

1 Nephi 16:23 "I, Nephi, did make out of wood a bow, and out of a straight stick, an arrow."

Most readers of the Book of Mormon remember vividly the story in 1 Nephi 16 of the slack and broken bows. The account is interesting and well told. Imbedded in this memorable narrative are several long-overlooked points that only now drive home the fact that Nephi's account is right on target.

The symbolic message of the broken bow, first detected by Alan Goff, was highlighted in the March 1984 issue of the F.A.R.M.S. newsletter: "Bows were symbols of political power. One thinks of Odysseus bending the bow to prove himself. An overlord would break the bow of a disobedient vassal to symbolically put the rebel in his place" (see also Jeremiah 49:35; 51:56).[1] That detail is significant in 1 Nephi 16. Nephi's bow broke, and the bows of Laman and Lemuel lost their springs, but when Nephi fashioned a new bow, making him the only one in camp with a bow, his brothers soon accused Nephi of having political ambitions (see 1 Nephi 16:37–38).

Once this point was detected, a further authentic detail about this particular account was soon noticed. It has to do with Nephi's arrows. Three times in his record, Nephi mentioned that he had broken his bow, but not once did he say that any of his arrows were damaged. Yet in 1 Nephi 16:23, Nephi says that he "did make out of wood a bow, and out of a straight stick, an arrow." Why would he need to make a new arrow if his old ones were still intact?

David S. Fox, in a letter to F.A.R.M.S., suggests an answer:

"An examination of Nephi's account shows that whoever wrote that account was familiar in some detail with the field of archery." Consider what happens to an arrow at the instant the string is released: the full force of the drawn string is applied to the end of the arrow, trying to accelerate it, but also tending to bend or buckle the arrow. If the bow's draw weight and the arrow's stiffness are not perfectly matched, the arrow will stray off the intended course or fall short of the mark. An arrow that is too flexible will leave the bow with a vibration that can cause the arrow to behave erratically. On the other hand, an arrow that is too stiff is probably too heavy for the bow.

Nephi's steel bow likely used heavier, stiffer arrows than his simply fashioned wooden bow could handle. Nephi was physically large (see 1 Nephi 2:16; 4:31), and he would have had little reason to use a bow made from metal if he did not have considerable strength. The arrows to match the steel bow used by such a man would undoubtedly have been quite heavy in order for them to be of adequate stiffness. One experienced archer reports, "The arrows from the steel bow when shot from the wooden bow would be like shooting telephone poles." Hence, it is accurate that Nephi should mention, in one and the same breath, the fact that he made an arrow as well as a bow. Bow wood and arrow wood from the same tree or area could be matched as well.

One doubts that such information was known to Joseph Smith or to many, if any, of his contemporaries. Archery, as a means of self-defense or as a serious method of hunting or warfare, went out of vogue among Europeans many years before the time of Joseph Smith. On the other hand, archery as a sport did not emerge until the latter half of the nineteenth century.

David Fox concludes: "Nephi's statement that he made an arrow out of a straight stick is an additional subtle but significant example of internal consistency within the Book of Mormon. Anyone unfamiliar with the field of archery would have almost certainly omitted such a statement." Another bull's-eye for the Book of Mormon.

The publication of this Update in July 1984 has continued to spark interest. Most recently, William Hamblin has written at length on "The Bow and Arrow in the Book of Mormon," in Stephen Ricks and William Hamblin, eds., Warfare in the Book of Mormon *(Salt Lake City: Deseret Book and F.A.R.M.S., 1990), 365–99. Hamblin concludes that the length of Nephi's old arrows may have been another, perhaps even bigger, problem than their weight or stiffness.*

Note

1. This newsletter article announced the reprint of Nahum Waldman, "The Breaking of the Bow," *Jewish Quarterly Review* 69 (October 1978): 82–88, which was introduced by Alan Goff and John W. Welch and entitled "The Breaking of the Bow" (F.A.R.M.S. reprint, 1984).

Chapter 12

LODESTONE AND THE LIAHONA

1 Nephi 16:28 "I, Nephi, beheld the pointers which were in the ball."

Why was Laman apparently of the opinion that his younger brother Nephi had made the Liahona? Nephi and Alma expressed the view that the Liahona was "prepared . . . by the hand of the Lord" (1 Nephi 18:12; 2 Nephi 5:12; Alma 37:38–39). However, shortly after the appearance of the Liahona at the door of Lehi's tent, Laman began complaining that Nephi "worketh many things by his cunning arts, that he may deceive our eyes, thinking, perhaps, that he may lead us away into some strange wilderness" (1 Nephi 16:38). After all, whenever fine workmanship and metallurgy had to be done, Nephi was the one who did it (1 Nephi 17:10–11, 16; 19:1; 2 Nephi 5:15–16). What does the study of ancient metallurgy tell us about the setting of Laman and Lemuel's point of view that Nephi made the Liahona?

According to the Book of Mormon, the word Liahona meant specifically "compass" (Alma 37:38), though it was also called a "ball" or "director"—based apparently upon its round form and its guiding function on both land and sea (1 Nephi 16:10, 16; 18:21; Mosiah 1:16; Alma 37:45). While the Book of Mormon does not tell us whether the Liahona functioned partly on geomagnetic principles, Nephi did say that it contained two spindles, one of which functioned as a directional pointer, and that the body was made of "fine brass" (1 Nephi 16:10, 28). Brass is an excellent noncorroding and nonmagnetic case for a compass. Those who are familiar with modern compasses might naturally ask whether the Liahona worked on a similar principle, with a magnetic function for one spindle, and a possible azimuth setting for the other. Perhaps part of Laman's skepticism was based on some familiarity with just such a technology.

But what sort of "cunning artifice" did Laman imagine Nephi employed in order to transmit divine messages to the surface of the ball-shaped Liahona (1 Nephi 16:26–29)? Moreover, as Laman and Lemuel later learned to their dismay, the Liahona functioned or failed based directly upon the faith, heed, and diligence given to it and to the Lord (1 Nephi 16:28–29; Mosiah 1:16; Alma 37:40–41, 44–45), all of which is very reminiscent of the mode in which the Nephite interpreters-directors-Urim and Thummim functioned best (Mosiah 8:13; Alma 37:23; D&C 9:7–9; 10:1–5; Joseph Smith—History 1:35).

Although we do not know specifically what Laman had in mind, it is worth noting that the function of magnetic hematite was well understood in both the Old and New Worlds before Lehi left Jerusalem. Magnetite, or *lodestone,* is, of course, naturally magnetic iron (Fe_3O_4), and the word *magnetite* comes from the name of a place in which it was mined in Asia Minor by at least the seventh century B.C., namely Magnesia.[1] Parenthetically, Professor Michael Coe of Yale University, a top authority on ancient Mesoamerica, has suggested that the Olmecs of Veracruz, Mexico, were using magnetite compasses already in the second millennium B.C. This is based on Coe's discovery during excavations at San Lorenzo-Tenochtitlán of a magnetite "pointer" which appeared to have been "machined," and which Coe placed on a cork mat in a bowl of water in a successful test of its function as a true floater-compass.[2] The Olmecs (Jaredites?) of San Lorenzo and their relatives in the Oaxaca Valley were utilizing natural iron ore outcroppings by the Early Formative period (c. 1475–1125 B.C.), and at the end of the San Lorenzo phase and in the Nacaste phase (c. 1200–840 B.C.). Mirrors and other items were also fashioned from this native magnetite (and ilmenite).[3]

Whatever the nature of the Liahona, it is intriguing to note that certain properties of compasses might have been familiar to those who were blessed with its guiding functions, and that those who were skeptical of Nephi and the Liahona might have logically turned to those characteristics in seeking to find a plausible rationalization.[4]

This Update was based on research by Robert F. Smith, March 1984. Nephi's great familiarity with metals was also explored by John A. Tvedtnes, in his paper "Was Lehi a Caravaneer?" (Provo: F.A.R.M.S., 1984), which argues against the suggestion made long ago by Hugh Nibley that Lehi was a merchant and presents evidence instead for the idea that Lehi was a skilled metallurgist and craftsman.

Notes

1. Thales of Miletus is the first known to have mentioned its strange properties, c. 600 B.C.

2. J. B. Carlson, "Lodestone Compass: Chinese or Olmec Primacy?" *Science* 189 (September 5, 1975): 753–60; R. H. Fuson, "The Orientation of Mayan Ceremonial Centers," *Annals of the Association of American Geographers* 59 (September 1969): 508–10; E. C. Baity, "Archaeoastronomy and Ethnoastronomy So Far," *Current Anthropology* 14 (October 1973): 443.

3. Kent V. Flannery and J. Schoenwetter, "Climate and Man in Formative Oaxaca," *Archeology* 23 (April 1970): 149; see also Kent Flannery, ed., *The Early Mesoamerican Village* (New York: Academic Press, 1976), 318.

4. For views of the Liahona that consider its possible nonmagnetic functions, see Hugh Nibley, "The Liahona's Cousins," reprinted in *Since Cumorah,* in *The Collected Works of Hugh Nibley* (Salt Lake City: Deseret Book and F.A.R.M.S., 1988), 7:251–63; and Gordon C. Thomasson, "Mosiah: The Complex Symbolism and the Symbolic Complex of Kingship in the Book of Mormon" (Provo: F.A.R.M.S., 1982).

Chapter 13

LEHI'S TRAIL AND NAHOM REVISITED

1 Nephi 16:34 "Ishmael died, and was buried in the place which was called Nahom."

Going well beyond what one could safely say about the Arabian peninsula in 1829, Joseph Smith's translation of the Book of Mormon included several details about Lehi's route through the desert. The text mentions a place "which was called Nahom," and it makes the astonishing claim that somewhere along the southern coast of Arabia, one can find a fruitful and bounteous haven with trees, garden spots, and honey. Such claims can now be checked better than ever before.

In 1976, Lynn M. and Hope Hilton traveled through Arabia and published an illustrated report in which they proposed that the place called Nahom, where Ishmael died and was buried, was around Al Kunfidah near the Red Sea coast of Saudi Arabia.[1] Ross T. Christensen soon suggested an alternative location for Nahom, based upon a map of Yemen prepared as a result of a 1762–64 exploration by Carsten Niebuhr for Danish King Frederick V.[2] To investigate these competing claims, Warren P. and Michaela J. Aston of Australia visited Yemen in November 1984, searching for additional evidence concerning Nahom and the route taken by Lehi and his party.

The Astons located a 1976 map at the University of Sana'a in the Yemen Arab Republic that showed "Nehem" located some thirty-five miles northeast of Sana'a (further south than the site proposed by the Hiltons). This appeared to be the same region Niebuhr listed as "Nehm." Moreover, the Nahm or Naham tribe has existed in the area since at least the tenth century A.D. If further work supports their tentative findings associating "Nehem" with the Book of Mormon "Nahom," several details of Lehi's route will need to be reassessed. In particular, the identification of the land Bountiful on the southern coast of the Arabian peninsula, from which the group set sail for the New World, probably needs to be moved westward from Salalah, the site proposed by the Hiltons (which also happens to keep it in the proper relationship "nearly eastward" [1 Nephi 17:1] with Nahom).

There are two Semitic language roots suggested by the Book of Mormon Nahom: *nhm* and *nḥm*. Either or both may stand behind the name Nahom in 1 Nephi 16. In 1950, Hugh Nibley noted that the name Nahom must come from a Semitic language root signifying lamenting and grieving (in Arabic as *naḥama*, "sigh, groan, moan, especially with another").[3] In Hebrew, the root *nḥm* is often used for "mourning" someone else's death or "consoling" the bereaved (Genesis 37:35; 38:12; 50:21; 2 Samuel 10:2–3; Isaiah 22:4; 51:19; Jeremiah 16:7).[4] Since the Astons found that a large zone of ancient tombs extends over many miles within the region of Nehem in Yemen, this could indicate the longtime use of this area as a burial ground, possibly making a name signifying "grieving" highly appropriate, if only as a play on similar roots.

The name of the area in Yemen now mapped as "Nehem" is pronounced by local inhabitants Nä-hum, derived from the Arabic root *nhm*, whose basic meaning is "growl, groan, roar; suffer from hunger; complain." The same root is found in biblical Hebrew (see Isaiah 5:29–30; Hosea 2:23) and in ancient Egyptian (*nhm*, "thunder, shout"; *nhmhm*, "roar, thunder"). Thus a ritual concomitant of mourning (groaning) is also associated with this root, as well as the sense of suffering from hunger, which is equally apt in the context of 1 Nephi 16:35, which reports much complaining, suffering, and hunger.

The Astons further found that current scholars plot out a more complicated trail system for the frankincense trade than was thought a decade ago. Those trails came farther south along the Red Sea coast before branching off eastward than the Hiltons' sources showed. And instead of there being only a single area, Dhofar (Zufar), producing frankincense, it now appears that an area some five hundred miles long along the south coast of the Arabian peninsula produced this precious substance.[5] It was shipped from the eastern areas (including the Salalah area favored by the Hiltons for Bountiful) in coastal vessels to Qana, thence northward along the trail toward the consuming centers in the Near East. These facts make it less likely than had appeared that Lehi's party would have reached the sea as far east as Salalah.

Instead, Lehi's group may have ended its desert journey between Salalah and the coastal Hadramawt area of modern South Yemen. In that region, William Hamblin has found pre-Islamic traditions about a prophet named Hud, whose tomb is located near the border between Oman and South Yemen.[6] Like Lehi, Hud reputedly prophesied against certain idol worshippers who were "renowned for their elaborate buildings" (compare 1 Nephi 8:26), was rejected because of the pride of the people (compare 1 Nephi 8:27), but escaped while the wicked were destroyed.[7] While probably not closely connected, Lehi and Hud seem to have been kindred spirits.

For centuries, the sands have blown across Lehi's trail. Perhaps additional clues yet remain about where Lehi's group might have traveled.

After the time of this Update in September 1986, which was based on research by Warren P. and Michaela J. Aston, Stephen D. Ricks, and John W. Welch, the Astons made other trips to south Arabia, traveling also into Oman. The most recent versions of their regularly updated and enhanced reports, "The Search for Nahom and the End of Lehi's Trail," "The Place Which Was Called Nahom," and "And We Called the Place Bountiful—The End of Lehi's Arabian Journey," can be ordered from F.A.R.M.S.

In particular, the Astons' examination of the central stretch of the south coast of the Arabian peninsula has produced exciting new results. A previously unexplored fertile valley called Wadi Sayq, tucked away on the south Arabian coast, seems the most likely candidate for the place of Lehi's Bountiful.

Notes

1. Lynn M. and Hope Hilton, *In Search of Lehi's Trail* (Salt Lake City: Deseret Book, 1976), 94; also published in *Ensign* 6 (September 1976): 33–54 and (October 1976): 34–63.

2. Ross T. Christensen, "Comment: The Place Called Nahom," *Ensign* 8 (August 1978): 73.

3. Hugh Nibley, "Lehi in the Desert," *Improvement Era* 53 (June 1950): 517. See *Lehi in the Desert and the World of the Jaredites* (Salt Lake City: Bookcraft, 1952), 90–91; in *The Collected Works of Hugh Nibley* (Salt Lake City: Deseret Book and F.A.R.M.S., 1988), 5:79.

4. See H. Van Dyke Parunak, "A Semantic Survey of *NḤM*," *Biblica* 56 (1975): 512–32, who compares Ugaritic *nḥm* "console."

5. Nigel Groom, *Frankincense and Myrrh: A Study of the Arabian Incense Trade* (London: Longman Group, 1981). See also Thomas J. Abercrombie, "Arabia's Frankincense Trail," *National Geographic* 168 (October 1985): 474–512.

6. William Hamblin, "Pre-Islamic Arabian Prophets," in Spencer Palmer, ed., *Mormons and Muslims* (Provo: BYU Religious Studies Center, 1983), 87–89.

7. See Qur'an 7:65–72; 11:50–60; 26:123–40.

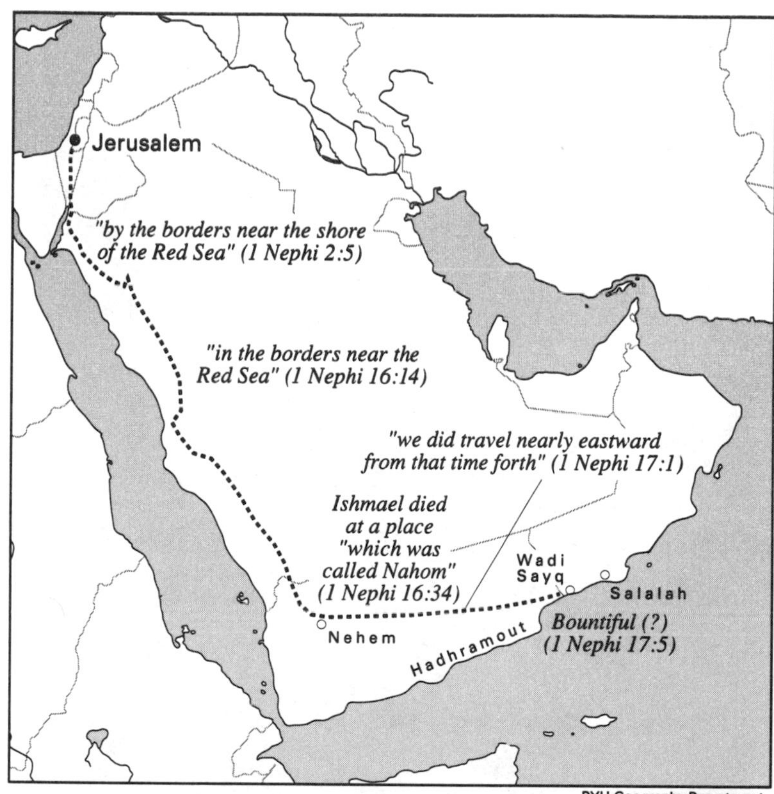

This map shows the probable route of Lehi from Jerusalem to the place he called Bountiful. His path followed the general route of the ancient frankincense trails, which pass through an area known for centuries as Nehem. Wadi Sayq, a verdant valley on the sea coast, has been explored only recently by Warren Aston. From The Encyclopedia of Mormonism, *courtesy Macmillan Publishing Company.*

The Wadi Sayq, on the southern coast of the Arabian peninsula. No Westerners in the 1820s knew that this pocket of vegetation existed, possibly the area where Lehi's group camped, built a ship, and set sail. Courtesy of Warren and Michaela Aston.

Chapter 14

WINDS AND CURRENTS: A LOOK AT NEPHI'S OCEAN CROSSING

1 Nephi 18:23 "We had sailed for the space of many days."

The Book of Mormon provides only fragmentary information about the voyage of Lehi's party from Arabia to America. But external sources help us grasp what might have been involved. If one were to sail from the southern coast of Arabia across the Indian Ocean and then across the Pacific to Central America (which seems to have been Lehi's most likely route), what combination of winds, currents, times, and distances would make the voyage feasible under the normally prevailing conditions?

From Arabia to Indonesia: Navigation on the Indian Ocean remained in many ways the same from very early times until the development of steamships.[1] Sailing there has always depended upon the monsoons. The word *monsoon* is from the Arabic *mawsim,* which literally means "the date for sailing from one port in order to reach another." According to Tibbetts, the end of March or beginning of April was the best time to head east from the south Arabian coast; if delayed too long after that, a ship would encounter huge, dangerous swells as it neared the west coast of India.[2]

The route would have gone essentially straight east at about fifteen degrees north latitude to the Indian coast, then south around Ceylon in time for the southwest monsoon, first felt in May in the Bay of Bengal. Sumatra would have been reached no later than September. The great storm noted in 1 Nephi 18:13–14 could have been either a cyclonic storm or a typhoon, which are violent in the Bay of Bengal. The "great calm" in 1 Nephi 18:21 may have been a doldrum. If Nephi's vessel continued through the Java and Flores Seas of modern Indonesia, the westerly winds from December to March could have taken it past those areas within the first year of the trip. This route is most likely, although there are other possibilities.

Since boats routinely had to be beached for repairs after storms, or to have their bottoms scraped, or to await favorable winds, it is reasonable to assume that Lehi's party would have stopped from time to time on their journey through these islands. The closeness of major islands and historical records of other voyaging in the area suggest further that travelling from Java to the Admiralty Islands off the north coast of New Guinea would not have been especially difficult.

Across the Pacific: Professor Ben Finney, an authority at the University of Hawaii on Pacific Island voyaging, has recently pointed out how early voyagers could have moved from Melanesia out into the broad Pacific to the east.[3] Until recently, he notes, scholars have been puzzled about easterly travel by Polynesians across the Pacific, since the normal trade winds would appear to have posed an almost insurmountable barrier to easterly movement. Finney reports that new information about the meteorological phenomenon known on the west coast of South America as El Niño now changes the picture.

When El Niño conditions prevail, warm surface water from the equatorial zone moves south down the coast of South America, upsetting many normal conditions.[4] It is now known that the trouble begins with a slackening of the normal trade winds. This causes a strong easterly flow of water from the western Pacific all the way to South America. That is accompanied by unusual westerly winds in place of the trades. Under these conditions, travel from Melanesia to South America is quite feasible. Finney proposes that the makers of Lapita pottery sailed out of Melanesia on such westerlies, reaching western Polynesia before

1000 B.C. Their descendants would have used the same winds to move, perhaps all the way to the Marquesas Islands from Tonga. Finney further suggests that the same winds might bear a vessel virtually to the Americas. Depending on conditions, the winds could then take a vessel either to South or Central America.[5] It seems likely that these spells of westerlies have occurred every seven to sixteen years throughout the past. Other combinations of winds and routes eastward are also possible, as Finney notes.

How long might Nephi's voyage have taken? From Tonga to the Marquesas is about 30 percent of the distance from the Bismarck Archipelago to Central America. Finney figures it could have taken about thirty days to sail this distance under El Niño conditions. Thus, the whole Pacific distance might be four or five times that, or, in other words, a little less than half a year; the entire journey from Arabia to Central America might have taken from one to two years, depending on the route and time allowed to stop for food, water, and repairs.

Of course, Nephi could not have explicitly planned such a voyage. He indicates that his group was guided by God through the Liahona (see 1 Nephi 18:12, 21–22). Divine knowledge of wind and sea conditions, within the range we now know to have existed, could indeed have permitted the successful crossing of two oceans – more than halfway around the earth – in a plausible period of time.

This Update was based on research by John L. Sorenson, April 1986. For further reflection on other aspects of Lehi's voyage, see Sorenson's "Transoceanic Crossings," in Monte Nyman and Charles Tate, eds., First Nephi *(Provo: Religious Studies Center, 1988), 251–70. A monumental reference work documenting and annotating hundreds of proposed or possible transoceanic connections between the Old and the New Worlds is John L. Sorenson and Martin H. Raish,* Pre-Columbian Contact with the Americas across the Oceans *(Provo: Research Press, 1990).*

Notes

1. See George Hourani, *Arab Seafaring in the Indian Ocean in Ancient and Early Medieval Times* (Princeton: Princeton University Press, 1951); G. R. Tibbetts, *Arab*

Navigation in the Indian Ocean before the Coming of the Portuguese, Oriental Translation Fund, new series, vol. 42 (London: Royal Asiatic Society, 1981), xi–50; Pliny the Elder, *Natural History* VI, 26, 101–6. Tim Severin, "In the Wake of Sindbad," *National Geographic* 162 (July 1982): 2–40, reports a modern reenactment of such a voyage.

2. Tibbetts, *Arab Navigation,* 360–71.

3. Ben Finney, "Anomalous Westerlies, El Niño, and the Colonization of Polynesia," *American Anthropologist* 87 (1985): 9–26.

4. For coverage of the most powerful El Niño on record, that in the winter of 1982–83, see Thomas Y. Canby, "El Niño's Ill Wind," *National Geographic* 165 (February 1984): 144–83.

5. See the chart in Finney, "Anomalous Westerlies," 13.

Chapter 15

DID LEHI LAND IN CHILE?

1 Nephi 18:23 "We did arrive at the promised land."

From the earliest days of the Church, the site of Lehi's landing in the New World has been a topic of discussion. Much of the debate has centered around the origin of a statement written by Frederick G. Williams, stating that Lehi "landed on the continent of South America in Chile thirty degrees south Lattitude."[1] This idea was so popular during the nineteenth century that Orson Pratt included it in his notes to the 1879 edition of the Book of Mormon and in several other publications. Where did this idea come from? A recent comprehensive examination of the original documents yields some new answers.

Franklin D. Richards, it seems, was the first author to attribute the specific Williams statement to Joseph Smith and to revelation. In 1882, Richards published a statement nearly identical to the wording of Williams's handwritten copy, adding the title "Lehi's Travels—Revelation to Joseph the Seer."

There is no solid historical evidence, however, attributing this statement to Joseph, let alone to revelation, and the assumption that such information was received by revelation is inconsistent with other evidence. An editorial in *Times and Seasons* gives another landing site for Lehi's party: "Lehi . . . landed a little south of the Isthmus of Darien,"[2] or modern Panama. If Joseph had received a revelation concerning Lehi's landing only a few years earlier (or if he knew of someone else's receiving such a revelation), it is unlikely that he would have allowed this contradictory statement to be published. Given the variety and sparsity of statements about Book of Mormon geography during Joseph's lifetime, it seems that, at least in his mind, the location of Lehi's landing remained indefinite.

The Williams handwritten document is the prime source of information about its own origin. His statement about Lehi's travels is found at the bottom of that sheet. The three items above it are separated by lines drawn across the page. Together, they give a possible context to the statement about Lehi's travels. The first item on the sheet, known today as Doctrine and Covenants 7, is a revelation given to Joseph Smith and Oliver Cowdery regarding John the Beloved. It was received in 1829 and published in 1833. The second item is entitled "Questions in English, Answers in Hebrew." It quotes from Jacob 5:13 ("For it grieveth me that I should loose [sic] this tree and the fruit thereof") and 7:27 ("Brethren, I bid you adieu"), and then below each statement gives "An[swers]," translating the English into rough Hebrew. The third item, headed "characters on the book of Mormon" and "the interpretion of Languages," gives two characters under each. The statement about Lehi's travels is then the fourth item on the sheet.

It appears likely that these statements were part of what was being studied at the School of the Prophets in Kirtland, since the first three deal with translation. This idea is corroborated by another known document, virtually identical to the second and third items on the Williams paper, with the signature "written and kept for profit and learning—by Oliver." The Cowdery paper, like the Williams document, appears to contain notes, written only for "profit and learning" as these men studied together in the School of the Prophets, sometimes held in the Kirtland Temple.

On the back of the Williams paper are other characters and a statement written by Ezra G. Williams, Frederick's son. It reads: "G. S. L. City, April 11, 1864. This paper is in the hand writing of my father, Fred G. Williams. The *characters* thereon *I believe* to be a representation of those shown to him at the dedication of the Kirtland Temple." This statement discloses several important facts: (1) While Ezra knows that the page is in his father's handwriting, (2) he only believes the characters had something to do with the dedication of the Kirtland Temple. (3) Nothing ties Ezra's statement on the back to any of the four items on the front (indeed, it makes no sense to link Doctrine and Covenants 7 from 1829 to the dedication of the Kirtland Temple in 1836). Furthermore, Ezra does not attribute the statement about Lehi's travels (4) to Joseph or (5) to revelation.

It is easy to understand, however, how the context of the statement on Lehi's travels could have been misunderstood. The error can possibly be traced innocently to the partial copy, made in 1845, of Joseph Smith's inspired translation of the Bible. John M. Bernhisel wrote the same statement on the last sheet of his copy, preceded by several blank pages. The isolated statement is given no context, heading, or comment, and it is not attributed to Joseph or anyone else. The mere fact that it was copied at the back of the Joseph Smith Translation, however, may have led people to assume that the Lehi statement was also an inspired statement by Joseph Smith. Bernhisel's source, however, appears to be the Williams document, since Bernhisel's copy has the identical wording and nearly the same spelling, capitalization, and punctuation as the Williams copy, with both misspelling the word "lattitude."

As early as 1909, B. H. Roberts doubted that the statement about Lehi's travels came from Joseph Smith. Even before that, George Q. Cannon, First Counselor in the First Presidency, issued a statement in the *Juvenile Instructor* urging students of Book of Mormon geography to avoid contention and confusion, and to exercise caution in "drawing all the information possible from the record which has been translated for our benefit."[3] If we had certain knowledge from a revelation of Book of Mormon geography, including Lehi's landing site, there would be neither speculation nor the need for such a caution. As it is, there is both.

This July 1988 Update, based on recent research by Frederick G. Williams

III was followed by an extensive treatment of this topic by Williams, edited by John W. Welch and John L. Sorenson, entitled "Did Lehi Land in Chile? An Assessment of the Frederick G. Williams Statement" (Provo: F.A.R.M.S., 1988). Further information may also be found in John L. Sorenson, "The Geography of Book of Mormon Events: A Source Book" (Provo: F.A.R.M.S., 1990).

Notes

1. For full documentation, see Frederick G. Williams III, "Did Lehi Land in Chile? An Assessment of the Frederick G. Williams Statement" (Provo: F.A.R.M.S., 1988).

2. *Times and Seasons* 3 (15 September 1842): 922.

3. George Q. Cannon, "The Book of Mormon Geography," *Juvenile Instructor* 25 (January 1, 1890): 19.

Notes from the School of the Prophets in Kirtland, Ohio. At the bottom is the statement by Frederick G. Williams. Courtesy of the Church Historical Department.

A revelation concerning John the beloved disciple

And the Lord said unto me John my beloved what desirest thou

And I said Lord give unto me power that I may bring souls

unto thee, and the Lord said unto me verily I say unto thee because

thou desirest this thou shalt tarry till I come in my glory

and for this cause the Lord said unto Peter if I will that he

tarry till I come what is that to thee for he desirest of me

that he might bring souls unto me, but thou desirest

that thou might speedily come unto me in my kingdom

I say unto thee Peter this was a good desire But my beloved

hath undertaken a greater work, verily I say unto you ye

shall both have according to your desires for ye hath joy in that

which ye have desired &c. &c. &c. — — — — — —

Question asked in English & answered in hebrew

For it grieveth me that I should lose this tree & the fruit thereof

Ans. Ofan Zimim ezmon E, Zer ones ifs veris etzer ensvonis

veneris — — — — — — — — — — — —

English Brethren I bid you adieu

Ans. Ifs E Zamtri

Characters on the book of Mormon

The book of Mormon — The interpreters of languages

L. CP — Onn — Cr.

The course that Lehi travelled from the city of

Jerusalem to the place where he and his family took

ship, they traveled nearly a south south east direction

untill they come to the nineteenth degree of North

Latitude, then nearly east to the sea of Arabia

then sailed in a south east direction and landed

on the continent of South America in Chile thirty

degrees south Latitude

Chapter 16

STATUTES, JUDGMENTS, ORDINANCES, AND COMMANDMENTS

2 Nephi 5:10 "And we did observe to keep the judgments, and the statutes, and the commandments of the Lord in all things, according to the law of Moses."

In 2 Nephi 5:10, Nephi records that his people were strict to observe "the judgments, and the statutes, and the commandments of the Lord in all things, according to the law of Moses." Why did he use so many words to convey what seems to us the simple idea that they kept the law?

Part of the answer comes from Hebrew, which uses several words to express different semantic aspects and subtle nuances of our word "law."[1] Those words may match the Book of Mormon usage of comparable English terms.

Torah. In Hebrew, the "law of Moses" is always the "*torah*" of Moses. It means more than "law" in any modern sense. *Torah* derives from the verb *yarah,* whose many meanings include "to show, to instruct, to teach." The *torah* thus embodies all God's instructions given to his people, implemented and taught through his priests. Only a rebellious people would fail to listen to the *torah* of the Lord (see Isaiah 30:9).

These ideas fit the frequently mentioned priestly function of "teaching" in the Book of Mormon (see, e.g., Jacob 1:17–19; Jarom 1:11; Mosiah 6:3; 12:25; Alma 8:24; Moroni 3:3). Isaiah's message also fits Benjamin's warning that anyone who transgressed "the law [*torah?*] of God contrary to his own knowledge, . . . the same cometh out in open rebellion against God" (Mosiah 2:33, 37).

Mishpat. Usually translated "judgment," this word not only means "to pronounce a verdict," but it also embraced most phases of a trial. It usually has something to do with the rules of governing properly. For example, the laws in Exodus 21–23 are called the *mishpatim*, giving standards of behavior required by God.

Likewise, in the Book of Mormon, when the term *judgments* appears by itself, it is in the context of judges who "judge righteous judgments" (Mosiah 29:29, 43), or it refers to the outcome of a court procedure (Alma 30:57), or to God's judgments upon his people.

Ḥuqqah and *ḥoq*. In this pair, the first is feminine, the second is masculine. Both, though, have substantially the same meanings, basically "custom, manner, decree, portion, order, prescription, limit, etc." Often these words are translated interchangeably as "statute" and "ordinance," but their meanings are very broad. Thus, when the word *ordinance* is used to translate these terms from an ancient text, we should understand that it includes more than priesthood ordinances. What is covered is a wide range of cultural rules.

Indeed, when the Book of Mormon speaks of ordinances in an outward sense, it generally seems to add the term *performances* (see 2 Nephi 25:30; Mosiah 13:30). Those words describe the kind of "outward performances" (Alma 25:15) that became unnecessary after the atonement of Christ (see 4 Nephi 1:12), not the idea of law or orderly conduct in general.

Mitzvah. This broad term has no technical meaning and is usually translated "commandment" or "precept." It is found frequently in Deuteronomy to signify divine commandments in general. Similarly, the use of the word *commandments* is broad and extensive in the Book of Mormon (see, e.g., 1 Nephi 3:7; Jacob 1:2).

Edut. Less common is this word, meaning "testimony, witness, or monument." Especially in the early biblical period, the law was thought of as a testimony or witness that God had established. The book of the "law" (*edut,* Deuteronomy 31:26) witnessed that God had established his law, by which mankind will be judged (see Psalms 78:5).

In the Book of Mormon, similar ideas are found, for example, in Benjamin's farewell speech (see Mosiah 3:23–24) and in Moroni's words concluding the monumental Nephite record (see Moroni 10:27).

Another part of the meaning of *edut* was the idea of "law" as in the expression "the book of the law." Besides the oral and ethical instruction of the *torah* and the prophets, law was also the written text (see Joshua 8:31; Exodus 24:3–7), as well as covenantal monuments denoting the covenant (see Joshua 8:32; 23:6; 24:24–26). Thus, the mysterious *edut* given to the king at his coronation may have been a copy of the law (see 2 Kings 11:12; also Deuteronomy 17:18; Mosiah 1:15–16). Lehi and his family risked much to obtain a copy of the written law, for in a literal sense one is without the "law" (*edut*) without a written copy.

These terms for "law" are often used cumulatively in the Hebrew Bible. Modern legal draftsmen sometimes do the same, multiplying words in pleonastic lists to cover all the bases (i.e., "rights, title and interest"). King David exhorted Solomon to keep God's "statutes [*ḥuqqot*], and his commandments [*mitzvot*], and his judgments [*mishpatim*], and his testimonies [*edot*], as it is written in the law [*torah*] of Moses" (1 Kings 2:3). Likewise, the terms *statutes, judgments, commandments,* and *ordinances* often cluster together in the Book of Mormon as in 2 Nephi 5:10 (see also 1 Nephi 17:22; Mosiah 6:6; Alma 8:17; 30:3; 58:40; Helaman 3:20; 15:5).

Interestingly, usage of the two Hebrew words *ḥoq* and *ḥuqqah* may correspond quite precisely with the Book of Mormon "ordinances" and "statutes." Due to the near identity of these Hebrew words, finding them both in the same sentence or pleonastic list would be odd. No Hebrew verse has been found containing both *ḥoq* and *ḥuqqah*. (When "statute" and "ordinance" occur together in the King James translation, the Hebrew word translated as "statute" is either *ḥoq* or *ḥuqqah,* but then the word for "ordinance" is *mishpat.*) Thus, it appears significant that "ordinance" and "statute" never appear as companions in the Book of Mormon. Indeed, they are the only two English equivalents of the Hebrew terms for law that never appear in the Book of Mormon in combination with each other.

Based on research by John W. Welch, June 1988.

Note

1. J. van der Ploeg, "Studies in Hebrew Law: The Terms," *Catholic Biblical Quarterly* 12 (1950): 248–59.

Chapter 17

KINGSHIP AND TEMPLE IN 2 NEPHI 5–10

2 Nephi 5:16 "And I, Nephi, did build a temple."

Several studies have recently demonstrated that kings and temples were closely connected in antiquity. Building (or renovating) a temple was an integral part in the legal formation of states and societies in the ancient Near East.[1]

Becoming a king, issuing laws or judgments, and performing many other acts of legal consequence in the ancient world were virtually unthinkable without a temple in which such acts could be solemnized in the presence of a god. A new king would announce interim legislation establishing himself as a king of justice (as in 2 Nephi 5:10), but as soon as possible in the first decade of his rule, "the king builds, renovates, or rededicates the main temple of his city, at which time the fuller version of the laws is decreed and elaborated into a stele by royal scribes."[2]

Temples were similarly prominent in the royal and legal landscapes of Nephite civilization. This invites the observation that Nephi's construction of a temple in the city of Nephi directly paved the way for him, two verses later, to become king (see 2 Nephi 5:16–18). Similarly, Mosiah II's coronation in the city of Zarahemla (see Mosiah 1:9–6:3) and Jesus' giving of the new law in Bountiful (see 3 Nephi 11–18) both took place at temples.

On such occasions in antiquity new kings would typically (1) cite their divine calling, (2) issue new laws, (3) ordain officers, (4) erect monuments, and (5) enter into a new legal order by way of covenant with a ritually prepared community.[3] Similar elements were present on several occasions in the Book of Mormon. Consider Nephi's account of the beginning of his reign:

1. Nephi established his legitimacy as ruler and teacher by citing the earlier promise given to him by the Lord that God had chosen him to be a ruler (see 2 Nephi 5:19; quoting 1 Nephi 2:22).

2. A new law was then issued that no Nephite should intermarry with the Lamanites. The penalty for anyone who might break this law was affliction with a curse (see 2 Nephi 5:23). This New World prohibition compares to the similar law given to the Israelites at the time of their conquest in the Old World: it prohibited them from intermarrying with the Canaanites (see Deuteronomy 7:3–4).

3. Nephi consecrated Jacob and Joseph to be priests and teachers (see 2 Nephi 5:26). An essential part of the accession of each new ruler was the installation (or reappointment) of priests and administrators to rule under the new king (see also Mosiah 6:3; 3 Nephi 11:21–22).

4. God next instructed Nephi to make a new set of plates (see 2 Nephi 5:30). The sequence of events here suggests that the Small Plates of Nephi were made in connection with the coronation of Nephi. Accordingly, they served as the "tablets of the law," or the pillar or *stele* that were traditionally set up as a monument to the creation of the new king's order. Nephi wrote on these plates things that were "good in [God's] sight, for the profit of [his] people" (2 Nephi 5:30). In addition to the religious purposes that these plates primarily served, they also acted as a founding constitutional and political document, as has been discussed by Noel Reynolds.[4]

5. Finally, the new legal order was traditionally submitted by way of covenant to a "ritually prepared community."[5] Significantly, Jacob's ensuing speech is a covenant speech: "I have read these things that ye might know concerning the covenants of the Lord" (2 Nephi 9:1). Jacob's purpose was to purify the people, to shake his garments of all iniquities and have his people turn away from sin (see 2 Nephi 9:44–45), to motivate them to act for themselves—"to choose the way of everlasting death or the way of eternal life" (2 Nephi 10:23). His words compare

closely with the covenant text of Joshua 24, where the Israelites were given the same choice as they established their new religious and social order under Joshua.

As Lundquist asserts, covenant ceremonies at temples were essential to the successful creation of ancient states. For a charismatic figure to merely become king did not assure or perpetuate the state. Without inward commitments and outward symbols of the temple, Nephi's little community looked like a mere splinter group, lacking divine and social sanction. With these observances, however, they laid an enduring foundation for the reign of Nephite kings for over four hundred years to come.

Based on research by John M. Lundquist and John W. Welch, November 1991.

Notes

1. See John M. Lundquist, "Temple, Covenant, and Law in the Ancient Near East and in the Old Testament," in A. Gileadi, ed., *Israel's Apostasy and Restoration* (Grand Rapids, Michigan: Baker Book House, 1988), 293–305.

2. Ibid., 296.

3. Ibid., 296–303.

4. Noel Reynolds, "The Political Dimension in Nephi's Small Plates," *BYU Studies* 27 (Fall 1987): 15–37.

5. Lundquist, "Temple, Covenant, and Law," 300.

Chapter 18

JACOB'S TEN COMMANDMENTS

2 Nephi 9:27 "But wo unto him."

In a lecture delivered at Brigham Young University in 1985, Professor William M. Brinner of the University of California at Berkeley analyzed two passages in the Qur'an that seem to contain Islamic versions of the "Ten Commandments." These are not copies of the biblical Decalogue, Brinner argued, although there are some resemblances that have led others to belittle the Qur'an as a poor copy of the Bible. Each religion, Brinner suggested, has its own summary of its most cherished principles, stated in terms relevant to its own cultural setting.

Similar observations might be made regarding ten statements made by Jacob in 2 Nephi 9:27–38. There Jacob summarizes ten essential principles and rules of Nephite religion. They may be paraphrased as follows:

> 1. Wo unto them who have God's law and commandments, who transgress them because they are learned and think they are wise. They hearken not unto the counsel of God, supposing they know of themselves. Therefore, their wisdom is foolishness, and they shall perish (vv. 27–29).
>
> 2. Wo unto the rich. Because they are rich, they despise the poor. Their treasure is their God, and their treasure shall perish with them (v. 30).
>
> 3. Wo unto the deaf who will not hear, for they shall perish (v. 31).

> 4. Wo unto the blind who will not see, for they shall perish also (v. 32).
>
> 5. Wo unto the uncircumcised of heart, for a knowledge of their iniquities shall smite them at the last day (v. 33).
>
> 6. Wo unto the liar, for he shall be thrust down to hell (v. 34).
>
> 7. Wo unto the murderer who deliberately kills, for he shall die (v. 35).
>
> 8. Wo unto them who commit whoredoms, for they shall be thrust down to hell (v. 36).
>
> 9. Wo unto those who worship idols, for the devil of all devils delights in them (v. 37).
>
> 10. Wo unto all those who die in their sins, for they shall return to God, behold his face, and remain in their sins (v. 38).

Jacob apparently had the Decalogue of Deuteronomy 5 or Exodus 20 in mind when he wrote these words. The prohibitions against worshiping images, committing murder or adultery, and bearing false witness (see Exodus 20:4–6, 13–14, 16) are clearly present in Jacob's sixth through ninth woes. Jacob's summary in these ten "woes" is much more than a thoughtless copy of the biblical ideals. Whereas the Decalogue gave the law, Jacob goes one step further by stressing the consequences of breaking the law. Furthermore, Jacob's principles have been tailored as revelation to his people and to their needs:

The first and second woes are heaped upon those who reject the counsel of God and make riches their God. In these verses Jacob basically reinterprets the first commandment against having any other gods (see Exodus 20:3) and mentions the rewards that will come to those who obey God (see Exodus 20:6).

Setting aside the counsels of God was a particular problem that Jacob had to confront, given the hardness of Laman and Lemuel. A broader problem was the persistence of the Nephites from the beginning to seek riches (see Jacob 2:13, 19–21). His curse upon those who despise the poor is like the third commandment of the Qur'an to give liberally to kinsmen, to the needy, and to travelers, and it may relate to the Israelite command against coveting (see Exodus 20:17).

In Jacob's third and fourth woes, he curses those who will not hear, see, or obey, perhaps intentionally expanding the commandment that one should hear and obey parents.

Lehi's contemporary, Jeremiah, was the one who commanded the Israelites to "circumcise [themselves] to the Lord, and take away the foreskins of [their] heart" (Jeremiah 4:4; see 9:26), a precept Jacob echoed here in his fifth wo.

Jacob expands the sixth prohibition against bearing false witness to include all liars, as in Leviticus and Proverbs (see Leviticus 19:11; Proverbs 6:17, 19). Jacob's wo also parallels the punishment associated in Proverbs with lying: "He that speaketh lies shall perish" (19:9; see 19:5).

Jacob's seventh command prohibits "deliberate" killing, that is, intentional or premeditated murder. Jacob could not likely have commented on the law of homicide without Nephi's slaying of Laban coming to mind. Since Nephi's killing of Laban can be considered unpremeditated and classified with nonculpable slayings under ancient Israelite law,[1] it seems that Jacob intentionally condemned only those who killed deliberately.

Jacob's eighth commandment is against whoredoms, not just the narrower crime of adultery. This reflects Lehi's teachings against whoredoms of any kind (see Jacob 2:33–34).

The ninth wo addresses idolatry, the refusal to hear the word and see the way of the Lord, which had been the downfall of the people in Jerusalem. On the other hand, listening to the Lord's word and following his way had resulted in the salvation of Lehi and his family (see 1 Nephi 1:6).

The threat in the tenth wo, that the unrepentant sinner will behold the face of God, seems to hark back to Moses, whose unrighteous people might have been destroyed if they had seen the face of God (see Exodus 19:21; Deuteronomy 5:4).

Jacob's woes are not formulated as "thou-shalt-not" statements, as in the Ten Commandments, but the "wo-unto" idiom is functionally equivalent to those prohibitions. Compare, for example, the set of twelve "cursed-be-he-that" woes in Deuteronomy 27:15–26, some of which also implement the interdictions of the Ten Commandments.

Thus, a new perspective of 2 Nephi 9:27–38 emerges. Jacob's inspiration formulates a set of principles relevant to his people and their cultural needs and concerns. His "ten woes" function as the equivalent of a contemporaneous Nephite set of ten commandments. His statement is an admirable summary of the basic religious values of the Nephites, cast in a form fully at home in ancient Israel and in the Near East.

Based on research by John W. Welch, March 1985.

Note

1. Exodus 21:12–14, part of the law in effect in Jerusalem at the time of Lehi and Nephi, defines certain slayings as nonculpable acts if (1) the slayer did not lie in wait to ambush or attack the victim and (2) God delivered the victim into his hands. Nephi's account in 1 Nephi 4 purposefully sets forth facts that satisfy these two conditions. For further discussion, see Fred Essig and H. Daniel Fuller, "Nephi's Slaying of Laban: A Legal Perspective" (Provo: F.A.R.M.S., 1982).

Chapter 19

WHAT DID CHARLES ANTHON REALLY SAY?

2 Nephi 27:6 "The Lord God shall bring forth unto you the words of a book."

In 1834, Professor Charles Anthon vehemently denied that he told Martin Harris that the Book of Mormon characters resembled Egyptian. A different story, of course, is found in the Pearl of Great Price (Joseph Smith—History 1:63–65). Who is telling the truth?

According to Martin Harris, Joseph Smith copied some of the Book of Mormon characters and Martin took them to New York. There he met with Charles Anthon, who certified to him that they were correct. Completely reassured, Harris returned to Harmony, told his friends about it, and later mortgaged his property to finance the publication of the Book of Mormon. This is very early concrete evidence that Martin Harris's version of his meeting with Anthon is accurate and that Anthon's later retraction was an attempt to save face, if not an act of downright dishonesty.

Shortly afterwards, in 1831 W. W. Phelps wrote a letter in which he reported that Anthon had translated the Book of Mormon characters and declared them to be "*the ancient shorthand Egyptian.*" This is a most telling clue, for where else, except from Anthon, would Harris and hence Phelps have gotten this precise phrase, the phrase *shorthand Egyptian?* It was not part of Harris's environment or education.[1] Indeed, the phrase is so singular that it appears only this one time in LDS history.

On the other hand, this precise term was known to scholars, Anthon included. In 1824, Champollion had used an equivalent term, "tachygraphie," in his landmark *Précis du système hieroglyphique des anciens Égyptiens* (a copy of which Anthon owned),[2] to describe hieratic Egyptian script. In June 1827, this book was reviewed in the *American Quarterly Review,* calling hieratic Egyptian script "short-hand" Egyptian.[3] Anthon knew this review: He owned a copy and he cited it in his *Classical Dictionary.*[4] Anthon would have read this review only months before Harris's visit.

Thus it becomes highly probable that Phelps indeed heard this peculiar phrase from Harris, who in turn got it from Anthon, the only person involved who was likely to have known it. Anthon probably mentioned shorthand Egyptian because he was struck by certain obvious similarities in the transcript to hieratic or demotic Egyptian. From this, what else can one conclude, except that Harris told the truth about what Anthon said on this point?

Anthon's side of the story breaks down in other ways, as has long been pointed out. For example, on whether he gave Harris a written statement: Anthon's 1834 letter to Eber D. Howe says that he *did not,* while his 1841 letter to T. W. Coit says that he *did*. On how convincing he had been, Anthon's 1834 letter simply says that Harris "took his leave," but his 1841 letter claims that Harris left with the "express declaration" that he would not mortgage his farm or have anything to do with printing the golden book.[5] In fact, in light of Harris's subsequent conduct (which was totally supportive of Joseph Smith and the Book of Mormon), Harris clearly left Anthon fully satisfied.

Moreover, a motive for Anthon's 1834 and 1841 behavior is not hard to find. Protecting his prestigious standing among his peers must have been Anthon's primary concern. It turned out to be a professional liability for Anthon to have been linked with the Mormons and with Smith's notorious "roguery"—as Anthon termed it. In 1868 (some forty years later!), in a *Commemorative Address,* Anthon's successor at Columbia College still spoke about the Harris-Anthon affair and admitted that it was a real threat to Anthon's reputation.

Caught on the horns of a dilemma, and having unwittingly fulfilled the prophecy of Isaiah 29, Anthon took the easy way out: He tore up the statement he had innocently given to Harris and denied Harris's story. Today Anthon's cover-up appears more blatant than ever.[6]

Based on research by Robert F. Smith, Gordon C. Thomasson, and John W. Welch, originally published May 1985 and revised 1990. Although the focus of this research has shifted to the evidence given by W. W. Phelps, now that the Salamander Letter is known to have been a forgery, the likelihood that Anthon was the source of the phrase "reformed Egyptian" or "shorthand Egyptian" remains a strong corroboration of Martin Harris's understanding of Anthon's original intent. For a recent restating of this historical information, see "Martin Harris's Visit with Charles Anthon: Collected Documents on Shorthand Egyptian" (Provo: F.A.R.M.S., 1990).

Notes

1. See Gordon Thomasson, "Daddy, What's a Frontier?" in Book of Mormon Symposium, BYU, Provo, 1970.

2. Jean-François Champollion, *Précis du système hieroglyphique des anciens Égyptiens,* 2 vols. (Paris, 1824, 1827–28), 2:18, 20, 355.

3. *American Quarterly Review* 1, no. 2 (June 1827): 450.

4. Charles Anthon, *Classical Dictionary,* 4th ed. (New York: Harper, 1845), 45.

5. See B. H. Roberts, *Comprehensive History of the Church,* 1:102–8; Richard Bushman, *Joseph Smith and the Beginning of Mormonism* (Urbana: University of Illinois, 1984), 87–88.

6. For further enlightening details, see Stanley B. Kimball, "The Anthon Transcript: People, Primary Sources, and Problems," *BYU Studies* 10 (1970): 325–52. Available as a F.A.R.M.S. reprint—revised June 1985.

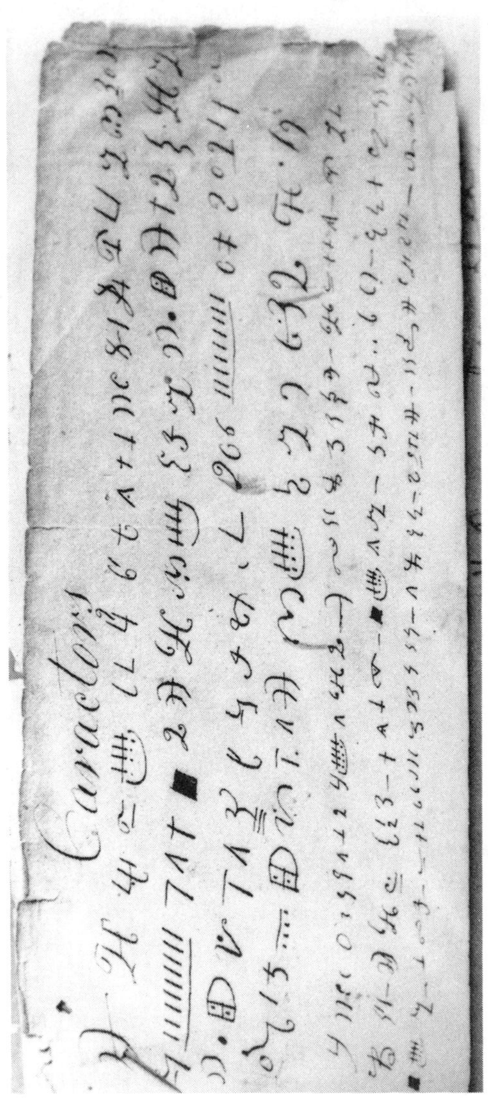

This document, which may be the original paper carried by Martin Harris to show Charles Anthon in New York City, presents some of the Book of Mormon characters. Courtesy Library Archives, Reorganized Church of Jesus Christ of Latter Day Saints, The Auditorium, Independence, Missouri.

Chapter 20

TEXTUAL CRITICISM OF THE BOOK OF MORMON

2 Nephi 27:14 "The Lord God will proceed to bring forth the words of the book."

Textual criticism seeks to render intelligent, scholarly judgment as to the most accurate and original form of a given text. It is an essential first step in the study of any text, including the Book of Mormon. The word "criticism" in this sense is taken from the Greek word *krisis,* meaning "judgment," for a critic is one who makes careful, informed decisions or judgments.

A number of interesting things have been learned from the textual criticism of the Bible and Book of Mormon over the years, and, with the publication by F.A.R.M.S. of the *Book of Mormon Critical Text,* it seems a good time to provide some examples:

Although the Book of Mormon generally agrees with the King James Version (KJV) of the Bible both in its acceptable scriptural idiom of translation and in its direct quotations from Isaiah, Joseph Smith's translation of the Isaiah texts in the Book of Mormon sometimes differs. At 2 Nephi 20:29, for example, Joseph dictated *Ramath* instead of the usual "Ramah" of the parallel King James Isaiah 10:29. Indeed, there is no "t" in the Hebrew text, the Greek Septuagint, or even in the Syropalestinian Aramaic version. The "t" appears, however, in the later Jewish Aramaic translation know as Targum Pseudo-Jonathan, as well as in the Christian Syriac Peshitta version. The words there are *Ramata* and *Rameta,* respectively (as is also evident in the Old Syriac *Rametha* for New Testament *Arimathea* in Matthew 27:57). Neither source was available to Joseph.

Another difference from the KJV came when Joseph was dictating from Isaiah 48:11 in 1 Nephi 20:11. Among other things, Joseph added an "it" that does not appear in the Greek or Hebrew texts. However, the "it" *is* in one Syriac manuscript, in one Jewish Aramaic Targum manuscript, and in a scribal correction to the large Isaiah Scroll from Qumran Cave One (the latter being the earliest Hebrew text of Isaiah).

King James "Ariel," a poetic term for Jerusalem, is not to be found in the 2 Nephi 27:3 quotation of Isaiah 29:7. However, it is also absent from the Jewish Aramaic Targum—which replaces it with "the City." The Book of Mormon reads *Zion* instead. This fits well, however, since "Mount Zion" appears at the end of the verse (Isaiah 29:8), and "Zion" and "Mount Zion" parallel each other here.

As noted long ago by the late Professor Sidney B. Sperry, the Jewish Targum and Greek Septuagint texts of Isaiah 2:16 confirm the authenticity of the reading "and upon all the ships of the sea" in 2 Nephi 12:16, even though the line is lacking in the Hebrew and King James texts.[1]

At 1 Nephi 7:11, the Original and Printer's Manuscripts of the Book of Mormon, as well as the 1830 edition of the Book of Mormon, all use the word *how,* which was changed in the 1837 and all subsequent editions to read *what*. However, even the King James translators could not decide, in translating a closely similar phrase in 1 Samuel 12:24, whether *how* or *what* was a more accurate translation of the Hebrew relative particle *'asher*. They thus placed the one in the text and the other in the margin (the reasons for marginal readings are explained at length in the introduction to their 1611 edition of the King James Version). Exactly the same variant readings occur in the texts we have of the Title Page of the Book of Mormon.

There is an interesting confusion between *things* and *words* at 2 Nephi 6:8 and 33:4. While the Printer's Manuscript reads *things* at both locations, all editions (except the 1830 at 2 Nephi 33:4) have changed this to read *words*. Either variant is a good reading, and the Hebrew word *d^ebarim* is accurately translated either "things" or "words."

The 1981 edition of the Book of Mormon has returned for the first time to the reading of the Printer's Manuscript *father* (singular) at Jacob 3:5, which of course refers directly to Lehi in the preceding Jacob 2:27, 34. The plural form *fathers,* which had been mistakenly used in all editions since 1830, suggested that Jacob attributed a restriction on plural marriage to earlier Israelite fathers, whereas historical evidence of any such legal restriction before Lehi is lacking.

These, and many other examples, show the significant and interesting things that textual criticism can teach us about the words of the Book of Mormon.

Based on research by Robert F. Smith, September 1984. The Book of Mormon Critical Text: A Tool for Scholarly Reference, *published by F.A.R.M.S. in three volumes (1984–87), has enjoyed widespread use. A further project is now being prepared by Royal Skousen, a professor in the English Department at Brigham Young University. See his article "Towards a Critical Edition of the Book of Mormon,"* BYU Studies *30 (Winter 1990): 41–69. In the course of his work, Professor Skousen has newly examined, in minute detail, improved photographs of the Original Manuscript of the Book of Mormon and the actual pages of the Printer's Manuscript. In addition, the major printed editions of the Book of Mormon have been entered into computer data bases and can be compared and analyzed now with great precision.*

Note

1. Sidney B. Sperry, *Answers to Book of Mormon Questions* (Salt Lake City: Bookcraft, 1967), 92–93.

Chapter 21

PARALLELISM, MERISMUS, AND DIFRASISMO

2 Nephi 31:3 "for he speaketh unto men according to their language"

Language is important to the scriptures. In order to communicate effectively, God speaks to mortals "according to their language" (2 Nephi 31:3). As tools for increasing one's appreciation and understanding of sacred texts, many types of literary studies are helpful.

In an interesting article, "Hebrew Poetry in the Book of Mormon, Part 1," Angela Crowell briefly describes twenty-three poetic devices found in both the Old Testament and the Book of Mormon.[1] One of the forms, chiasmus, is by now fairly well known. At the most direct level, the existence of these literary features provides insight to readers of the Book of Mormon enabling them to read it more sensitively—as ancient poetry as well as history. At another level, believers in the scripture will undoubtedly take such materials as further support for the idea that Joseph Smith did not originate the volume.

Several of the forms of *parallelism* that Crowell discusses also appear in ancient American literature. For example, Munro Edmonson's introduction to his translation of the *Popol Vuh* notes that it is written "in poetry, and cannot be accurately understood in prose."[2] The *Popol Vuh* is entirely composed in parallelistic couplets. Edmonson maintains, moreover, that present-day speakers of Quiche (the original language of the *Popol Vuh*) "speak to each other, at least most of the time, in the same poetic form." What one says, one says doubly: for example, "this is my word, . . . is what I say." This device was used anciently in

Mesoamerica. J. E. S. Thompson, the late great Mayanist, said, "There are close parallels in Maya transcriptions of the colonial period, and, I am convinced, in the hieroglyphic texts themselves to the verses of the Psalms, and the poetry of Job."[3]

Two other recent papers—one by Richard A. DeLong, the other by Allen J. Christensen—also explore several possible chiastic structures in early Mesoamerican texts, especially in the *Annals of the Cakchiquels* and the *Popol Vuh*.

Another form noted by Crowell, called *merismus,* allowed Hebrew poets to express a broad concept by a pair of narrower adjectives: young and aged = everybody (see Job 29:8); sea and dry land = the universe (see Psalms 95:5); flesh and blood = sacrificed animals (see Psalms 50:13). Crowell notes in Alma 37:37 the use of "night" and "morning" to convey the concept "all the time."

In Mesoamerica the same device is known as *difrasismo* or *kenning*. Among the Aztecs, for example, skirt and blouse signified the sexual aspect of woman, flower and song meant poetry and art, and face and heart signified personality.[4] My hand, my foot meant my body; while in the clouds, in the mist conveyed the idea mystery.[5] Thus, Edmonson comments on "the extraordinary difficulty" in reading such texts. The "obvious" meaning of an expression frequently must be modified to extract its "synthetic or esoteric meaning," and a translator is faced with "complex puns, metaphors, and traditional religious symbolisms." Furthermore, "these [religious] texts are purposely obscure. They are not intended to make sense to outsiders—and they don't." They were meant to be "read and pondered rather than skimmed over or recited."[6]

Such statements and comparisons recall what Nephi said about Jewish prophecies: "Isaiah spake many things which were hard for many of my people to understand; for they know not concerning the manner of prophesying among the Jews" (2 Nephi 25:1). Their manner of speaking was not readily apparent to his brothers (see 1 Nephi 15:2–3, 7; 22:1) or to Nephi's children (see 2 Nephi 25:5–6). Accordingly, one might expect to find vestiges of such mannerisms in the Book of Mormon as we have it today.

Although such intercultural studies raise many questions about how such similarities may have occurred, how they may have been transmitted, and what significance they may or may not have, they also add, piece by piece, to our appreciation of the depth of the Book of Mormon and of the ancient cultures with which it had contact.

This Update was based on research by John L. Sorenson, Angela Crowell, and Allen J. Christensen, December 1986. Christensen's extensive research has been published by F.A.R.M.S., and shorter articles have appeared in the Ensign *and in the journal* Latin American Indian Literature *(see pp. 233 to 235 in this volume).*

Work continues steadily on the literary characteristics of the Book of Mormon. A massive three-part listing by Donald W. Parry of different types of parallelisms found in the Book of Mormon was published by F.A.R.M.S. in 1988 (see pp. 167 to 169 and 290 to 292 in this volume). In 1989 other papers were released dealing with the criteria used to evaluate the presence of chiasmus, as well as its presence in Alma 36.

Notes

1. Angela Crowell, "Hebrew Poetry in the Book of Mormon, Part 1," *Zarahemla Record,* Nos. 32–33 (1986): 2–9.

2. Munro Edmonson, *The Book of Counsel: The Popol Vuh of the Quiche Maya of Guatemala,* Tulane University, Middle American Research Institute, Publication 35 (1971), xi.

3. J. E. S. Thompson, *Maya Hieroglyphic Writing: Introduction* (Washington, D.C.: Carnegie Institute of Washington, 1950), 61–62.

4. Miguel Leon Portilla, *Pre-Columbian Literatures of Mexico* (Norman: University of Oklahoma, 1969), 77.

5. Charlotte McGowan, "The Philosophical Dualism of the Aztecs," *Katunob* 10 (December 1977): 45.

6. Munro Edmonson, *The Ancient Future of the Itza: The Book of Chilam Balam of Tizimin* (Austin: University of Texas, 1982), xiii–xv.

Chapter 22

VIEW OF THE HEBREWS: "AN UNPARALLEL"

2 Nephi 33:2 "Wherefore, they cast many things away which are written and esteem them as things of naught."

The claim has been made before, and has recently been raised again, that Joseph Smith specifically copied the main structure and many details in the Book of Mormon from Ethan Smith's 1823 *View of the Hebrews*. Alleged parallels between these two books have led some to esteem the Book of Mormon lightly, "as a thing of naught."

Since the alleged points of contact are scattered throughout *View of the Hebrews* and in some cases are claimed to be quite specific, this assertion becomes plausible only if we assume that Joseph knew *View of the Hebrews* quite well and implicitly accepted it as accurate. If he did so, then he should have followed it—or at least should have not contradicted it—on its major points.

But this does *not* turn out to be the case. Since several people have pointed out alleged "parallels" between the Book of Mormon and *View of the Hebrews,* consider the following "unparallels" that weaken, if not completely undermine, the foregoing hypothesis:

1. *View of the Hebrews* begins with a chapter on the destruction of Jerusalem by the Romans.[1] It has nothing to say, however, about the destruction in Lehi's day by the Babylonians.

2. *View of the Hebrews* tells of specific heavenly signs that marked the Roman destruction of Jerusalem. Joseph Smith ignores these singular and memorable details.

3. Chapter 2 lists many prophecies about the restoration of Israel, including Deuteronomy 30; Isaiah 11, 18, 60, 65; Jeremiah 16, 23, 30–31, 35–37; Zephaniah 3; Amos 9; Hosea and Joel.[2] These scriptures are essential to the logic and fabric of *View of the Hebrews,* yet, with the sole exception of Isaiah 11, none of them appear in the Book of Mormon.

4. Chapter 3 is the longest chapter in *View of the Hebrews.*[3] It produces numerous "distinguished Hebraisms" as "proof" that the American Indians are Israelites. Hardly any of these points are found in the Book of Mormon, as one would expect if Joseph Smith were using *View of the Hebrews* or trying to make his book persuasive. For example, *View of the Hebrews* asserts repeatedly that the Ten Tribes came to America via the Bering Strait, which they crossed on "dry land." According to *View of the Hebrews,* this opinion is unquestionable, supported by all the authorities.

From there *View of the Hebrews* claims that the Israelites spread from north to east and then to the south at a very late date. These are critical points for *View of the Hebrews,* since Amos 8:11–12 prophesies that the tribes would go from the north to the east. Population migrations in the Book of Mormon, however, always move from the south to the north.

5. *View of the Hebrews* reports that the Indians are Israelites because they use the word "Hallelujah." Here is one of the favorite proofs of *View of the Hebrews,* a dead giveaway that the Indians are Israelites. Yet the word is never used in the Book of Mormon.

Furthermore, a table showing thirty-four Indian words or sentence fragments with Hebrew equivalents appears in *View of the Hebrews.*[4] No reader of the book could have missed this chart. If Joseph Smith had wanted to make up names to use in the Book of Mormon that would substantiate his claim that he had found some authentic western hemisphere Hebrew words, he would have jumped at such a ready-made list! Yet not one of these thirty-four Hebrew/Indian words (e.g., *Keah, Lani, Uwoh, Phale, Kurbet,* etc.) has even the remotest resemblance to any of the 175 words that appear for the first time in the Book of Mormon.

6. *View of the Hebrews* says the Indians are Israelites because they carry small boxes with them into battle. These are to protect them against injury. They are sure signs that the Indians' ancestors knew of the Ark of the Covenant! How could Joseph Smith pass up such a distinguished and oft-attested Hebraism as this?! Yet in all Book of Mormon battle scenes, there is not one hint of any such ark, box, or bag serving as a military fetish.

7. The Indians are Israelites because the Mohawk tribe was a tribe held in great reverence by all the others, to whom tribute was paid. Obviously, to Ethan Smith, this makes the Mohawks the vestiges of the tribe of Levi, Israel's tribe of priests. If Joseph Smith believed that such a tribe or priestly remnant had survived down to his day, he forgot to provide for anything to that effect in the Book of Mormon.

8. The Indians are Israelites because they had a daily sacrifice of fat in the fire and passed their venison through the flame, cutting it into twelve pieces. This great clue of "Israelitishness" is also absent from the Book of Mormon.

9. *View of the Hebrews* maintains that the Indians knew "a distinguished Hebraism," namely "laying the hand on the mouth, and the mouth in the dust." Had Joseph Smith believed this, why is the Book of Mormon silent on this "sure sign of Hebraism" and dozens of others like it?

10. According to *View of the Hebrews,* the Indians quickly lost knowledge that they were all from the same family. The Book of Mormon tells that family and tribal affiliations were maintained for almost one thousand years.

11. *View of the Hebrews* claims that the righteous Indians were active "for a long time," well into recent times, and that their destruction occurred about A.D. 1400, based upon such convincing evidence as tree rings near some of the fortifications of these people. The Book of Mormon implicitly rejects this notion by reporting the destruction of the Nephites in the fourth century A.D.

12. *View of the Hebrews* argues that the Indians are Israelites because they knew the legends of Quetzalcoatl. But the surprise here is that *View of the Hebrews* proves beyond doubt that Quetzalcoatl was none other than—not Jesus—but Moses! "Who could this be but *Moses,* the ancient legislator in Israel?"[5] Quetzalcoatl was white, gave laws, required penance (strict obedience), had a serpent with green plumage (brazen, fiery-flying serpent in the wilderness), pierced ears (like certain slaves under the law of Moses), appeased God's wrath (by sacrifices), was associated with a great famine (in Egypt), spoke from a volcano (Sinai), walked barefoot (removed his shoes), spawned a golden age (seven years of plenty in Egypt—which has nothing to do with Moses, by the way), etc. Besides the fact that the *View of the Hebrews*'s explanation of Quetzalcoatl as Moses is inconsistent with the Book of Mormon, none of these hallmark details associated with Quetzalcoatl are incorporated into the account of Christ's visit to Bountiful in 3 Nephi.

The foregoing twelve points could be multiplied literally seven times over. In the face of these differences, the few vague similarities pale. Both speak of long migrations for religious reasons; both report wars; both say the people knew how to write and work with metals; and both praise generosity and denounce pride. *View of the Hebrews* speaks of Indian lore that they left a "lost book" back in Palestine. But these points are rather general and inconsequential.

The question has been asked: "Can such numerous and startling points of resemblance and suggestive contact be merely coincidence?" The answer is "yes," not only because the points of resemblance are neither numerous nor startling, but also because the differences far outweigh the similarities. Why would Joseph have contradicted and ignored *View of the Hebrews* at virtually every turn, if indeed he gave it basic credence?[6]

An expanded version of this October 1985 research by John W. Welch was published that same year by F.A.R.M.S., entitled "An Unparallel." It and Spencer Palmer's and William Knecht's 1964 article in BYU Studies *are now available together under the title "View of the Hebrews: Substitute for Inspiration?"*

Notes

1. Ethan Smith, *View of the Hebrews: The Tribes of Israel in America,* 2nd ed. (Poultney, Vermont: Smith and Shute, 1825), 2–46. This book argues that the American Indians originated from the lost ten tribes.

2. Ibid., 47–66.

3. Ibid., 67–225.

4. Ibid., 90–91.

5. Ibid., 206, italics in original.

6. Further discussion is available in Spencer Palmer and William Knecht, "View of the Hebrews: Substitute for Inspiration?" *BYU Studies* 5 (1964): 105–13; and Hugh Nibley, "The Comparative Method," *Improvement Era* 62 (October-November 1959), 744–47, 759, 848, 854, 856, reprinted in *The Collected Works of Hugh Nibley* (Salt Lake City: Deseret Book and F.A.R.M.S., 1989), 8:193–206.

Chapter 23

NO, SIR, THAT'S NOT HISTORY!

2 Nephi 33:2 "Wherefore, they cast many things away which are written and esteem them as things of naught."

The recent publication of B. H. Roberts's personal papers on similarities between the Book of Mormon and the *View of the Hebrews*[1] has raised again a question that has circulated for several years among certain critics: Did B. H. Roberts lose faith in the Book of Mormon? The editor of the Roberts studies, Brigham Madsen, reports that the record is "mixed," that "whether or not Roberts retained his belief in the Book of Mormon may never be determined."[2] A closer look at the evidence, however, yields a much different assessment.

A critical issue is determining *when* Roberts wrote *Studies*. This is important because the earlier that Roberts wrote it, the less evidence there is that he worked on it for a long time as a serious and troubling project. The editor figures it was an ongoing project for Roberts during his mission presidency in New York (1922–1927). Newly discovered evidence, however, proves that position false. This evidence—obvious only on the original documents themselves—shows definitively that Roberts began the study in January 1922 and finished it (except for a few minor proofreading changes) *before* he left for the Eastern States Mission on May 29, 1922.

Consider these points:

1. The first page of Roberts's typescript originally read: "A number of years ago—thirteen years ago, to be exact—in . . . *New Witnesses for God,* I discussed . . . ." Since *New Wit-*

nesses was published in 1909, thirteen years later was 1922. Roberts says, "thirteen years ago, *to be exact.*" The newly printed version of the study, however, omits this crucial phrase, apparently because when Roberts proofread the typescript, he crossed these words out. Still, this telltale phrase clearly dates the writing of the study to 1922.

2. We can tell that Roberts wrote the study before he knew the date of the first edition of *View of the Hebrews.* At that time he had only the second edition and could only speculate that the first was published around 1820. In five handwritten changes, Roberts later changed "1820" to "1823." When did Roberts learn of the date of the first edition of *View of the Hebrews?* From notes he took in a New York Library, we know he learned this shortly after his arrival in New York, in June 1922.

3. In a letter from Roberts dated October 24, 1927, to Apostle Richard R. Lyman, Roberts says he "dropped" the study when his mission call came. On March 14, 1932, Roberts wrote of the study that it "was from research work I did *before going to take charge of the Eastern States Mission.*"

All these facts and several other similar points show that one should not view the study as a long-time project of Roberts while in New York.

Moreover, the record of Roberts's testimony is far from "mixed." His service to the Church from 1922 to his death in 1933 was uninterrupted and unambiguous. He frequently testified of the truthfulness of the Book of Mormon as an ancient American scripture. He praised its divinity. He based most of his numerous mission and conference talks on its messages. He wrote in May 1922 of "the tremendous truth" of the Book of Mormon.[3] He said in 1924 that the Saints build upon the Book of Mormon, "wherein is no darkness or doubt."[4] He spoke at general conference, April 1928, of the "hundred more such glorious things that have come to the world in that book to enlighten the children of men."[5] He spoke repeatedly of the historicity of the book. In 1928 he glorified God for the account of Jesus' visit to the Nephites in Bountiful: "And now, O Lord Jesus, if thou couldst but come into the consciousness of our souls this day, as thou didst come into the vision of the ancient Nephites in the Land of Bountiful, we would join their great song of praise and worship, saying—'Hosanna! Hosanna! Blessed be the name of the Most High God!' And we, like them, would fall down at the feet of Jesus and worship him this Easter day! Amen."[6] This does not sound like a person who had lost faith in the Book of Mormon.

Although Roberts had an "unshaken and unshakable" faith in the Book of Mormon (as he wrote in a cover letter accompanying *Studies*), he knew that as a debater and researcher he had asked questions that might cause some people to wonder about his views. He spoke to this general issue at October Conference in 1929, saying: "After bearing testimony to the fundamental things of this work, and my confidence in it, *I hope that if anywhere along the line I have caused any of you to doubt my faith in this work, then let this testimony and my indicated life's work be a correction of it.*"[7]

In sum, it seems plain; the evidence is neither "enigmatic" nor "mixed." Rather, it is quite overwhelming. There is no significant evidence (Wesley Lloyd's diary included) of "late-in-life doubts." Questions, yes; uncertainty about weak archaeological evidences, yes; but doubts? This man, who gave fifty-four years of his life in full-time service to his church and to his God, remained firm and true in his testimony of the antiquity and divinity of the Book of Mormon.

This Update was based on research by John W. Welch, November 1985. An expanded treatment appeared a few months later, and a summary appeared in John W. Welch, "B. H. Roberts: Seeker after Truth," Ensign *16 (March 1986): 56–62. That article was reprinted in* A Sure Foundation: Answers to Difficult Gospel Questions *(Salt Lake City: Deseret Book, 1988), 60–74.*

Further details and documentation are given in "Did B. H. Roberts Lose Faith in the Book of Mormon?" and "Finding Answers to B. H. Roberts' Questions" (Provo: F.A.R.M.S., 1985). A substantial collection of all known statements made by Roberts about the Book of Mormon from 1922 until his death in 1933, "B. H. Roberts: His Final Decade: Statements about the Book of Mormon," has also been published by F.A.R.M.S. in 1985.

Notes

1. B. H. Roberts, *Studies of the Book of Mormon* (Urbana: University of Illinois, 1985). For reviews of this book in academic journals, see Thomas G. Alexander, in *Dialogue* 19 (Winter 1986): 190–93; Marvin S. Hill, in *Church History* 55 (December 1986): 546–48; and John W. Welch, in *Pacific Historical Review* 55 (November 1986): 619–23.
2. Roberts, *Studies,* 29–30.
3. B. H. Roberts, "Why Mormonism," Tract No. 4 (1922), 60–61.
4. B. H. Roberts, "A New Outlook upon Mormonism," Radio Broadcast (1924), 4.
5. *Conference Report* (April 1928): 112.
6. Ibid., 113.
7. *Conference Report* (October 1929): 90; italics added.

B. H. Roberts, about the time that he served as president of the Eastern States Mission. Courtesy Special Collections Department, University of Utah Libraries.

Chapter 24

SEVEN TRIBES: AN ASPECT OF LEHI'S LEGACY

Jacob 1:13 "They were called Nephites, Jacobites, Josephites, Zoramites, Lamanites, Lemuelites, and Ishmaelites."

Several years ago it was observed that the descendants of Lehi's party consistently divided themselves into seven tribes. Three times in the Book of Mormon these seven are mentioned, each time in the rigid order of "Nephites, Jacobites, Josephites, Zoramites, Lamanites, Lemuelites, and Ishmaelites" (Jacob 1:13; 4 Nephi 1:38; Mormon 1:8). Significantly, these references come from the earliest as well as the latest periods of Nephite history, indicating the importance and persistence of kinship as a basic element in this society.[1] Now it has been discovered that the origin of this stable societal structure can be traced back to the words of Lehi himself.

One of the many enduring legacies of Lehi's last will and testament appears to be the organization of his descendants into seven tribes. After speaking to several of his sons collectively (see 2 Nephi 1:1–29), Lehi spoke first to Zoram (see 2 Nephi 1:30–32), second to Jacob (see 2 Nephi 2), third to Joseph (see 2 Nephi 3), fourth to the children of Laman (see 2 Nephi 4:3–7), fifth to the children of Lemuel (see 2 Nephi 4:8–9), sixth to the sons of Ishmael (see 2 Nephi 4:10), and seventh to Nephi and Sam together (see 2 Nephi 4:11). This seems to be the precedent that established the social and legal order that lasted among these people for almost one thousand years. The seven groups recognizable here are exactly the same as those listed in Jacob 1:13, 4 Nephi 1:38, and Mormon 1:8.

Several interesting things can be said about this arrangement:

1. The list was widely used. As a rule, most people named in the Nephite record can be clearly identified as belonging to one of these seven groups. This is a rather amazing element sustained almost imperceptibly throughout the Book of Mormon.

2. The structure was enduring. Though different forms of government might come and go in Nephite history, the underlying family fabric of this society remained permanent. Even in the darkest days of political collapse, all the people still had "much family," and the tribal structure was present to supplant the collapsed government (see 3 Nephi 7:2–4).

3. The arrangement was also foundational. Only the idea that Lehi originated this tribal organization can comfortably explain why it persisted so long and was recognized both by the Nephites and by the Lamanites. This is evidence that Lehi's last words to his sons were taken as being constitutionally definitive. Thus, there are Jacobites and Josephites, but never Samites, in the Book of Mormon.

4. In many ways, Lehi is acting here like Jacob of old. Both Jacob and Lehi pronounced their blessings to "all [their] household," who had gathered around them shortly before they died. The aim was to organize a household of God in a new land of promise (see 2 Nephi 4:12; Genesis 49). Both organized their posterity into tribal groups in the patriarchal tradition of ancient Israel. The claim that Lehi chose that patriarchal role is borne out by the fact that to the end the Nephites remembered Lehi as "Father Lehi." As the Israelites speak of Abraham as "Father Abraham," so the Nephites, including Enos, Benjamin, Alma, Helaman, Nephi, and Mormon, uniformly remembered Lehi as "our father Lehi" (Enos 1:25; Mosiah 1:4; 2:34; Alma 9:9; 18:36; 36:22; 56:3; Helaman 8:22; 3 Nephi 10:17). Indeed, Lehi is the *only* figure in Nephite history called "our father," apparently in reference to his position at the head of Nephite society and religion.

5. Division of these people into kin-based tribes served several functions—religious, military, political, and legal. The Is-

raelite tribe of Levi was given priestly duties (see Numbers 3:6), as was the family of Jacob and his recordkeeping posterity in the Book of Mormon (see 2 Nephi 2:3). The armies of Israel were numbered according to tribe (see Numbers 1), much like the Nephite practice that "numbered" allies as members of their group (see 3 Nephi 2:13–14).

Land law also was fundamentally interrelated with the tribal structure of Israelite society. Lands of inheritance could not be permanently sold outside of a given tribe, according to a ruling dating back to Moses himself (see Numbers 36:7). Indeed, a "land of inheritance" was unthinkable under the law of Moses without a family structure and a legal system that gave rights of family foreclosure, redemption, and preemption to next of kin. Since Nephi reports that his people observed the law of Moses "in all things" (2 Nephi 5:10), they apparently followed the law of Moses regarding their land laws—another function served by Lehi's division of his family into these seven paternal groups.

Thus, the sevenfold division of the people was an important feature of Nephite civilization. It may even have set a pattern for other Nephite organizations. After all, Alma established "seven churches in the land of Zarahemla" (Mosiah 25:23), and traditions claim that ancient Mesoamericans sprang from seven "caves" or lineages.[2]

This Update reflects the work of John L. Sorenson, John A. Tvedtnes, and John W. Welch in November 1987. This research has been developed further in John W. Welch, "Lehi's Last Will and Testament: A Legal Approach," in Monte Nyman and Charles Tate, eds., Second Nephi: The Doctrinal Structure *(Provo: Religious Studies Center, 1989), esp. 68–70; and John A. Tvedtnes, "Book of Mormon Tribal Affiliation and Military Castes," in Stephen Ricks and William Hamblin, eds.,* Warfare in the Book of Mormon *(Salt Lake City: Deseret Book and F.A.R.M.S., 1990), 296–326.*

Notes

1. See John L. Sorenson, *An Ancient American Setting for the Book of Mormon* (Salt Lake City: Deseret Book and F.A.R.M.S., 1985), 310–13.

2. Mentioned in ibid., 313, and Ross T. Christenson, "The Seven Lineages of Lehi," *New Era* 5 (1975): 50–51.

Chapter 25

ANTENANTIOSIS IN THE BOOK OF MORMON

Jacob 4:8 "despise not"

An interesting figure of speech used in the Book of Mormon is called *antenantiosis*. It is the practice of stating a proposition in terms of its opposite. The result is to express the positive in a very high degree, or as the biblical scholar E. W. Bullinger puts it, "We thus emphasize that which we seem to lessen."[1]

For instance, when Jacob counsels to "despise not the revelations of God" (Jacob 4:8), he is not merely saying that one should not despise the revelations; he is actually urging the righteous to hold the revelations of God in the highest esteem. The unexpected negative increases the force of the idea that it apparently understates. It seems to make us notice and dwell on the expression, so that we can learn more from it.

Thus in the promise, "if ye do this, and endure to the end, ye will *in nowise be cast out*" (Mormon 9:29), Moroni is actually promising that the faithful who endure will be blessed beyond measure. When Mosiah says, "It is not expedient that such abominations should come upon you" (Mosiah 29:24), he is not merely saying that the people should not commit or allow such abominations, he is forcefully admonishing the people to prevent them. When Amulek warns that "he [the devil] rewardeth you no good thing" (Alma 34:39), he does not mean just the lack of a good reward, but the surety of tremendously evil results—torment, captivity, and damnation.

Other Book of Mormon uses of antenantiosis appear in Mosiah 2:9; 19:17; Alma 12:14; 30:21; 34:39; 46:30; 50:27; and 3 Nephi

5:1; 6:18; 7:18. It is an interesting figure of speech, drawn to our attention by biblical scholarship, that helps illuminate the forceful effectiveness of many of the prophetic messages of the Book of Mormon.

This Update was published in the F.A.R.M.S. newsletter, Insights, *no. 4* (1991), and is based on research submitted by Gail Call.

Note

1. See *Figures of Speech Used in the Bible* (Baker Book House: Grand Rapids, 1989), 159–64.

Chapter 26

ONCE MORE: THE HORSE

Enos 1:21 "and also many horses"

A question frequently asked about the Book of Mormon is why so little evidence exists for the presence of horses in the Pre-Columbian Western Hemisphere. Thinking about this question requires us to begin by reflecting on the Book of Mormon text itself.

Is "horse" in the Book of Mormon merely a matter of labeling by analogy some other quadruped with the name *Equus,* the true horse, or does the scripture's use of "horse" refer to the actual survival into very recent times of the American Pleistocene horse (*Equus equus*)? If, as most zoologists and paleontologists assume, *Equus equus* was absent from the New World during Book of Mormon times, could deer, tapir, or another quadruped have been termed "horse" by Joseph Smith in his translating?

John L. Sorenson has suggested the latter possibility[1] and has pointed to archaeological specimens showing humans riding on the backs of animal figures, some of which are evidently deer. Also Mayan languages used the term *deer* for Spanish horses and *deer-rider* for horsemen.[2] Indians of Zinacantan, Chiapas, believe that the mythical "Earth Owner," who is supposed to be rich and live inside a mountain, rides on deer.[3] In addition, the Aztec account of the Spanish Conquest used terms like *the-deer-which-carried-men-upon-their-backs, called horses.*[4]

Another explanation has been to hold that true horses, which are well-documented for the late glacial age in America,[5] survived into Book of Mormon times. Archaeologist Paul S. Martin, for example, saw no theoretical reason why "pockets" of horses and other Pleistocene fauna could not have survived as late as 2000

B.C.[6] Dr. Ripley Bullen thought horses could have lasted until 3000 B.C. in Florida,[7] and J. J. Hester granted a possible 4000 B.C. survival date.[8]

Various Argentine natural scientists have even maintained that the herds of horses on the pampas were native, not from Spanish imports, but they have lacked strong evidence for that view. Horse remains found in a Missouri Indian mound some decades ago were assumed to date after European horses were in the area—even though there was nothing specific in the circumstances of the find to indicate that it was post-Columbian.[9] This sort of feeble evidence and argument has hampered acceptance of the Pleistocene survival view.

Yet there exists better evidence, universally ignored these days but deserving careful attention. Excavations at the Post-Classic site of Mayapan in Yucatan in 1957 yielded remains of horses in four lots. Two of these specimens are from the surface and might have been remains of Spanish animals. Two other lots, however, were obtained from excavation in Cenote [water hole] Ch'en Mul "from the bottom stratum in a sequence of unconsolidated earth almost 2 meters in thickness." They were "considered to be pre-Columbian on the basis of depth of burial and degree of mineralization. Such mineralization was observed in no other bone or tooth in the collection although thousands were examined, some of which were found in close proximity to the horse teeth." Clayton E. Ray somewhat lamely suggests that the fossil teeth were of Pleistocene age and "could have been transported . . . as curios by the Mayans."[10]

In southwest Yucatan, Mercer found horse remains in three caves associated with potsherds and other artifacts, and with no sign of fossilization.[11] Excavations of 1978 at Loltun Cave in the Maya lowlands turned up further horse remains.[12]

A careful study of the reported remains—examining museum lots, associated bones, pottery, and other artifacts—still remains to be done. Radiometric dating might also be worthwhile. Full references to related material are available to any qualified persons who desire to carry out such a study. But in the meantime, the few references to horses in the Book of Mormon should not be counted as erroneous or unhistorical.

Based on research by John L. Sorenson, June 1984.

Notes

1. See John L. Sorenson, *An Ancient American Setting for the Book of Mormon* (Salt Lake City: Deseret Book and F.A.R.M.S., 1985), 295–96.

2. See John L. Sorenson, "Wheeled Figurines in the Ancient World" (Provo: F.A.R.M.S., 1981).

3. See E. Z. Vogt, *The Zinacantecos of Mexico* (New York: Holt, Rinehart and Winston, 1970), 6.

4. See Bernardino de Sahagun, *The War of Conquest: How It Was Waged Here in Mexico,* trans. A. J. Anderson and C. E. Dibble (Salt Lake City: University of Utah Press, 1978), 28, 35, 55, 60.

5. See Gordon Smith, "E. Equus: Immigrant or Emigrant?" *Science* 5, no. 3 (April 1984): 78, 80.

6. See Paul S. Martin, "The Discovery of America," *Science* 179 (1973): 974 n. 3.

7. See Robert A. Martin, in S. David Webb, ed., *Pleistocene Mammals of Florida* (Gainesville: University of Florida, 1974), 132, 144.

8. See Paul S. Martin and H. E. Wright, Jr., eds., *Pleistocene Extinctions,* Proceedings of the VII Congress, International Association for Quaternary Research (New Haven: Yale University Press, 1967), 183, 186.

9. See Carl Chapman, "Horse Bones in an Indian Mound," *Missouri Archaeologist* 7, no. 1 (April 1941): 3–8.

10. Clayton E. Ray, "Pre-Columbian Horses from Yucatan," *Journal of Mammalology* 38 (1957): 278; Harry E. D. Pollock and Clayton E. Ray, "Notes on Vertebrate Animal Remains from Mayapan," *Current Reports* 41 (August 1957): 638 (Carnegie Institution, Washington, D.C., Dept. of Archaeology).

11. See Henry Chapman Mercer, *The Hill-Caves of Yucatan: A Search for Evidence of Man's Antiquity in the Caverns of Central America* (Philadelphia: Lippincott, 1896), 172.

12. See Institute of Maya Studies, Miami Museum of Science, *Newsletter* 7, no. 11 (November 1978): 2.

Chapter 27

LOST ARTS

Jarom 1:8 "We multiplied exceedingly, and spread upon the face of the land, and became exceedingly rich in . . . fine workmanship of wood, in buildings, and in machinery, and also in iron and copper, and brass and steel, making all manner of tools of every kind to till the ground, and weapons of war."

The Book of Mormon claims that groups such as the Nephites and the Jaredites migrated from one area to another. That suggestion has sometimes been rejected because a particular idea or technological feature in the area of origin has not been found in the destination area. The absence of such "obviously useful" cultural items is used to argue that no migration took place.

In some cases, it is possible that technology was simply lost. It may have lost its usefulness in the new location, or it may have been forgotten as certain people became less cultured or less civilized. In other cases, the archaeological evidence may simply be incomplete or unrecognized.

The true arch is often cited to support the idea that there was no contact between the pre-Columbian Eastern and Western Hemispheres. Professor Linton Satterthwaite had accepted that view, but then found himself having to change: "It has been usual to suppose that the principle of the true arch was unknown to the American Indian, though here and there in some particular structure it has been argued that the principle, though not obvious, was really present." Yet finally, on the basis of a field reconnaissance, Satterthwaite was left with "no doubt that the

Maya at La Muñeca roofed a long room with the true arch, and that they knew exactly what they were doing."[1]

Earlier, Alfred Tozzer had reported that at Nakum, Guatemala, "two lateral doorways have what may be truthfully called concrete arches, . . . the only examples of the true arch which I have met with in Maya buildings."[2] E. G. Squier had reported an arch of adobe bricks from Pachacamac, Peru, in the 1870s.[3] There are other examples that either are not complete arches or have questionable pre-Columbian dates. But a single good example proves the point without multiplying cases.

The potter's wheel is another feature long supposed to have been entirely absent from the New World. That notion too has now had to change. Samuel Lothrop reported decades ago seeing in an archaeological context in Peru what "seemed to be" just such a device.[4] Then in the early 1970s, Terence Grieder settled the matter. In the grave of a high-status woman near the Peruvian site of Pashash, he found scores of wheel-turned hemispherical ceramic cups. These offerings accompanied the burial of an aristocratic woman (although cups of the same shape in commoners' graves showed no evidence of being made on the wheel). Furthermore, the grave offerings showed fifteen stone cups evidently turned on a "lathe," perhaps consisting of a wooden shaft with a flywheel attached that could be set in motion by pulling a cord wrapped around the shaft. Archaeological evidence of these wheeled devices for processing clay and stone lasted a maximum of two hundred years, then totally disappeared.[5]

The arch and potter's wheel join other examples to warn us that even what we might consider "obviously useful" devices may be lost to a people.

Example: Pioneer settlers of Eastern Polynesia brought pottery with them and used it for centuries, yet by the time European explorers arrived, their descendants knew nothing of ceramics.[6]

Example: The Greeks had a complex, clocklike, astronomical "computer" for calculations in astronomy, but that fact was totally unknown until 1900 when sponge divers pulled one from a shipwreck (dated ca. 65 B.C.) off the Aegean island of Antikythera.[7]

Example: As is generally known, the wheel probably was invented in the Near East, possibly as early as the beginning of the third millennium. It continued in use for over three thousand years and was bequeathed to other cultures, where it was further developed. However, by about A.D. 200, the wheel began a decline in the Near East that eventually led to its complete disappearance from the entire area. It was not reintroduced until Western imperial powers became involved in the Near East during the nineteenth century.[8]

Example: The Parthians, who inhabited the Baghdad area for several centuries around the time of Christ, made electric batteries! Asphalt served to fasten and insulate an iron rod from within a copper tube filled with an unknown electrolyte (acid). The makers may have used their discovery to electroplate jewelry, but not to do anything "useful." Their basic idea was only rediscovered nearly two thousand years later.[9]

Example: The discovery of an apparently ground rock-crystal lens in the ruins of Assyrian Nineveh has made scholars wonder what they might have seen through such a magnifier.[10]

Obviously, archaeological remains discovered at any given moment give only a partial record of ancient life and thus of migrations. Future finds by archaeologists may further challenge the anthropological orthodoxy that New World civilizations were essentially independent of the Old World.

Based on research by John L. Sorenson, July 1985. Paul Y. Hoskisson later added the information about the wheel in the Near East.

Notes

1. Linton Satterthwaite, Review of Ruppert and Denison, *Archaeological Reconnaissance in Campeche, Quintana Roo, and Peten,* in *American Antiquity* 10 (1944): 217; see also Harumi Befu and Gordon F. Ekholm, "The True Arch in Pre-Columbian America?" *Current Anthropology* 5, no. 4 (1964): 328–29.

2. Alfred Tozzer, "A Preliminary Study of the Prehistoric Ruins of Nakum, Guatemala," *Memoirs, Peabody Museum, Harvard,* 5, no. 3 (1913): 167.

3. See Ephraim G. Squier, "The Arch in America," *Journal of the Anthropological Institute of New York* 1 (1871–72): 78–80; *Peru: Incidents of Travel and Exploration,* 2nd ed. (New York: Harper and Bros., 1878), 70.

4. See Samuel Lothrop, "¿Conocieron la Rueda los Indigenas Mesoamericanos?" *Cuadernos Americanos* 25, no. 1 (1946): 201.

5. See Terence Grieder, "Rotary Tools in Ancient Peru," *Archaeology* 28 (1975): 178–85; "Lost Wheels," *Scientific American* 233 (October 1975): 54.

6. See Peter Bellwood, "The Prehistory of Oceania," *Current Anthropology* 16, no. 1 (1975): 12–14.

7. See Derek J. de Solla Price, "Unworldly Mechanics," *Natural History* 71 (March 1962): 8–17; L. Sprague de Camp, *The Ancient Engineers* (1974), 167ff.

8. See R. W. Gulliet, *The Camel and the Wheel* (Cambridge, Mass.: Harvard University Press, 1975).

9. See Rushwarth M. Kidder, *Christian Science Monitor* (June 14, 1985): 20; Harry M. Schwalb, "Electric Batteries of 2,000 Years Ago," *Science Digest* 41 (April 1957): 17–19; see also Colin G. Fink on Egyptian "electroplating" of copper with antimony, *1933 Annual Log* (New York: Scientific American Publishing Co., 1933), 85.

10. See Sir David Brewster, "On the Form of Images Produced by Lenses and Mirrors of Different Sizes," *American Journal of Science* 2, no. 15 (1853): 122–23.

Chapter 28

WHAT WAS A "MOSIAH"?

Omni 1:12 "I will speak unto you somewhat concerning Mosiah."

In 1965, John Sawyer published an article titled "What was a Môšia^c?"[1] He argues that the term *mosiah* was an ancient Hebrew term, like *gō'ēl* ("redeemer, or avenger of blood"), or *ṣedeq* ("victor, savior"). Such terms originally had meaning in Hebrew daily life and culture but came to be used among their titles for God. The word *môšia^c* (pronounced moe-**shee**-ah) is a word peculiar to Hebrew, a "word invariably implying a champion of justice in a situation of controversy, battle or oppression."[2]

Sawyer's analysis sheds interesting light on the name Mosiah in the Book of Mormon. Several subtle reasons show why Nephites, who continued to speak Hebrew in the New World, would have been attracted to the use of such a name or title.

Apparently the form of the word Mosiah is a "hiphil participle" in Hebrew. It occurs in the Hebrew in Deuteronomy 22:27; 28:29; Judges 12:3; Psalms 18:41; and Isaiah 5:29—texts that in all probability were on the Plates of Brass. This word, however, was not transliterated into the English by the King James translators, and thus the Hebrew would not have been known to Joseph Smith. It was, however, known and used as a personal name in the Book of Mormon, as well as by people in the Jewish colony at Elephantine in the fifth century B.C.

The key meaning of the word *môšia^c* was "savior." People in danger cry out, "But there is no *môšia^c*" (Deuteronomy 22:27). After examining all occurrences of this term in the Hebrew Bible, Sawyer concludes that the term applied to a particular kind of person or role and was sometimes a title designating "a definite office or position."[3] Typical of this office are the following traits:

1. The *môšia*ᶜ is a victorious hero appointed by God.

2. He liberates a chosen people from oppression, controversy, and unjustice after they cry out for help.

3. Their deliverance is usually accomplished by means of a nonviolent escape or negotiation.

4. The immediate result of the coming of a *môšia*ᶜ was "escape from unjustice, and a return to a state of justice where each man possesses his rightful property."[4]

5. On a larger scale, "final victory means the coming of *môšiᶜim* [plural, pronounced moe-shee-**eem**] to rule like Judges over Israel."[5]

Thus the term also had judicial, legal, or forensic connotations, similar to the word *advocate.*" A *môšia*ᶜ gives refuge to those on his "right hand" from their accusers in court (Psalm 17:7).

The exact derivation of the Book of Mormon name Mosiah is unknown, but it appears the same as *môšia*ᶜ, which derives from the Hebrew *yaša*ᶜ ("to be wide open, free, deliver, rescue, preserve, save"). It is thus quite different from the Hebrew word *mašiah* (anointed, "messiah," Greek *christós*). The Nephite word *mosiah* might also contain a theophoric element (-iah), thus meaning "the Lord is a *môšia*ᶜ."

Interestingly, the term *môšia*ᶜ applies perfectly to the Mosiahs in the Book of Mormon. King Mosiah I was a God-appointed hero who delivered the chosen people of Nephi from serious wars and contentions by leading them in an escape from the land of Nephi (see Omni 1:12–14). It is unknown whether he was called Mosiah before he functioned as a *môšia*ᶜ of his people or whether he gained this well-earned title afterward, perhaps as a royal title, but either is possible.

Indeed, the themes of God's salvation and the deliverance of his people are strong in the book of Mosiah. It tells of one *môšia*ᶜ after another. Alma was a God-inspired *môšia*ᶜ who peaceably saved his people from king Noah and the Lamanites. Zeniff tried to return to the land of Nephi to repossess the rightful property of the Nephites. His efforts failed, however, and his grandson Limhi eventually functioned as a *môšiaᶜ* by leading his people in their escape back to Zarahemla. At the end of the book of Mosiah, the reign of judges was established, a fitting development for a people that had been well served by *môšiᶜim* for over a century. Thus, the book of Mosiah, like the book of Judges in the Old Testament, appears to have been meaningfully named.

Finally, the Hebrew term *môšiaᶜ* also was used as a divine title. God was and is such a savior, who would come down and bring salvation (see Mosiah 3:9). The Book of Mormon adds support to Sawyer's idea that the divine title *môšiaᶜ* was also at home in a cultural context. It seems to preserve traces of a broader usage when it says that "the knowledge of *a* Savior shall spread throughout every nation" (Mosiah 3:20; italics added), "in other words *a* Savior of the world" (1 Nephi 10:4; italics added).

Ultimately this term, as a divine title, was applied exclusively to God. As Isaiah 43:11 states, "I . . . am the Lord; and beside me there is no *môšiaᶜ*." Likewise, the angel to Benjamin affirmed the unique work of the Savior, the only way and means whereby salvation comes to mankind (see Mosiah 3:17). Thus, in several respects, the Book of Mormon usage of this term is quite remarkable, meaningful, and wholly consistent with Hebrew usage.

Based on research by John W. Welch, April 1989. The Sawyer article from the Old Testament journal Vetus Testamentum *became available as a F.A.R.M.S. reprint in 1989.*

Notes

1. John Sawyer, "What Was a Môšiaᶜ?" *Vetus Testamentum* 15 (1965): 475–86.
2. Ibid., 476.
3. Ibid., 477.
4. Ibid., 480.
5. Ibid., 482.

Chapter 29

ANCIENT EUROPEANS IN AMERICA?

Omni 1:16 "They journeyed in the wilderness, and were brought by the hand of the Lord across the great waters."

The Nephites were not the only people who lived in the Western Hemisphere in antiquity. The Jaredites (Ether 6:4–12) and the Mulekites (Omni 1:16) also came from the Old World to the New. The archaeological record attests that many others came as well, although how, when, and where they came from remains obscure.

In the past fifteen years, popular publications have claimed that ancient inscriptions in west European or North African writing systems exist in remote locations throughout much of the United States and Canada. The best known of these publications are by Barry Fell. If such inscriptions could be shown to be authentic, they would prove that voyagers crossed the Atlantic before Columbus's day, a point of interest to many believers in the Book of Mormon.

Despite wide enthusiasm for these claims, most archaeologists have found such flaws in the evidence as to reject the claims. (Incidentally, Fell "translated" the "new copy of the Anthon transcript" immediately after Mark Hofmann claimed to find that forgery. His "reading" sounded a good deal like 1 Nephi 1, although Fell asserted that it was written in Arabic of the twelfth or thirteenth century A.D. Of course, it has since been established that the document was a forgery.)

Many former associates of Fell have distanced themselves from his exaggerated statements while retaining belief that some of the inscriptions are genuine. Among these are W. R. McGlone and P. M. Leonard, authors of *Ancient Celtic America* (Leonard is a resident of Kamas, Utah). For ten years they have studied inscriptions in caves or rock shelters in southeastern Colorado and the panhandle of Oklahoma.

To draw the attention of reputable scholars to these inscriptions, they hosted a seminar in Springfield, Colorado, September 20–25, 1989, at the time of the equinox. A small number of enthusiasts were joined by an invited group of friendly, though cautiously skeptical, scholars (including John Sorenson), plus outright antagonists.

Among dozens of sites where Ogam writing (known chiefly from Ireland in medieval times) appears, two caves in Colorado were especially examined. At Crack Cave, rays of the sun at the moment of its rising on fall equinox morning strike the cave's inside wall at precisely the point where an inscription says, when read as Old Gaelic, "Sun strikes [implied, "here"] on the day of Bel." (*Bel* is a name of the Gaelic sun god.) The limit of the sun's rays fits precisely with a curved line at the indicated spot.

In nearby west-facing Anubis Cave, another Ogam inscription has been read as, "Instructions for the Druid. In clear weather the projecting piece of rock eclipses the [mark] at sunset. The shadow will reach nearly to the jaw of the image of the doglike divinity." Precisely that happened at sunset at the fall equinox. The divinity petroglyph is very similar to the jackal-with-threshing-flail-atop that represented the Egyptian god known to the Greeks as Anubis, who was guardian of the equinoxes.

All the visitors, including the most skeptical, were struck by what they observed. However, exactly what one is to make of these inscriptions in historical terms is not apparent. The cultural knowledge represented in them is foreign to anything known among American Indians at the time European explorers reached Colorado. McGlone and Leonard have evidence that both Ogam writing and Egyptian religious elements could have been present in Spain and Portugal around A.D. 100–400. They suppose voyagers reached America from there. Very preliminary evidence from a new chemical (cat-ion) method of dating these inscriptions agrees that such a date is possible. The idea that the inscriptions are modern fakes is hard to believe.

Professor David Kelley, noted contributor to the decipherment of Mayan (who attended the Colorado seminar), is currently preparing a thorough review of both these matters and all of Fell's work, to be published in the important quarterly *Review of Archaeology*. He is finding that many (but not all) of the North American inscriptions in apparent European script, like those described here, are credible. This includes the remarkable petroglyph scene at Rochester Creek in east-central Utah, which displays dozens of astronomically connected Egyptian and Celtic elements. Kelley's highly informed view is that, despite flaws in the work of Fell and others, conventional scholars are on the verge of being forced to backtrack on their fundamental belief that no important contacts across the ocean took place in ancient times.

Based on research by John L. Sorenson, November 1989. In this connection, see also Cyrus H. Gordon's article about the Bat Creek inscription in Tennessee, "A Hebrew Inscription Authenticated," in John Lundquist and Stephen Ricks, eds., By Study and Also by Faith, *2 vols. (Salt Lake City: Deseret Book and F.A.R.M.S., 1990), 1:67–80. Kelley's extremely informative review was published Spring 1990, pages 1–10.*

Chapter 30

"LATEST DISCOVERIES"

Omni 1:20 "There was a large stone brought unto him with engravings on it."

The Book of Mormon reports the fact that inhabitants of ancient America other than Nephites left stone inscriptions. Particularly, when the Nephites joined the Mulekites in the city of Zarahemla about 200 B.C., a large engraved stone was brought to King Mosiah that merited special mention in the Nephite records (see Omni 1:20). Presumably this was part of a tradition of stone-monument erection, not a lone case.

Many ancient American monuments continue to baffle archaeologists and linguists. It seems, however, that with increasing frequency the press trumpets with great certitude some "new archaeological discovery," particularly in the Americas. These typically brief reports stem from press releases by discoverers acting on the modern rule that the one who gets the most publicity likely will get funding. A word of general explanation and reflection about such claims is in order.

The general problem with "latest discovery" press releases is that those who issue them can say what they wish. Only when fuller reports are made can other scholars formulate adequate critiques of the purported finds. Thus when a F.A.R.M.S. reader asks what we think about this or that newspaper or magazine report—especially as it may bear on the Book of Mormon—the answer usually has to be that no responsible person will know what to think for perhaps years. Short of that, speculation based on inadequate information could mislead. Hence, patience!

For example, in the spring of 1988, the Associated Press and *New York Times,* among other outlets, reported the discovery of a stone slab from the state of Veracruz in Mexico. It contained "inscriptions in an unknown language," supposedly by some "mysterious people." (The actual discovery was in 1986.) Aside from the extravagant journalistic language employed ("fertility-rite," "crocodiles infest the region," "fierce-looking bearded man"), there are outright errors in the report (e.g., "previously unknown system of hieroglyphics"). Actually, the glyphs on the new find are in the same system used on the Tuxtla Statuette, first published in 1907,[1] which is related to other finds analyzed at length in a 1987 article by S. Méluzin.[2]

The Veracruz find indeed promises to be of major importance because of the length of its text (577 characters), its date (second century A.D.), and its location (in or near what many Latter-day Saints believe to have been a Nephite land at that time). But what is actually to be made of it must await careful studies and publications by experts like Méluzin.

Some finds can be put into better context than others, even with limited information. For example, reports a few months ago about "ten-story high" temples in Peru that may date to 3000 B.C. or before would not be wholly without basis. G. Engel in Peru and Ecuadorean and North American archaeologists on Ecuador's north coast have made previous lesser finds of that period.

Similarly, the "jungle-shrouded city" of Nakbe in northern Guatemala that Richard Hansen (a BYU graduate now at UCLA) and Don Forsyth (BYU professor) reported in the press in September 1989 could date as early as the sixth and fifth centuries B.C. and indeed could "push the beginning of Maya civilization back further into the past." But it is by no means "one of the oldest in the Americas," based on comparison with substantially earlier non-Maya sites in Mexico, Ecuador, and Peru, some of which would have to be considered seeds for what happened at later Nakbe.

Most recently, "explorer" Gene Savoy has reported finding inscribed slabs in caves in Peru on which are "Hebrew-like" characters that may date to the time of King Solomon. Savoy's claims of major discoveries some years ago have never been adequately reported to the scientific community for evaluation. So it may be a long time before informed judgment can be rendered on these inscriptions known to the world so far only from photographs exhibited at a press conference.

This is an interesting time, when information about ancient American civilizations is expanding notably. If the latest finds prove genuine, we should learn all we can about them. Meanwhile, patience and restrained comment are called for.

Based on research by John L. Sorenson, January 1990. For further information about writing in ancient Mesoamerica, see the discussion and references in John L. Sorenson, "The Book of Mormon as a Mesoamerican Codex" (Provo: F.A.R.M.S. Reprint, 1976); "Digging into the Book of Mormon," Ensign *14 (September 1984): 26–37, and (October 1984): 12–23; and John L. Sorenson,* An Ancient American Setting for the Book of Mormon *(Salt Lake City: Deseret Book and F.A.R.M.S., 1985).*

Notes

1. William H. Holmes, "On a Nephrite Statuette from San Andres Tuxtla, Vera Cruz, Mexico," *American Anthropologist* 9 (1907): 691–701.

2. "The Tuxtla Statuette: An Internal Analysis of Its Writing System," in Gary Pahl, ed., *The Periphery of the Southeastern Classic Maya Realm,* (Los Angeles: UCLA Latin American Center, 1987), 67–113.

Chapter 31

THE IDEOLOGY OF KINGSHIP IN MOSIAH 1–6

Mosiah 1:10 "I shall proclaim unto this my people out of mine own mouth that thou art a king and a ruler over this people, whom the Lord our God hath given us."

A vital feature of almost every ancient and medieval society was divine kingship, that is, rule by god-appointed kings. This was true of Egyptian and Mesopotamian cultures, as well as of Israelite, Nephite, and Lamanite societies during much of their history. Only recently have scholars noted a common pattern in the ideology of kingship in Israel and the rest of the ancient Near East. Interestingly, we now find in the Nephite ideology of kingship, elements of which are recorded in Mosiah 1–6, striking parallels to the kingship ideology in Israel and elsewhere in the ancient Near East.

Four of the most significant features follow:

1. *Accession to the Throne*. The king in ancient Israel was deemed chosen by God in that his accession showed God's choice. Similarly, Benjamin affirmed that Mosiah was chosen by the Lord to succeed him when he said: "On the morrow I shall proclaim unto this my people out of mine own mouth that thou art a king and a ruler over this people, whom the Lord our God hath given us" (Mosiah 1:10; see also 2:11, 30).

The eldest son of the king in ancient Israel was generally entitled to the throne (see 2 Chronicles 21:3), although he does not always seem to have been obligated to do so (see 2 Kings 23:31, 36; 2 Chronicles 11:21–22). It is never explicitly stated that Mosiah was Benjamin's firstborn son, but this seems likely, since his name is given first among the names of Benjamin's sons (see Mosiah 1:2).

In early Israel both Solomon and Jotham became king while their fathers were still alive and ruling (see 1 Kings 1:32–40; 2:1–10; 2 Kings 15:5). Three years before he died, Benjamin too installed his son Mosiah as king (see Mosiah 6:5): "[Benjamin] waxed old, and he saw that he must very soon go the way of all the earth; therefore, he thought it expedient that he should confer the kingdom upon one of his sons" (Mosiah 1:9). During these three years, Benjamin and his son may have administered the kingdom jointly.

2. *Ambivalent View of Kingship*. In Mesopotamian and Egyptian societies, kingship was the primary form of government, and the king was viewed as being divine or at least as being the adopted offspring of deity. In Israelite and Nephite societies, however, the king did not view himself as divine, and kingship itself was viewed rather ambivalently. Benjamin clearly stated at the beginning of his address, "I have not commanded you to come up hither . . . that ye should think that I of myself am more than a mortal man" (Mosiah 2:10). Further, while both the Old Testament and the Book of Mormon note that there are very positive aspects of kingship (see 1 Samuel 12:12–15; Mosiah 29:13–15), they also observe that there are negative and even dangerous features of it (see 1 Samuel 8:11–18; Mosiah 29:16–17).

3. *The King as Protector of the Weak*. Kings in the ancient Near East, including Israel, were obligated to maintain justice and to protect the rights of the weakest members of society. Indeed, these qualities were invariably mentioned in descriptions of good kings. In his address, Benjamin detailed his efforts to maintain justice during his rule: "Neither have I suffered that ye should be confined in dungeons, nor that ye should make slaves one of another, nor that ye should murder, or plunder, or steal, or commit adultery" (Mosiah 2:13). Benjamin further told his people that their concern for the poor and the needy was essential to retain a remission of their sins (see Mosiah 4:26): "Ye will not

suffer that the beggar putteth up his petition to you in vain, and turn him out to perish" (Mosiah 4:16).

4. *The King and the Covenant of the Lord.* Unlike kings of other peoples of the ancient Near East, the king in Israel had the responsibility of acting as the guardian of the covenant between the Lord and his people. The king in ancient Israel was one "from among the people of Yahweh who, because of the singular privilege of being anointed to kingship, bore a special responsibility of guardianship for the faith of the nation."[1]

In a similar manner, kingship and covenant are inextricably connected in Benjamin's speech (see Mosiah 2:29–30). Benjamin commanded his son to gather the people together in order that he might proclaim his son king and "give this people a name" (Mosiah 1:10–11). This "name" is "the name of Christ," to be accepted by all "that have entered into the covenant with God that [they] should be obedient unto the end of [their] lives" (Mosiah 5:8). Much of Benjamin's address is concerned with admonishing the people to keep the covenant. Kingship, covenant, and the observance of commandments are again connected in Mosiah 6:3 which states that Benjamin appointed priests "to teach the people, that thereby they might hear and know the commandments of God, and to stir them up in remembrance of the oath which they had made."

It is impossible to understand ancient Near Eastern cultures and societies without appreciating their attitude toward kingship. The king in Israel was central; he had both sacral and political roles. Many customs defined the king's roles and duties. As the foregoing examples from Benjamin's speech illustrate, this rich and complex ideology is accurately reflected in the Book of Mormon.

Based on research by Stephen D. Ricks, August 1987.

Note

1. Helen A. Kenik, "Code of Conduct for a King: Psalm 101," *Journal of Biblical Literature* 95 (1976): 391.

Chapter 32

"THIS DAY"

Mosiah 2:9 "Hear my words which I shall speak unto you this day."

The phrase "this day" may be very significant in the scriptures. This solemn and emphatic concept appears, for example, in the famous covenantal text at the end of the book of Joshua: "Choose you *this day* whom ye will serve. . . . Ye are witnesses against yourselves that ye have chosen you the Lord, to serve him. And they said, We are witnesses. . . . So Joshua made a covenant with the people *that day*" (Joshua 24:15–25). It seems that words of this nature were especially used in antiquity in reference to religious or ceremonial holy days.

The words "this day" appear eighteen times in the Book of Mormon. Six occurrences are regular expressions meaning "at this time," and one in Alma 30:8 quotes Joshua 24:15. But the remaining eleven all appear in conjunction with holy Nephite gatherings at their temples.

King Benjamin uses the phrase "this day" five times in his monumental speech, and each time it occurs at ritual and covenantal highpoints in the text: He enjoins the people to give heed to "my words which I shall speak unto you *this day*" (Mosiah 2:9). He calls the people as "witnesses *this day*" that he has discharged his duties as king according to the law and has a pure conscience before God "*this day*" (Mosiah 2:14–15; compare Deuteronomy 17:14–20). He declares "*this day*" that his son Mosiah is their new king (Mosiah 2:30). He affirms that "*this day* [Christ] hath spiritually begotten you" (Mosiah 5:7). These usages are important covenantal markers. It seems likely that Benjamin is using this phrase not as a mere literary embellishment, but as a term with legal and religious import.

All Israelites were commanded to assemble at their temple "before the Lord God" three times a year on their high holy days (see Exodus 23:17). The Nephites were "exceedingly strict" in observing the law of Moses (in their looking forward to the Christ whom that law typified; see 2 Nephi 5:10; 11:4; Jarom 1:5; Alma 30:3). It thus follows that they also regularly gathered in holy assemblies on such days. Indeed, the following texts may be read as evidence that they marked those occasions with special reference to "this day."

Jacob tells of coming "up into the temple *this day*" to rid his garments of the people's sins and to declare the word of God (Jacob 2:2–3). He pronounces a curse upon those who remain impure on this particular day: "Wo, wo, unto you that are not pure in heart, that are filthy *this day* before God" (Jacob 3:3). Why "this day"? Is it because Jacob chose a holy day, perhaps even the purifying Day of Atonement, on which to preach his powerful sermon against unchastity and greed, and to rid his people of sin and wickedness?

Similarly, when Alma delivers his most powerful sermon on the Atonement in the city of Gideon, he requires the people to witness their righteousness to God "*this day* by going into the waters of baptism" (Alma 7:15). Elsewhere, the phrase "this day" also appears in connection with Limhi's assembly (Mosiah 7:12; 7:21). Jacob's farewell sermon also seems to be set in a ritual context, and he asks his audience, "Yea, *today,* if ye will hear his voice [a liturgical image], harden not your hearts; for why will ye die?" (Jacob 6:6).

Beyond Joshua 24:15, further corroboration for these pointed uses of "this day" in the Book of Mormon can be found in Hebrew literature. In Hebrew the word *etzem* is significant. It appears, for example, in Exodus 12:17, "Ye shall observe the feast of unleavened bread; for in *this selfsame day* [*b'etzem hayom hazeh*] have I brought your armies out of the land of Egypt." Abraham Bloch has recently concluded that "this descriptive word was not a mere literary flourish" but a technical term of art with some unknown special significance.[1]

For further insight, Bloch turns to the medieval Jewish jurist Nahmanides, who "noted with great amazement that *etzem* ['self-same'] was used only in connection with the observance of Yom Kippur [the Israelite festival of the Day of Atonement] and Shavuot [the biblical festival of the Firstfruits, or Pentecost]."[2] The implication is that this term was used to indicate that these high holy days in and of themselves produced a binding legal effect or holy religious status.

Evidently, in Nephite language and rhetoric, the phrase "this day" often indicated the covenantal and legal status of a holy day, much as "this day," "today," or "this selfsame day" did in Hebrew.

Based on research by John W. Welch, Donald W. Parry, and Stephen D. Ricks, April 1990.

Notes

1. Abraham Bloch, *The Biblical and Historical Background of the Jewish Holy Days* (New York: KTAV, 1978), 114.

2. Cited in ibid.

Chapter 33

BENJAMIN'S SPEECH: A CLASSIC ANCIENT FAREWELL ADDRESS

Mosiah 2:28 "at this period of time when I am about to go down to my grave"

Scholars have recently taken an interest in the similarities that exist in the farewell speeches of many ancient religious and political leaders. Certain themes appear consistently in these farewell addresses, as if the speakers were following a customary pattern. These themes are to be found to an equal or greater extent in the farewell speeches of the Book of Mormon.

William S. Kurz has published a detailed study comparing twenty-two addresses from the classical and biblical traditions.[1] He has found that in Greco-Roman writings, the dying speaker, usually a philosopher or statesman, was concerned with suicide, the meaning of death, and life after death. However, in biblical farewell addresses, the speaker, typically a man of God, focused on God's plan, his people, and covenants, or on theological interpretations of history. While some elements are peculiar to one or the other tradition, Kurz has identified twenty elements common to the farewell addresses in general (listed on following pages).

Although Kurz knows no single speech that contains all of these elements, some contain more than others. Moses' farewell speech contains sixteen elements (see Deuteronomy 31–34); Paul's, fourteen (see Acts 20); and Socrates', eleven.

It is remarkable that King Benjamin's oration contains as

many or more elements of the ancient farewell address than any of Kurz's examples. Unlike those other texts, Benjamin's speech was recorded in full and was precisely preserved. The report of Benjamin's address is not a paraphrase and is longer and more detailed than such addresses found in biblical accounts. Sixteen elements of the ideal ancient farewell address appear directly and others may be implied.

Kurz signals four of his twenty elements as particularly common to Hebrew farewell addresses in the Old Testament and in the Old Testament Apocrypha: (1) the speaker proposes tasks for successors, (2) reviews theological history, (3) reveals future events, and (4) declares his innocence and fulfillment of his mission. These elements all appear in the Benjamin account. Furthermore, the emphasis in Benjamin's address, as in the Israelite tradition, is on God's relationship to man, the speech ending with a covenant renewal. No trace of the Greco-Roman preoccupation with death occurs. Benjamin's speech thus fits illustriously into the Israelite tradition of farewell addresses.

Recent research finds Benjamin's speech to be the most complete example of this speech typology yet found anywhere in world literature. It captures the essence of the traditional Israelite farewell sermon. By understanding this tradition, the Western mind can more deeply appreciate yet another dimension of the salutary words of King Benjamin.

Those interested in comparing Benjamin's address with any of the twenty-two addresses that Kurz examined in his study may consult the detailed chart in his article. A skeleton outline of those elements in Benjamin's speech is as follows:

Kurz's Twenty Elements of Ancient Farewell Addresses	References for the Same Elements in Benjamin's Speech
1. The speaker summons his successors	1:9-10; 2:1, 9
2. He cites his own mission as an example	2:12-14, 18

3. He states his innocence and the fact that he fulfilled his duty	2:15, 27-31
4. He refers to his impending death	1:9; 2:26, 28
5. He exhorts his audience	2:9, 40-41; 4:9-10; 5:12
6. He issues warnings and final injunctions	2:31-32, 36-39; 3:12, 25; 4:14-30; 5:10-11
7. He blesses his audience	Not clearly found, but see "blessed" in 2:41
8. He makes farewell gestures	Possibly implied in 2:28; see 2 Nephi 9:44
9. He names tasks for his successors	1:15–16; 2:31; 6:3
10. He gives a theological review of history	2:34-35; 3:13-15
11. The speaker reveals future events	3:1, 5-10
12. Promises are given	2:22, 31; 4:12; 5:9
13. He appoints/refers to successor	1:15-16; 2:31; 6:3
14. Rest of people bewail loss of leader	Not found
15. Future degeneration addressed	3:23-27; 4:14-15
16. Sacrifices and covenants are renewed	2:3; 5:1-7
17. Care is given for those left	4:14-26; 6:3
18. Consolation is given to inner circle	5:15
19. Didactic speech is made	3:16-21
20. *Ars moriendi*	Possibly in 2:28

Based on research by John W. Welch, assisted by Daryl R. Hague, June 1987.

Note

1. William S. Kurz, "Luke 22:14–38 and Greco-Roman and Biblical Farewell Addresses," *Journal of Biblical Literature* 104 (1985): 251–68.

King Benjamin delivered his farewell address from a tower near the temple in the city of Zarahemla. Painting by Minerva Teichert, courtesy of Museum of Fine Arts, Brigham Young University.

Chapter 34

THE CORONATION OF KINGS

Mosiah 2:30 "I should declare unto you this day, that my son Mosiah is a king and a ruler over you."

Closely associated with the ideology of kingship is the coronation of the king. It is the central ritual act connected with kingship. In Mosiah 1–6 is found a fascinating text surrounding the coronation of Benjamin's son, Mosiah. A comparison of that text with the coronation ceremonies recorded in the Old Testament and with enthronement rituals among other peoples of the ancient Near East reveals striking parallels. For example:

1. *The Sanctuary as the Site of the Coronation.* Sacred space is the natural and necessary location for the sacral act of regal coronation. Following the construction of the temple in ancient Israel, the temple site always served as the site of coronations. Thus, during his coronation, Joash is mentioned as standing in the temple "by a pillar, as the manner was" (2 Kings 11:14). Similarly, the temple at Zarahemla was the site chosen for Benjamin's address to the people and for the "consecration" of his son Mosiah as king (Mosiah 1:18).

2. *Investiture with Insignia.* In ancient Israel, various tokens of kingship seem regularly to have been given to the new monarch at the coronation. These included such things as the law the king was required to have and read (see Deuteronomy 17:18–19), the diadem, and other material symbols of power. Similarly, Benjamin, in the course of transferring power to his son Mosiah, "gave him charge concerning the records which were engraven

on the plates of brass; and also the plates of Nephi; and also, the sword of Laban, and the ball or director, which led our fathers through the wilderness" (Mosiah 1:15–16). Although not explicitly stated, these things were clearly given to Mosiah because of his responsibility as king and because they were symbols of law, power, and leadership.

3. *Anointing*. Anointing the king with oil is a significant element in the coronation ceremonies in ancient Israel and in the ancient Near East generally. The Bible records the anointings of six Israelite kings: Saul, David, Solomon, Jehu, Joash, and Jehoahaz. In the Book of Mormon, following Benjamin's address and the renewal of the covenant by the people, Benjamin "consecrated his son Mosiah to be a ruler and a king over his people" (Mosiah 6:3). The text does not indicate whether this "consecration" included anointing. However, some ritual act was clearly involved. Other instances in Nephite history indicate that the coronation included anointing. Jacob records that his brother Nephi "began to be old, and he saw that he must soon die; wherefore, he anointed a man to be a king and a ruler over his people now, according to the reigns of the kings" (Jacob 1:9).

4. *Receipt of a Regnal Name*. At the time of his accession to the throne, the king usually also received a new name, either a title or a name possessed by a predecessor. Examples of this abound in Egypt, Mesopotamia, and ancient Israel. Similarly, in the Book of Mormon, Jacob describes the giving of regnal names in his day: "Whoso should reign in [Nephi's] stead were called by the people second Nephi, third Nephi, and so forth, according to the reigns of the kings; and thus they were called by the people, let them be of whatever name they would" (Jacob 1:10–11). Whether Mosiah similarly had a regnal name is difficult to determine. He is invariably referred to as "Mosiah" (i.e., Mosiah 6:4–7), so it is unknown if this was a given name or a coronation name. The latter is possible, since the name Mosiah may be a title meaning "savior, deliverer."[1] Evidently between the time that Jacob made his record and Mosiah acceded to the throne, the practice of using Nephi as a regnal name had been changed,

perhaps because the kingdom was no longer located in the land of Nephi. It is also possible that Mormon, the editor of this particular part of the history, used only one name for Mosiah in order to eliminate further confusion about multiple "Nephis."

5. *Other Elements*. Other factors in Mosiah's enthronement that were typically present at coronations of ancient Israelite kings can also be mentioned: for example, sacrifices of thanksgiving (see Mosiah 2:3–4); acceptance of the new monarch by the people agreeing to obey him and God (see Mosiah 2:31; 5:5); and the reappointment of priests and reconstitution of officers under the new regime (see Mosiah 6:3).

From the evidence at hand, we can see that the Nephite coronation ceremony quite appropriately consisted of elements similar to those used in ancient Israel. This aspect of kingship is fully and properly represented in the royal record of the Nephites.

Based on research by Stephen D. Ricks, July 1989.

Note

1. See chapter 28, pp. 105–7, in this book.

Chapter 35

"O MAN, REMEMBER, AND PERISH NOT" (Mosiah 4:30)

Mosiah 2:41 "O remember, remember that these things are true; for the Lord God hath spoken it."

The Book of Mormon constantly reminds its readers to remember. Nephi concluded his account of Lehi's prophecies by saying, "Therefore *remember,* O man, for all thy doings thou shalt be brought into judgment" (1 Nephi 10:20). King Benjamin punctuated his covenantal speech with the plea, "O *remember, remember* that these things are true; for the Lord God hath spoken it" (Mosiah 2:41). Jesus himself placed the Nephites in Bountiful under covenant to "always remember" him and to keep the commandments that he had given them (3 Nephi 18:7, 11; Moroni 4–5).

From numerous statements like these, it is evident that "remembering" is a saving principle of the gospel. Just as faith looks forward in Christ to actualize the present power of his redemption, so remembrance looks back on covenants and gifts from God and keeps the past alive.

Several recent scholarly studies have analyzed the meanings of remembrance in the Bible, and some of this research can help us appreciate the important meanings of remembrance in the Book of Mormon. By placing emphasis on the concept of "remembering," the Book of Mormon significantly captures one of the most distinctive aspects of Israelite mentality.

Brevard S. Childs has shown that various forms of the Hebrew verb *zakhor* (to remember) occur in the Old Testament well over two hundred times. He shows that what the Old Testament understands by "memory" goes well beyond the mere mental recall of information, though of course that is part of its meaning. To remember often means to be attentive, to consider, to keep divine commandments, or to act.[1] The word in Hebrew thus carries a wider range of meaning than is common with the verb *remember* in English. Indeed, to remember involves turning to God, or repenting, or acting in accordance with divine injunctions.[2]

Not only man, but also God "remembers." He remembers covenants he has made with Noah (see Genesis 9:15–16), with Abraham, Isaac, and Jacob (see Exodus 2:24; Leviticus 26:42), and with all of Israel (see Ezekiel 16:60; Luke 1:72).

Conversely, the antonym of the verb *to remember* in Hebrew—*to forget*—does not merely describe the passing of a thought from the mind, but involves a failure to act, or a failure to do or keep something. Hence, failing to remember God and his commandments is the equivalent of apostasy.

Interestingly, words for memory and remembrance also occur well over two hundred times in the Book of Mormon. This high density is not noticed by casual readers, but it vividly reflects a religious sensitivity on the part of Book of Mormon prophets that is similar to that of other Israelite prophets. Though the range of uses of remembering in the Book of Mormon is perhaps not quite as extensive as that identifiable in the Old Testament, the idiom of remembrance in both books includes warnings, promises, threats, pleas, and complaints, and the same deep connection between memory and action can be found in both. To remember is to hearken (see, e.g., Jacob 3:9–11), to awaken, to see, to hear, to believe, to trust.

One remembers only through a faithful response to the terms of the covenant. But rebellious Israel has always been "quick to do iniquity, and slow to remember the Lord their God; therefore there was a law given them, yea, a law of performances and of ordinances, a law which they were to observe strictly from day to day, to keep them in remembrance of God and their duty towards him" (Mosiah 13:29–30).

It is therefore common to find remembering linked to the

demand to "keep his commandments" (see, e.g., 1 Nephi 15:25; Mosiah 2:41; 4:30; Alma 7:16; 9:13–14; 18:10; 36:1–2; 46:23; 58:40; compare Numbers 15:39–40; Psalms 103:18). For example, King Lamoni praised Ammon, "For even he doth remember all my commandments to execute them" (Alma 18:10). Likewise, Alma constructs an elegant parallelism based upon this linkage:

> O, remember, my son,
> and learn wisdom in thy youth;
> yea, learn in thy youth
> to keep the commandments of God.
> (Alma 37:35)

In such ways the Book of Mormon shows a clear link between the ways of remembrance or forgetfulness and the blessings or cursings associated with the covenant people of God. Since one of the main purposes of the Book of Mormon, as stated on its Title Page, is to show that God remembers the covenants he has made with his people (see also 1 Nephi 19:15–16; 2 Nephi 29:1–2; 3 Nephi 16:11), it is especially appropriate that the renewal of covenants includes a commitment to "always remember him, and keep his commandments," as the faithful affirm their willingness to take upon them the name of Jesus Christ (Moroni 4:3).

Based on research by Louis C. Midgley, March 1990. A fuller treatment of this topic by Midgley can now be found as "The Ways of Remembrance," in John Sorenson and Melvin Thorne, eds., Rediscovering the Book of Mormon *(Salt Lake City: Deseret Book and F.A.R.M.S., 1991), 168–76.*

Notes

1. *Memory and Tradition in Israel* (London: SCM, 1962), 9–10, 50–54.

2. See also Hayim Yerushalmi, *Zakhor: Jewish History and Jewish Memory* (Seattle: University of Washington Press, 1982).

Chapter 36

BARLEY IN ANCIENT AMERICA

Mosiah 7:22 "one half of our corn, and our barley, and even all our grain of every kind"

The December 1983 issue of the popular magazine *Science 83* reported the discovery in Phoenix, Arizona, by professional archaeologists of what they supposed to be pre-Columbian domesticated barley. That same month, F.A.R.M.S. carried a preliminary notice of the discovery. This Arizona find is the first direct New World evidence for cultivated pre-Columbian barley in support of the Book of Mormon. Mosiah 9:9 lists barley among several crops that were cultivated by the Nephites in the land of Nephi, and Alma 11:7 singles out barley as the primary grain into which silver and gold were converted in the Nephite system of weights and measures.

That there are copious samples of cultivated barley at pre-Columbian sites in Arizona seemed a first for the Western Hemisphere, but Professor Howard C. Stutz of the BYU Department of Biology tells us that three types of *wild* barley have long been known to be native to the Americas. The real surprise is that this barley is of a cultivated ("naked") type, although the ethnobotanist for the Arizona project, Dr. Vorsila Bohrer (Eastern New Mexico University, Portales), says that it is not yet clear whether the samples were truly naked (unhulled) or simply naturally degraded in context.

Archaeologists have been analyzing the barley samples retrieved from the Phoenix area and say that they are associated with material and strata generally dated c. A.D. 900. The same sort of naked *hordeum pussilum* was seen years ago in the Snaketown excavation of Dr. Emil Haury (University of Arizona, now retired). The Snaketown samples and more recent samples from archaeological contexts in Southern Illinois are said to be dated from A.D. 1 through 900.

Samples of similarly naked barley have also been found in context in eastern Oklahoma, although hulled samples from a cave in the Tonto National Monument raise questions (Dr. Bohrer suggests rodent activity may be involved in this instance). However, none of these samples has yet been radiocarbon dated, and it is not yet clear where the samples lie in the process of cultivation to true domestication. We await with interest further excavations, dating, and morphological examination to determine *when* and *how* the cultivation of this barley was begun, as well as its taxonomic relationship to New or Old World wild barleys.

The barley samples mentioned in *Science 83* (as well as the earlier Snaketown samples) were taken from recent "salvage" excavations into the remains of the very important culture—the Hohokam—that existed in southern Arizona from approximately 300 B.C. to around A.D. 1450 (dates well established via C–14). After appearing in the area, possibly as immigrants from Mesoamerica, those people constructed a vast irrigation network (using water from the Gila and Salt rivers) that eventually covered ten thousand square miles and twenty-two "cities" and served a population estimated at from one hundred thousand to one million persons. At least forty thousand of these people lived in the immediate area of Phoenix. Pima Indians and even nineteenth-century Mormons have made use of some of the remnant Hohokam canals.

These recent excavations are known as "salvage" excavations because they were sponsored with federal funds in order to recover archaeological data being destroyed by construction in Phoenix. One of these Hohokam excavations, operated by Arizona State University and completed in 1983, was at the site of a new interchange on the Papago Freeway—a site long known as La Ciudad, "The City." The Arizona State University archaeologists found 205 houses, a Mesoamerican-style ball court, and complete pottery vessels and other artifacts within a few feet of the surface! From oral descriptions given by Dr. Glenn Rice of Arizona State University, there was clearly wide-ranging trade with northern Mexico, with which Hohokam culture had much in common.[1]

What happened to ancient American people such as the Hohokam demands better explanation than we now have. How the information from Arizona, or indeed from Illinois, Oklahoma, Louisiana, or Peru, fits with the Book of Mormon cultural information needs to be spelled out. Were the Hohokam and their barley directly or indirectly related to the Nephites and their barley? Perhaps the shipping activities of Hagoth, who sailed north from the Nephite narrow neck of land (see Alma 63:6–10), will play a role in that explanation.

Based on research by John L. Sorenson and Robert F. Smith, December 1984. For further information about the role of barley in the ancient Egyptian and Mesopotamian systems of weights and measures, see the F.A.R.M.S. paper, "Weights and Measures in the Time of Mosiah II" (1983).

Note

1. For an informative article on the Hohokam ruins at Snaketown and elsewhere, see Emil W. Haury, "First Masters of the American Desert: The Hohokam," and Kenneth F. Weaver, "Magnetic Clues Help Date the Past," *National Geographic* 131 (May 1967): 670–95 and 696–701.

Chapter 37

DECORATIVE IRON IN EARLY ISRAEL

Mosiah 11:8 "all manner of precious things, of gold, and of silver, and of iron"

At various times when iron was scarce, it was used as a precious decorative metal. So concludes a recent article, "King Og's Iron Bed—Fact or Fancy?"[1] Here, Alan R. Millard documents archaeological evidence for the early use of iron to *decorate* beds (see Deuteronomy 3:11) and thrones, as well as bracelets and jewelry, weapons and royal swords. Such beds or jeweled boxes were not of solid iron, but they were plated, veneered, or studded with the metal.

The article features pictures illustrating how, in the second millennium B.C., iron was "highly prized," like other precious metals and the semi-precious blue stone, lapis lazuli. "At a time when iron was hard to obtain, the product of a difficult technique, a bed or a throne decorated with it could be a treasure in a king's palace."[2]

With such a point in mind, we can reread the account of King Noah, who built many elegant buildings and "*ornamented* them with fine work of wood, and of all manner of precious things, of gold, and of silver, and of *iron*[!]" (Mosiah 11:8; emphasis added). Although a person today would not normally think of using iron as a precious decoration, we can now see that this was actually done in antiquity.

Thus, though iron was present in the city of Nephi in Noah's time, it was apparently rare and precious then, just as it was in the early Iron Age in Palestine. This was probably always the case in Book of Mormon society, for all New World references to iron in the book mention it together with gold and silver and other precious things (see 2 Nephi 5:15; Jarom 1:8; Ether 10:23). Perhaps this metal was especially prized among the Nephites due to the great symbolic and spiritual value of the "rod of iron" in Lehi's vision in 1 Nephi 8.

Based on research by John W. Welch, appearing in Insights, *no. 2 (1990).*

Notes

1. Alan R. Millard, "King Og's Iron Bed—Fact or Fancy?" *Bible Review* 6 (April 1990): 16–20.
2. Ibid., 20.

Chapter 38

ABINADI AND PENTECOST

Mosiah 13:5 "His face shone with exceeding luster, even as Moses' did while in the mount of Sinai, while speaking with the Lord."

Fifty days after Passover on the ancient Israelite calendar was the festival of Pentecost or Shavuot ("Weeks"), which the law of Moses required the children of Israel to observe (see Exodus 23:16). Recent research has probed the possibility that Abinadi delivered his prophetic message in the city of Nephi on this festive occasion.

Pentecost marked the concluding phase of Passover.[1] It was also an agricultural holiday sometimes called the Day of the Firstfruits (see Numbers 28:26). It was a pilgrimage festival, with a "holy convocation" (Leviticus 23:21), rejoicing in the bounty of the spring, especially the new wheat (see Deuteronomy 16:9–12; 26:5–11). Just as Passover marked a time of poverty and bondage, Pentecost exulted in a time of bounty, with offerings of leavened bread baked from the new crop of wheat (see Leviticus 23:17) and of the choicest firstfruits.

About this same time of the year was the day when Moses received the Ten Commandments on Mount Sinai (see Exodus 19:1). Thus, Pentecost probably also celebrated the giving of the law by God to Moses. The connection between Pentecost and the giving of the law is well-documented in the Talmud.[2] When this connection was first established is a matter of historical debate. A recent opinion of Professor Moshe Weinfeld of the Hebrew University of Jerusalem is that this connection was made very early in Israelite history, as evidenced by Psalms 50 and 81, which he concludes were sung at Pentecost.[3]

Psalm 50:16–21 shows that Pentecost also became a day of stern admonition: "What hast thou to do to declare my statutes, . . . seeing thou hatest instruction[?] . . . When thou sawest a thief, then thou consentedst with him, and hast been partaker with adulterers" (vv. 16–18). A warning like this must have been especially potent on a day when the people were venerating the law.

Against this, the story of Abinadi in Mosiah 11–17 now comes vividly to life. Consider the following points:

1. Timing would have been important to Abinadi. He had already been expelled once from the city, two years earlier (see Mosiah 11:28–12:1). His reentry on a festival day would have given him a ready audience.

2. Both of Abinadi's speeches deal with the themes of Pentecost. He reversed the festival's blessings and rejoicing, and turned them into curses and predictions of gloom. At the time when a bounteous grain season would have been at hand, Abinadi cursed the crops: he prophesied that hail, dry winds, and insects shall ruin "their grain" (Mosiah 12:6). While Israel's deliverance from bondage was traditionally being celebrated, Abinadi called upon Exodus terminology to proclaim that bondage and burdens would return to the wicked people in the city of Nephi: "They shall be brought into bondage; . . . and none shall deliver them" (Mosiah 11:21, 23), "and I will cause that they shall have burdens lashed upon their backs" (Mosiah 12:2, 5; compare Exodus 1:11).

3. At precisely the time when Noah's priests would have been hypocritically pledging allegiance to the Ten Commandments (and indeed they professed to teach the law of Moses; see Mosiah 12:27), Abinadi rehearsed to them those very commandments (see Mosiah 12:33). On any other day this might have seemed a strange defense for a man on trial for his life, but not on Pentecost – the day on which the Ten Commandments were on center stage!

4. Indeed, the connection with Pentecost could hardly have been more graphic than when Abinadi's "face shone with ex-

ceeding luster, *even as Moses'* did while in the mount of Sinai, while speaking with the Lord" (Mosiah 13:5, italics added; compare Exodus 34:29–30). This divine manifestation was quintessentially pentecostal.

5. There are further connections between Abinadi and Exodus 19. For example, cursing Noah to be like a "garment in a hot furnace" may well recall the fact that Mt. Sinai became a furnace (see Exodus 19:18) and that people whose garments were not clean were not "ready" for the Lord (see Exodus 19:10–15). The tongues of fire that appeared when the apostle Peter spoke on the Feast of Pentecost in Acts 2–3 likewise recall the burnings on Mt. Sinai.

6. The ancient festival appears to have been a three-day event (see Exodus 19:11), which may explain why Abinadi's trial was postponed for "three days" (Mosiah 17:6).

7. Finally, there are intriguing parallels between Abinadi's piercing rebukes and Psalm 50, identified by Weinfeld as a psalm of Pentecost.

For example, Psalms 50:3 begins: "Our God *shall come,* and shall not keep silence" (italics added). Compare Exodus 19:11: On "the third day *the Lord will come down* in the sight of all the people" (italics added). So Abinadi's main message is how "God himself shall come down among the children of men" (Mosiah 15:1).

In Psalms 50:4–7, God is bringing a lawsuit against his people, just as Abinadi's words take the form of a "prophetic lawsuit."[4]

Psalms 50:13–14 makes it clear that the Lord prefers thanksgiving from the heart over sacrifices. Likewise, Abinadi requires the commandments of God to be "written in your hearts" (Mosiah 13:11).

Psalms 50:16 asks what a person must do in order to teach the law. The answer is to *keep the law,* otherwise God will "tear you in pieces, and there be none to deliver" (Psalms 50:22, italics added; compare Mosiah 11:23). This is exactly Abinadi's point:

"And again he said unto them: If ye teach the law of Moses why do ye not keep it?" (Mosiah 12:29).

Both Abinadi and Psalm 50 particularly condemn those who wrongfully become rich and those who commit whoredoms (compare Psalms 50:18; Mosiah 12:29).

All together these details lead to one conclusion: No other day on the ancient Israelite calendar fits the message, words, and experience of the prophet Abinadi more precisely than does the ancient Israelite festival of Pentecost.

Based on research by John W. Welch, Gordon C. Thomasson, and Robert F. Smith, September 1985.

Notes

1. Abraham Bloch, *Biblical and Historical Background of the Jewish Holy Days* (New York: KTAV, 1978), 179.

2. Ibid., 186–88, citing esp. *Shabbat* 86b.

3. Moshe Weinfeld, "The Decalogue in Israel's Tradition," in Edwin Firmage, Bernard Weiss, and John Welch, eds., *Religion and Law: Biblical/Judaic and Islamic Perspectives* (Winona Lake, Indiana: Eisenbrauns, 1990), 38–47; see also Moshe Weinfeld, "Pentecost as Festival of the Giving of the Law," *Immanuel* 8, no. 7 (Spring 1978): 7–18.

4. See Richard McGuire, "Prophetic Lawsuits in the Hebrew Bible and Book of Mormon" (Provo: F.A.R.M.S., 1983).

Chapter 39

DANCING MAIDENS AND THE FIFTEENTH OF AV

Mosiah 20:1 "There was a place in Shemlon where the daughters of the Lamanites did gather themselves together to sing, and to dance."

Just as the month of February means Valentine's Day (and sometimes Bachelors' Leap Year Day) to many Americans, the 15th of Av had significance to the ancient Israelites. On that day in the fifth month of the Israelite calendar (which fell originally on midsummer's day), the maidens of Israel would gather to dance. This was, among other things, a "matrimonial holiday for youth."

This ancient holiday is described by Abraham P. Bloch.[1] Bloch concludes that this unnamed holiday was of very early origin, dating back to Moses according to one rabbi.[2] In those days, the festival was primarily a matrimonial holiday, very much like the Jewish *Lag Ba'Omer* of springtime. Following the conclusion of their summer chores in the fields, youths would turn their attention to "bride-hunting," and the dance of the maidens was "designed to meet that end."[3] The dancing took place outside a temple city—during the period of the Judges, the dances were in the fields outside Shiloh. During later times they were at Jerusalem.

After the return of the Jews from their captivity in Babylon, the holiday took on a much different character. It became a festival of wood-gathering and of offerings of wood for the altar of the temple. This practice ended with the destruction of the Second Temple in Jerusalem by the Romans. The holiday briefly reappeared around A.D. 140 as a day to commemorate the termination of the Hadrianic persecutions of the Jews and to glorify the young Jewish patriots.[4]

Lehi and his people, of course, would only have known the earlier traditions of "dancing and bride-hunting," and perhaps this sheds light on the time when the priests of Noah carried off twenty-four Lamanite daughters to be their wives.

Mosiah 20:1 tells that "there was a place in Shemlon where the daughters of the Lamanites did gather themselves together to sing, and to dance, and to make themselves merry." This seems to say that the place was a customary one. The place may have been at an outlying shrine or sacred spot. It was not in the wilderness as such, for the priests went from there into the wilderness (see Mosiah 20:5), but neither was it inside a city.

There the priests found the young women, hid themselves and watched, and sprang out of their hiding places, taking the young women into the wilderness (see Mosiah 20:2–5). The Hebrew idiom translated "lying in wait" usually connotes premeditation and planning, implying that the priests may well have known of this place and the custom for young women to be there. Indeed, the young women apparently became the priests' wives willingly enough; at least we find no indication that any of them tried to escape, and all of them later pled with their brothers and fathers not to kill their husbands (see Mosiah 23:33).

This suggests that the Lamanite daughters had gathered to dance in celebration of a vestige of something like the preexilic Israelite festival of the 15th of Av. Is that how the priests of Noah knew where to go and when to be there? Is that why the young women accepted the priests as husbands? After all, they would have been dancing to attract husbands.

The Old Testament records one similar occurrence. During the period of the Judges, a feast of Jehovah was held "yearly" at Shiloh, which was then the religious center of Israel. One year, the men of Benjamin purposefully went to Shiloh on this feast day, laid in wait in the vineyards, caught "every man his wife of the daughters of Shiloh," and took them to the land of

Benjamin (Judges 21:16–23). Although the Hebrew account is somewhat unclear, the Benjaminite men apparently planned to defend themselves when the men of Shiloh came after them by arguing that they had done the best thing: By taking the young women, they had not asked the Shilohites to give them their daughters, which would have violated the oath of Judges 21:18; furthermore, they had not taken the young women by bloodshed.

This isolated biblical account, however, does not give the whole picture. It does not convey the point that this celebration was probably a widespread festival observed for many centuries among the ancient Israelites. Furthermore, the "matrimonial character" of the dances is only identified "in later talmudic traditions."[5] There are several other famous incidents in history following similar lines: for example, the abduction of the Sabine women by the Romans. Many such ancient practices and attitudes may have been relevant also to Book of Mormon peoples.

Based on research by John W. Welch, Robert F. Smith, and Gordon C. Thomasson, February 1985.

Notes

1. Abraham P. Bloch, *The Biblical and Historical Background of the Jewish Holy Days* (New York: KTAV, 1978), 215–19.
2. See Babylonian Talmud, *Baba Batra* 121a.
3. Bloch, *The Biblical and Historical Background of the Jewish Holy Days,* 216.
4. Ibid., 217–18.
5. Ibid., 216.

Chapter 40

NEW INFORMATION ABOUT MULEK, SON OF THE KING

Mosiah 25:2 "There were not so many of the children of Nephi, or so many of those who were descendents of Nephi, as there were of the people of Zarahemla, who was a descendant of Mulek."

Mulek, the son of Zedekiah, is mentioned several times in the Book of Mormon (see Mosiah 25:2; Helaman 6:10; 8:21) but not in the Bible—at least not in a way that people have recognized, until just recently. Biblical scholarship now bears out this Book of Mormon claim: King Zedekiah had a son named *Mulek*.

In the summer of 586 B.C., when the troops of King Nebuchadrezzar breached the walls of Jerusalem, King Zedekiah of Judah and a large company of warriors attempted to escape by night to the East. Babylonian troops caught up with them in the plains of Jericho. Many presumably escaped, but Zedekiah himself was seized and taken to Nebuchadrezzar's operational headquarters at Riblah (on the Orontes River, just south of Kadesh, in what is now Syria). There, as punishment for breaking his sacred oath of fealty to King Nebuchadrezzar, the Babylonians forced Zedekiah to witness the execution of his captured sons, had his eyes put out, and took him in bronze fetters to Babylon (see 2 Kings 25:4–7; 2 Chronicles 36:13).

According to the Book of Mormon, that was not the end of the matter. One son named Mulek escaped (see Omni 1:15–16; Helaman 8:21), even though the details remain shadowy. Since he landed first at the land of Desolation on the east coast (see Alma 22:30–31; Helaman 6:10), he probably journeyed to Mesoamerica via the Mediterranean, Atlantic Ocean, and Caribbean, perhaps with Phoenician help.

The first clue of the existence and escape of Mulek, son of Zedekiah, can be found in 2 Kings 25:1–10, which reports that Nebuchadrezzar and "*all* his host" scattered "*all* the men" and "*all* [the king's] army" and burnt "*all* the houses of Jerusalem," and with "*all* the army" they destroyed the walls. In the midst of all this, however, 2 Kings 25:7 omits the word *all* when it reports only that "the sons" of Zedekiah were killed, leaving open the question whether all of his sons were slain.

Biblical scholars have recently had interesting things to say about a person named *Malchiah.* Jeremiah 38:6 speaks of a "dungeon of Malchiah the son of Hammelech . . . in the court of the prison." But the Hebrew name here, *MalkiYahu ben-hamMelek,* should be translated "MalkiYahu, son of the king," the Hebrew word *melek* meaning "king."

Was this MalkiYahu a son of King Zedekiah? Several factors indicate that he was. For one thing, the title "son of the king" was used throughout the ancient Near East to refer to actual sons of kings who served as high officers of imperial administration.[1] The same is certainly true of the Bible, in which kings' sons ran prisons (see 1 Kings 22:26–27; Jeremiah 36:26; 38:6) or performed other official functions (see 2 Kings 15:5; 2 Chronicles 28:7). Moreover, in view of the fact that the name MalkiYahu has been found on two ostraca from Arad (in southern Judah), the late head of the Department of Archaeology at Tel Aviv University, Yohanan Aharoni, said that "Malkiyahu is a common name and was even borne by a contemporary son of king Zedekiah."[2]

But was this MalkiYahu the same person as Mulek? Study of these names tells us he may very well be. In the case of Baruch, scribe of Jeremiah, for example, the long form of his name, BerekYahu, has been discovered on a seal impression by Nahman Avigad of the Hebrew University in Jerusalem.[3] The full name has been shortened in Jeremiah's record to Baruch.

In view of this shortening, as in many other biblical names, there is no reason why a short form such as Mulek might not be possible. Indeed, the archaic Hebrew *qutl*-form could account for it, and *mulk* actually appears in Ugaritic and Phoenician, meaning "royal, princely-sacrifice; tophet-vow" (= Punic *molk*/ Hebrew *molek* [see Leviticus 18:21; 2 Kings 16:3]; child-sacrifice [see Acts 7:43]), and in Arabic meaning "reign, sovereignty, dominion" (Amorite *Muluk* = Akkadian and Eblaite *Malik*). One might, incidentally, be led to compare this with Mayan *Muluc*, the red-Bacab of the East, whom David H. Kelley correlates with "blood" and "devourer of children."[4]

A prominent non-Mormon ancient Near Eastern specialist declared recently of the Book of Mormon's naming "Mulek" as a son of Zedekiah, "If Joseph Smith came up with that one, he did pretty good!" He added that the vowels in the name could be accounted for as the Phoenician style of pronunciation. He found himself in general agreement that "MalkiYahu, son of the King" might very well be a son of King Zedekiah, and that the short-form of the name could indeed be *Mulek*.

Based on research primarily by Robert F. Smith, February 1984 and supplemented by Benjamin Urrutia in Insights, *February 1985. For the latest statements about Mulek and the Mulekites, see the entry on Mulekites by Curtis Wright in Macmillan's* Encyclopedia of Mormonism *(1991) and the article by John L. Sorenson, "The Mulekites,"* BYU Studies *30 (Summer 1990):* 6–22.

Notes

1. Anson Rainey, "The Prince and the Pauper," *Ugarit-Forschungen* 7 (1975): 427–32.

2. Yohanan Aharoni, "Three Hebrew Ostraca from Arad," *Bulletin of the American Schools of Oriental Research,* 197 (February 1970): 22.

3. Nahman Avigad, "Jerahmeel and Baruch: King's Son and Scribe," *Biblical Archeologist* 42 (Spring 1979): 114–18.

4. David H. Kelley, "Calendar Animals and Deities," *Southwestern Journal of Anthropology* 16 (1960): 317–37.

Chapter 41

FOUR QUARTERS

Mosiah 27:6 "abroad upon the face of the earth, yea, on the north and on the south, on the east and on the west, building large cities and villages in all quarters of the land"

Book of Mormon writers commonly spoke of their land as being divided into four quarters (i.e., Mosiah 27:6; Alma 43:26; 52:10; 56:1; 58:30). They similarly thought of the earth as being divided into four quadrants (i.e., 1 Nephi 19:16; 22:25; 2 Nephi 10:8; 21:12; 3 Nephi 5:24; 5:26; 16:5; Ether 13:11). Accordingly they described each area of their lands by reference to the cardinal directions, such as "the land northward" and "the land southward." Recent research by Diane E. Wirth, pursuing a topic explored earlier by Steven L. Olsen, shows that similar ideas existed in pre-Columbian America and the Old World.[1]

Good evidence exists that ancient Americans divided their territorial lands into four quadrants for administrative purposes. For example, the Inca had four governors, each presiding over a quarter of the state: "This makes a striking parallel to the administration in other high cultures in the Old World where the kingdom was divided into four provinces linked with the cardinal points."[2]

In an effort to keep the traditions of their fathers alive, the Nahua and Maya nations established four rulers, four governors, or four chiefs, each responsible for one quadrant of land.[3] "In Mexico we find that the four executive officers were the chiefs or representatives of the four quarters of the City of Mexico. . . . The entire dominion of Mexico was also divided into four equal quarters, the rule administration of which was attended to by four lords. . . . The Spaniards also found in Cuzco [Peru] a large, beautifully-polished stone-cross which evidently symbolized, as in Mexico, the four quarters."[4]

In Guatemala, records speak of "four nations, four provinces, four capitals, [and] four Tullans."[5] Mesoamerican accounts of their ancestry told that they descended from seven tribes (as in Jacob 1:13) who came from across the sea, but only four were considered fundamental.

Additionally, these records likewise envisioned the world and the heavens divided into quadrants. The Mayan *Lord of Totonicapan* speaks of "the four parts of the world."[6] Mesoamerican art commonly portrays four godlike creatures (*bacabs* and/or *chacs*) holding up the four corners of the earth and sky. Likewise, Ixtlilxochitl, *Obras Historicas* I, and Sahagun, as Bruce Warren reports, refer to the seas surrounding central Mexico as the Seas South (SW near Oaxaca), the Sea North (NE by Tampico), the Sea East (SE near Tabasco), and the Sea West (NW around Puerto Vallarta).

Similar references from the Old World can be cited. Cities such as Ebla and Jerusalem were divided into quarters, and the ancient Egyptian determinative glyph for "city" was a circle divided diagonally into four quarters.

In the Bible, the immediate land is divided into quarters (see, i.e., Joshua 15:5; 18:14–15; Isaiah 47:15; 56:11; Mark 1:45; Acts 9:32). Likewise, the heavens (see Jeremiah 49:36) and the earth (see Genesis 19:4; Revelation 7:1; 20:8) are seen in quadrants. In Egyptian texts, four beings or creatures often depicted the four cardinal points of the earth. Commenting on these figures, represented as canopic jars on the Lady Meux Hypocephalus, Budge explained: "These jars were under the protection of Isis, Nephthys, Neith and Serqet, and represented the south, north, east and west respectively."[7]

How the land was divided could vary in Mesoamerica. *North* rarely referred to true north. It often meant a direction about eighteen degrees east of true north, apparently based on the solstitial axis. A significant example of this comes from Río Azul, Guatemala, where a Mayan tomb has been found with the directional glyphs painted on the walls and oriented about eighteen degrees east of the cardinal points.[8]

Such may have been the conceptual base for the frequent use of the intercardinal point, depicted at forty-five degrees (as in the famous Aztec Calendar Stone), which we would call *northeast*. Correspondingly, the Anhuac region south of Mexico City was divided into Northeastern, Southeastern, Southwestern, and Northwestern quadrants (as in Jerusalem). Tombs, buildings, and plazas were often oriented toward directions other than the cardinals; and the heavens could be oriented differently from the earth.

These points may bear on several further aspects of the Book of Mormon. For example, some ancients thought of the north as dark and sinister; correspondingly, the Nephites called the land northward the Land of Desolation. As above, the Nephite generals Helaman, Teancum, and Moroni (see Alma 46–58) may have had separate quarters of the land under their command. In a Mesoamerican fashion, the Nephite "north" need not have been oriented toward our precise north.

While further research is warranted, apparently the traditions of the "four," which are more or less present in many cultures, were strongly represented in both the Old and the New worlds, including the Book of Mormon. Knowledge of this world view may help us in understanding these records.

Based on research by Diane E. Wirth and Steven L. Olsen, August 1986. More recently, see Appendix C to John L. Sorenson, "The Geography of Book of Mormon Events: A Source Book" (Provo: F.A.R.M.S., 1990), on directions in the Book of Mormon.

Notes

1. Steven L. Olsen, "Cosmic Urban Symbolism in the Book of Mormon," *BYU Studies* 23 (1983): 87.

2. Ake Hultkrantz, *The Religions of the American Indians,* trans. Setterwall (Berkeley: University of California Press, 1979), 187.

3. Ralph L. Roys, *The Book of Chilam Balam of Chumayel* (Norman: University of Oklahoma Press, 1973), 139 n. 5.

4. Zelia Nuttall, *The Fundamental Principles of Old and New World Civilizations* 2, Archaeological and Ethnological Papers of the Peabody Museum-Harvard University (Salem, Massachusetts: Salem Press, 1901), 75, 136.

5. Ibid., 494.

6. English version by Delia Goetz, *Lords of Totonicapan* (Norman: University of Oklahoma Press, 1974), 169.

7. E. Wallis Budge, *Gods of the Egyptians, or Studies in Egyptian Mythology* 1 (1904/rpt. 1969): 210. Compare Joseph Smith's comments on the four figures on Facsimile 1, Figs. 4–7, and on Facsimile No. 2, Fig. 6, of the Book of Abraham that represent "this earth in its four quarters."

8. See Ian Graham, "Looters Rob Graves and History," *National Geographic* 169 (April 1986): 456.

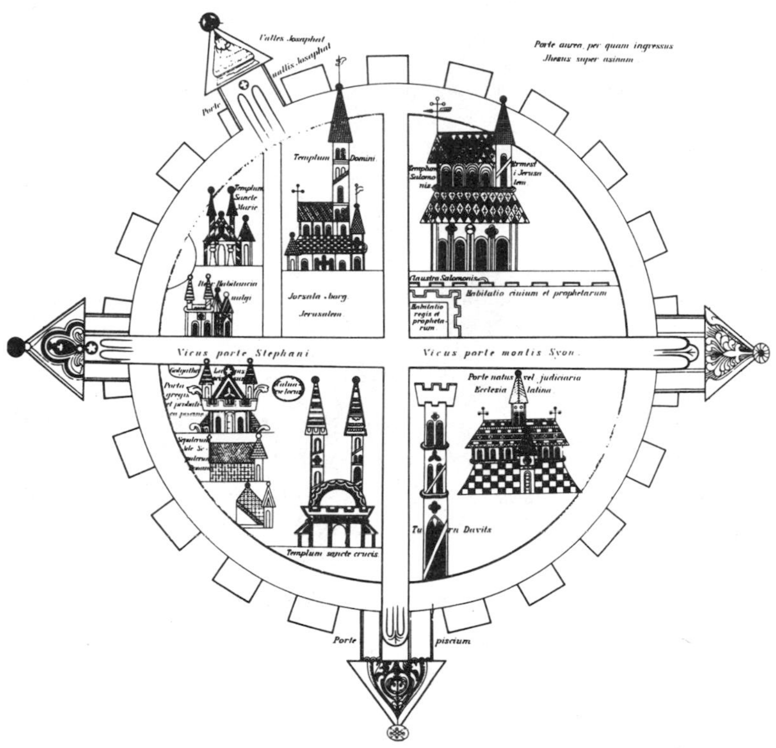

Medieval representation of the city of Jerusalem showing it divided into four quarters.

Chapter 42

THREE ACCOUNTS OF ALMA'S CONVERSION

Mosiah 27:23 "The limbs of Alma received their strength, and he stood up and began to speak unto them."

Not all readers are aware that the Book of Mormon contains three accounts of the conversion of Alma the Younger. Mosiah 27:8–37 gives a contemporary account of how Alma had agitated against the church of God and of his extraordinary conversion. In Alma 36:4–26 and 38:6–8, Alma twice recounts his conversion story as he blesses his sons Helaman and Shiblon. Interesting results come from a careful comparison of these three texts.

It is apparent that these three accounts all originated from the same man. For example, in Mosiah 27, Alma used many distinctive phrases as he described his conversion. He said, "The Lord in mercy hath seen fit to snatch me out of an everlasting burning, and I am *born of God*. My soul hath been redeemed from *the gall of bitterness* and bonds of iniquity. I was in the darkest abyss; but now I behold the *marvelous light* of God. *My soul* was *racked with eternal torment;* but I am snatched, and my soul is *pained no more*" (Mosiah 27:28–29). The emphasized terms here are just a few that could be mentioned.

Years later, Alma again used these same phrases. In Alma 36 he said, "God did *rack my soul*" (Alma 36:14) "*with eternal torment*" (Alma 36:12). "I cried . . . have mercy on me, who am in *the gall of bitterness*" (Alma 36:18). "I could remember my *pains no more*" (Alma 36:19). "What *marvelous light*" (Alma 36:20). "I had been *born of God*" (Alma 36:23).

Likewise, Mosiah 27:11 describes the voice of the angel as "a *voice of thunder,* which caused the *earth to shake* upon which they stood," while Alma 36:7 states: "He spake unto us, as it were the *voice of thunder,* and the whole *earth did tremble* beneath our feet." See also Alma 38:7; compare Alma 29:1: "O that I were an angel . . . and [could] speak . . . with a voice to *shake the earth.*"

There are many other such phrases that run in parallel, but not identically, through these three accounts. The repetitions show that a single person was the author of all three and suggest that Alma had told his story many times and had grown accustomed to using these characteristic words and phrases.

Furthermore, it is impressive that the specific details in the accounts remain accurately consistent. For example, all five of those present fell to the earth before the angel, but only Alma was told to "arise" (Mosiah 27:12–13; Alma 36:7–8) and to "remember the captivity of thy fathers" (Mosiah 27:16; Alma 36:2, 28–29), precisely the same in both accounts.

Even what superficially appears to be a difference is not. Alma 36:16 states that Alma was racked for three days and three nights. Mosiah 27:23, however, says the priests fasted for two days and two nights. This is because, under Nephite practice, the fast would not have begun until the morning of the next day after the decision to fast (Helaman 9:10).

Where there are differences between the accounts, they are understandable. For example, there is more emphasis in Mosiah 27:18 and 32 on the involvement of the four sons of Mosiah in the appearance of the angel than in Alma 36; this is understandable since King Mosiah is the one reporting the events in Mosiah 27, whereas Alma is speaking in Alma 36 and 38.

The psalm of Alma in Mosiah 27:24–31 bears the literary characteristics of a spontaneous utterance. These are the kind of words a person would speak unrehearsed. They are full of emotion and rejoicing; they are direct, first-person declarations.

Alma 36 and 38, however, show signs of thoughtful reflection, of years of thinking about his momentous conversion. For instance, in the later accounts Alma has placed his words into the context of his religious tradition. Instead of thinking only about the deliverance of his father from the land of Helam (as the angel mentions in Mosiah 27:16), Alma now speaks of older parallels of the deliverance of Lehi from Jerusalem and, beyond that, of the Israelites from Egypt (see Alma 36:28–29).[1] And in Alma 36:22, Alma has incorporated twenty-one words that are quoted verbatim from the vision of Lehi (see 1 Nephi 1:8). He has also applied his spiritual experience to his readers' daily religious practice, drawing lessons about trusting in the Lord throughout one's trials, troubles, and afflictions (see Alma 36:3, 27; 38:5), and about living a moral, righteous life (see Alma 38: 9–15).

To coincide with this thoughtful development, Alma's accounts have evolved structurally as well. The abrupt antithetical parallelisms in Mosiah 27:29–30 ("I was X, but now I am Y," repeated four times) have been rearranged into one masterfully crafted chiastic composition in Alma 36:1–30. It centers on the turning point of Alma's life, which was when he called upon Jesus Christ for forgiveness, and groups the negative attributes from Mosiah 27:29–30 into the first half of the chiasm and their positive opposites into the second half.[2] Expanding on the research of John W. Welch, Lowell Tensmeyer and others have recently worked out full chiastic analyses of chapter 36.[3]

Alma 38 is equally interesting. It presents essentially the first half of the chiasm found in Alma 36, up to the climactic turning point, before shifting into hortatory speech admonishing his second son. Having given the doubled version to his eldest son, Helaman, in Alma 36, Alma evidently felt no need to give the fully repeated structure to Shiblon in Alma 38.

The three accounts also consistently reflect different vantage points in Alma's life. In Mosiah 27, Alma is a young man, spontaneously overwhelmed by the power of the angel and terrified by the prospect of the day of judgment (see Mosiah 27:31). Later in Alma's life, it is clear that the older man has faithfully and successfully served his Lord and his people all the rest of his days (see Alma 36:24–26) so that he now emphasizes his longing to be present with God (see Alma 36:22).

Despite the fact that Mosiah 27 is separated from the accounts in Alma 36 and 38 by the many words, events, sermons, conflicts and distractions reported in the intervening one hundred pages of printed text, these three accounts still profoundly bear the unmistakeable imprints of a single distinctive person, who throughout his adult lifetime had lived with, thought about, matured through, and insightfully taught by means of his powerful and beautiful conversion story.

This October 1986 Update was based on research by John W. Welch, who has since continued his research on Alma 36. For an extensive discussion of Alma 36, approaching the text at various levels, see John W. Welch, "Chiasmus in Alma 36" (Provo: F.A.R.M.S., 1989) and a summary of that paper in "A Masterpiece: Alma 36," in John Sorenson and Melvin Thorne, eds., Rediscovering the Book of Mormon *(Salt Lake City: Deseret Book and F.A.R.M.S., 1991), 114–31.*

Notes

1. Regarding such typological comparisons, see George Tate, "The Typology of the Exodus Pattern in the Book of Mormon," in Neal Lambert, ed., *Literature of Belief* (Provo: Religious Studies Center, Brigham Young University, 1981), 246–62; Terrence L. Szink, "Nephi and the Exodus," in John Sorenson and Melvin Thorne, eds., *Rediscovering the Book of Mormon* (Salt Lake City: Deseret Book and F.A.R.M.S., 1991), 38–51; S. Kent Brown, "The Exodus Pattern in the Book of Mormon," *BYU Studies* 30 (Summer 1990): 111–26.

2. See John W. Welch, "Chiasmus in the Book of Mormon," in John W. Welch, ed., *Chiasmus in Antiquity* (Hildesheim: Gerstenberg, 1981), 206–7.

3. For a collection of these analyses, see John W. Welch, "Chiasmus in Alma 36" (Provo: F.A.R.M.S., 1989).

Chapter 43

JOSEPH SMITH: "AUTHOR AND PROPRIETOR"

Mosiah 28:14 "for the purpose of interpreting languages"

Joseph Smith repeatedly testified during his lifetime that he translated the Book of Mormon through the gift and power of God. At the bottom of the Title Page and in the Testimony of the Eight Witnesses of the 1830 edition of the Book of Mormon, Joseph Smith is identified as *"Author and Proprietor,"* and the publisher's line reads "PRINTED BY E. B. GRANDIN, FOR THE *AUTHOR*." Are these references to Joseph Smith as author inconsistent with his role as translator? Recent research into early federal copyright laws clearly explains that this terminology is not a problem because it is consistent with early nineteenth-century practice.

On June 11, 1829, Joseph Smith deposited a copy of the Title Page of the Book of Mormon with R. R. Lansing, clerk of the Northern District of New York. He did this in compliance with federal law enacted in 1790. That law required "every person who shall . . . claim to be the *author or proprietor* of any maps, charts, book or books," who wishes to assert a copyright, to perfect that copyright (1) by "recording the title thereof in the clerk's office," (2) by publishing within two months in a United States newspaper a copy of the clerk's record, (3) by inserting the clerk's record "at full length in the title-page or in the page immediately following," and (4) by delivering a copy of the book to the Secretary of State within six months after its publication.[1]

The 1790 statute even spelled out the words that the district clerk should write in his book: "*Be it remembered,* that on the

____ day of ____ in the ____ year of the independence of the United States of America, A. B. of the said district, hath deposited in this office the title of a map, chart, book or books (as the case may be) the right whereof he claims as *author or proprietor* (as the case may be). . . . " Those who complied held a fourteen-year copyright (renewable one time for another fourteen years). The Book of Mormon copyright thus was to expire in 1843, one year to the month before Joseph Smith was killed.

In 1831 the law was expanded so that copyright could be claimed by "authors" of any "musical composition, print, cut, or engraving" as well as any books, maps, or charts.

With this background, the following points are clear:

1. Joseph Smith complied with the law by depositing the required information with the district clerk and by publishing the clerk's record on the back of the Title Page of the Book of Mormon. The need for protection was real. Indeed, the book's copyright was soon violated by Abner Cole's *Palmyra Reflector,* forcing Joseph to return to Palmyra to assert his copyright.

2. The wording of the statute did not require him to claim *to be* the author, but simply to claim "the *right* whereof . . . *as* author." Moreover, the statute only allowed two options: the claimant had to identify himself either as "author" or as "proprietor." Since the word "proprietor" referred to those who purchased materials *"from authors,"*[2] Joseph could not claim to be a proprietor (since he had not purchased the book from anyone else). Thus he had to declare himself as "author" for official purposes.

Where he had a choice, he followed the statutory language and called himself *both* "author and proprietor," perhaps because Joseph felt that neither of these legal categories applied squarely in his case, or perhaps to prevent any other person (e.g., printer E. B. Grandin or Martin Harris—who had rights to the book's first sales proceeds) from claiming an assigned copyrightable interest in it as a proprietor.

3. Joseph fits comfortably, in any event, within the broad legal meaning of the word *author.* Musical composers, cartog-

raphers, etchers, engravers, and designers were all authors within the meaning of that term in this statute.

A *translator* also qualified, for copyright purposes, as the author of a book he had translated.[3] Indeed, other translators called themselves "authors." An 1824 printing of a King James Version of the Bible (Huddersfield, England) listed the Reverend B. Boothroyd as "the author."

4. On the same Title Page where the phrase "author and proprietor" appears, Joseph made it clear that he had translated the Book of Mormon. The title reads: "The Book of Mormon: An Account Written by the Hand of Mormon, Upon Plates Taken from the Plates of Nephi." In the preface to the 1830 edition, Joseph also wrote, "I would inform you that I translated, by the gift and power of God, and caused to be written [the Book of Mormon]." He speaks of translating the book *six* times in this thirty-five line preface, making his role as translator unmistakable.

To prevent confusion, Joseph changed the word "author" to "translator" in the second edition of the Book of Mormon, printed in 1837. It has appeared that way ever since.

Based on research by Miriam A. Smith and John W. Welch, August 1985.

Notes

1. 1 *Statutes* 124 (1790), as amended by 2 *Statutes* 171 (1802); italics added.

2. See the marginal note to 1 *Statutes* 124 (1790) and the Supreme Court decision of *Mifflin v. R. H. White Co.*, 190 U.S. 260, 262 (1903), so holding.

3. See, e.g., *Lesser v. Sklarz,* Federal Case No. 8276a (C.C.S.-.N.Y. 1859), holding that an English translation of portions of the Old Testament was copyrightable; see also *Wyatt v. Barnard,* 3 V. & B. 77, 35 *English Reports* 408 (1814).

Northern District of New York } To wit:

Be it remembered, That on the eleventh day of June in the fifty third year of the Independence of the United States of America, A. D. 1829 Joseph Smith Junior of the said District, hath deposited in this Office the title of a Book the right whereof he claims as author in the words following, to wit: The Book of Mormon; an account written by the hand of Mormon upon plates taken from the plates of Nephi. [illegible]

In conformity to the act of the Congress of the United States, entitled "An act for the encouragement of learning, by securing the copies of Maps, Charts, and Books, to the authors and proprietors of such copies, during the times therein mentioned;" and also, to the act entitled "An act supplementary to an act entitled 'An act for the encouragement of learning, by securing the copies of Maps, Charts, and Books, to the authors and proprietors of such copies during the times therein mentioned,' and extending the benefits thereof to the arts of Designing, Engraving and Etching historical and other prints."

R. R. Lansing Clerk of the United States Dist. Court for the Northern Dist. of New York.

Copyright application for the Book of Mormon, filed in the Federal District of New York, June 11, 1829. The application uses the Title Page of the Book of Mormon as the book's description, showing that the Title Page had been translated probably the end of May. Courtesy LDS Church Historical Department.

Chapter 44

THE LAW OF MOSIAH

Mosiah 29:11 "And we will newly arrange the affairs of this people."

Important changes occurred in Nephite law and society with the establishment and promulgation of the law of Mosiah in 92 B.C. Interestingly, several details about this significant legal reform are faithfully preserved in the Book of Mormon. This subtle and sometimes technical information embedded in the narrative of the Book of Mormon shows that "the law of Mosiah" (Alma 11:1) was solidly rooted in ancient Near Eastern ideas and legal tradition. Here is a sketch of some salient and noteworthy points:

King Mosiah established specific laws (Alma 1:1). In so doing, he was acting like other ancient lawgivers, such as the famous Babylonian lawgiver Hammurabi or the great Israelite leader Moses. In antiquity, such leaders personally acted to issue laws for the express purpose of establishing "justice and equity" among their people.[1] Likewise, one of Mosiah's main motives was that all would be "equal" (Mosiah 29:38; Alma 1:26), and their judges were praised for filling their judgeships with "justice and equity" (Helaman 3:20, 37).

Although the law of Mosiah allowed the people to select judges, it does not appear that these judges had the power to create law itself. The law that they applied was "given them" by Mosiah (Mosiah 29:39), and the laws under which they acted were remembered several generations later as the "laws of Mosiah" (Helaman 4:22).

Like other ancient lawgivers, who often drew on divine sources in legitimizing their laws, Mosiah gave the laws "which the Lord commanded him to give unto the people" (Helaman 4:22). For example, Moses issued the laws that Jehovah revealed to him, and Hammurabi claimed on his stele that the god Marduk had "called" him "to make justice to appear in the land" and commanded him "to set forth truth and justice" by establishing his laws.

The law of Mosiah primarily made procedural changes and probably did not make radical changes in the substantive rules of the law of Moses. Mosiah instructed the new Nephite judges to judge "according to the laws . . . given you *by our fathers*" (Mosiah 29:25; italics added), and twenty-two years later the Nephites were still "strict in observing the ordinances of God, according to the law of Moses" (Alma 30:3). In its procedural and administrative enactments, the law of Mosiah can well be compared with the Israelite legal reform of King Jehoshaphat in 2 Chronicles 19:5–11.

Moreover, like other ancients, Mosiah was outspoken against kings who "teareth up the laws of those who have reigned in righteousness before [them]" and who enact their own laws (Mosiah 29:22–23). Ancient legal presumptions in general did not encourage new substantive legislation, and basic rules of law tended to remain rather constant over the centuries.

The law of Mosiah made changes in the judicial system. It abolished the kingship and instituted judges and officers (see Alma 11:1–2; compare Deuteronomy 16:18, which mentions officers). It also established an innovative procedure whereby a judge could be judged by a "higher judge" if he did not judge according to the law (Mosiah 29:28). It further established a procedure for expelling unjust higher judges. If they did not judge righteously (that is, according to the law given by the fathers), a small number of the lower judges could be authorized by the people to judge the higher judges and remove them from office (see Mosiah 29:29).

The law of Mosiah departed most significantly from traditional law by providing that judges would be paid for their services (see Alma 11:1). This is not paralleled in other Near

Eastern systems, although the fixing of wages for various other laborers was one of the main subjects of several ancient Near Eastern law codes.

In order to set statutory wages of any kind, it was often necessary for ancient laws to recognize a system of legal exchange equivalents. Thus, the law of Mosiah gave exchange ratios for gold, silver, barley, and all kinds of grain (see Alma 11:7). Prior to the law of Mosiah, Nephite weights and measures had been altered "according to the minds and the circumstances of the people, in every generation" (Alma 11:4), but in the law of Mosiah they were standardized by decree of the king. Much the same thing can be found in the Mesopotamian laws of Eshnunna, which began with a list of thirteen exchange equivalencies (e.g., "1 *kor* barley for 1 shekel silver"). The laws of Eshnunna established fixed silver values for oil, salt, wool, copper, sesame oil, and lard, as well as prices for the services of harvesters, boatmen, and other workers.[2]

The law of Mosiah also dealt with other issues. We know that it prohibited slavery in the land of Zarahemla, for Ammon assured his converts that "it is against the law of our brethren, which was established by my father, that there should be any slaves among them" (Alma 27:9). Previously it had been only by royal benevolence that slavery was not allowed in Zarahemla (see Mosiah 2:13).

The law of Mosiah appears to have also contained a provision defining delinquent debtors as thieves (see Alma 11:2), but we cannot be sure, for the case of the delinquent debtor may have been an old law simply used in Alma 11:2 to illustrate how a case was to proceed through the new judicial system.[3]

The law of Mosiah probably also provided that the governor alone had jurisdiction over capital offenses (see 3 Nephi 6:22), but this regulation may have been introduced a few generations later. Either way, it was not unknown in ancient Near Eastern law for kings to retain jurisdiction over capital cases. Section 48 in the laws of Eshnunna allowed cases of up to one mina in value to be litigated, but "a matter of life [belongs] to the king himself."

Mosiah's judicial reform remained solid for sixty-two years, but then his laws were "altered and trampled under their feet" (Helaman 4:22). The majority of the people chose evil (see Helaman 5:2), Nephi had to deliver the judgment-seat to Cezoram (see Helaman 5:1), and judicial corruption soon ensued (see Helaman 8:4; 3 Nephi 6:23). We are left to wonder in how many ways the laws of Mosiah were altered. The right of the lower judges to remove the higher judges may have been taken away. Exclusive jurisdiction over capital punishment may have been taken at this time by the governor. The judges certainly colluded and began to rule contrary to the laws handed down from the fathers, with the result that the eventual corruption of Mosiah's system of justice became one of the major causes of the collapse of the Nephite republic.

Research into the laws and jurisprudence of the ancient Near East sheds light on the legal provisions and procedures reflected in the Book of Mormon. It is amazing that the writers of the Book of Mormon could weave into their records so many accurate and consistent details about their legal and political institutions without diverting attention from their main religious purposes. Whoever wrote the Book of Mormon was intimately familiar with the workings of ancient Israelite law and with the Nephite legal system that derived from it.

Based on research by John W. Welch, March 1987.

Notes

1. See, e.g., the Prologue and Epilogue to the Code of Hammurabi, in James B. Pritchard, ed., *Ancient Near Eastern Texts Relating to the Old Testament,* 3rd ed. (Princeton: Princeton University Press, 1969), 164–65, 177–80.

2. See Laws of Eshnunna 1–11, in ibid., 161–63; Reuben Yaron, "The Laws of Eshnunna," *Israel Law Review* 5 (1970): 327–36, and *The Laws of Eshnunna* (Jerusalem: Magnes Press, 1988).

3. Regarding the ancient law of theft and robbery in the Book of Mormon, see John W. Welch, "Theft and Robbery in the Book of Mormon and Ancient Near Eastern Law" (Provo: F.A.R.M.S., 1985).

Chapter 45

POSSIBLE "SILK" AND "LINEN" IN THE BOOK OF MORMON

Alma 1:29 "They began to be exceedingly rich, having . . . abundance of silk and fine-twined linen, and all manner of good homely cloth."

The question has arisen from both believers and nonbelievers in the Book of Mormon, what can be meant by the reference in Alma 1:29 to "silk and fine-twined linen"? Some critics have maintained that neither silk nor linen was known in pre-Columbian America. At the other extreme, one LDS writer has maintained that the actual East Asian complex of getting silk from worms eating mulberry leaves must have been known among the Nephites.[1] The question invites us to look at the possible meanings of the Nephite terms from which these two words may have been translated. Both English words are broad enough to cover types of cloths present in the Americas during Book of Mormon times.

Linen is defined as a cloth, often quite stiffish and hard-wearing, made of fibers from flax or hemp plants prepared by soaking and pounding. Although the flax plant was apparently not known in pre-Spanish America, several fabrics were made from vegetable fabrics that look and feel much like European linen. One was made from fibers (called *henequen*) of the leaf of the ixtle (maguey or agave plant), but fibers from the yucca and other plants gave similar results. Conquistador Bernal Diaz said of *henequen* garments that they were "like linen."[2] Bark cloth, made by stripping bark from the fig tree and soaking and pounding it, was common in Mesoamerica and also has some of the characteristics of linen.[3]

Dictionaries define *silk* as a "fine, lustrous fiber produced by the larvae of certain insects." It refers especially to the fiber from which an Asian moth, *Bombyx mori,* spins its cocoon, but also to cloth more generally "something silklike." Silk from cocoons gathered from the wild in Mexico and spun into expensive cloth at the time of the Spanish conquest provides the most literal parallel to Asiatic "silk."[4]

Interestingly, problems of labeling and of variant faunal sources are encountered in interpreting references in early Greek sources to "silk." William Forbes has argued that the description of the silkworm in Aristotle and other sources actually represents a conflation of two types of silkworm native to southeastern Europe (with no direct connection to the Far East). The fibers were prepared by carding rather than by reeling them off the cocoon.[5] Gisela Richter holds that the thin, soft, diaphanous cloth called by the classical Greeks *amorginon* was in fact silk produced by wild silk moths on only two small Greek islands.[6] So the term *silk* may describe a number of fine, silky fabrics.

Silklike fiber (*kapok*) from the pod of the Ceiba (or "silk-cotton") tree was gathered in Yucatan and spun; this seems to be what Landa referred to as "silk."[7] Father Clavigero said of this *kapok* that it was "as soft and delicate, and perhaps more so, than silk."[8]

Furthermore, the silky fiber of the wild pineapple plant was prized in tropical America; it yielded a fiber, "finer and perhaps more durable than agave (*henequen*), derived from the *pita floja* ('silk-grass,' *aecmea magdalenae*)."[9]

Moreover, a silklike fabric was made by the Aztecs from fine rabbit hair.[10] But even cotton cloth was sometimes woven so fine that specimens excavated at Teotihuacan and dating to the fourth century A.D. have been characterized as "of irreproachable evenness, woven . . . exceedingly fine," and "of gossamer thinness."[11] Aztec cloths "like damask" (a figured fabric of silk, linen, or wool) were inventoried by the Spaniards.[12]

Mesoamerica evidently exhibits almost an embarrassment of riches for the "silk" and "linen" of Alma 1:29. All but the most trivializing critics should be satisfied with the parallels. There is no need to look beyond the mark to seek traces in ancient America of the flax plant or mulberry trees.

Based on research by John L. Sorenson, November 1988.

Notes

1. Maurice W. Connell, "The Prophet Said Silk," *Improvement Era* 65 (May 1962): 324–35.

2. See Alfred Maudslay, trans., *Bernal Diaz del Castillo, The Discovery and Conquest of Mexico* (New York: Farrer, Straus and Cudahy, 1956), 24.

3. Irmgard W. Johnson, "Basketry and Textiles," *Handbook of Middle American Indians* 10, no. 1 (1971): 301–21.

4. Johnson, "Basketry and Textiles," 312; Matthew Wallrath, "Excavations in the Tehuantepec Region, Mexico," *American Philosophical Society Transactions* 57, no. 2 (Philadelphia, 1967): 12.

5. William T. M. Forbes, "The Silkworm of Aristotle," *Classical Philology* 25 (1930): 22–26.

6. Gisela M. A. Richter, "Silk in Greece," *American Journal of Archaeology* 33 (1929): 27–33. See also *New Bible Dictionary*, 2nd ed. (Wheaton, Illinois: Inter-Varsity, 1982), 1112, mentioning a species of moth that feeds on cypress and oak trees on the island of Cos from which an ancient silk industry arose.

7. Alfred M. Tozzer, ed., *Landa's Relacion de las Cosas de Yucatan*, Paper 18 (Cambridge, Massachusetts: Harvard University Peabody Museum of American Archaeology and Ethnology, 1941), 201; he used the same term "silk" for that introduced by the Spaniards, 205.

8. Francesco Saverino Clavigero, *History of Mexico* 1, Charles Cullen, trans. (Philadelphia: Thomas Dobson, 1817), 41.

9. Felix W. McBryde, "Cultural and Historical Geography of Southwest Guatemala," Smithsonian Institute, Institute of Social Anthropology, 4 (1947): 149; William E. Safford, "Food Plants and Textiles of Ancient America," *Proceeding of the 19th International Congress of Americanists* (1917): 17.

10. Johnson, "Basketry and Textiles," 312.

11. Elisabeth Stromberg, in Sigvald Linné, ed., *Mexican Highland Cultures*, Stockholm Ethnographic Museum of Sweden Publications 7 (1942): 157–60.

12. Marshall Saville, *The Goldsmith's Art in Ancient Mexico*, Heye Foundation, Indian Notes and Monographs (New York: Museum of the American Indian, 1920), 79.

Chapter 46

EPANALEPSIS IN THE BOOK OF MORMON

Alma 3:1: "After having buried those who had been slain—now the number of the slain were not numbered, because of the greatness of their number—after they had finished burying their dead . . . "

Epanalepsis is the name of a significant literary device known in antiquity. It occurs where an author repeats certain words in the course of a lengthy sentence, to pick up a previous train of thought after a parenthetical aside, to remind the reader of the original idea of the sentence. This technique was noted in antiquity by Demetrius, and it is sometimes called "resumptive repetition."

Epanalepsis is well illustrated in Alma 3:1: "And it came to pass that the Nephites who were not slain by the weapons of war, *after having buried those who had been slain*—now the number of the slain were not numbered, because of the greatness of their number—*after they had finished burying their dead* they all returned to their lands, and to their houses, and their wives, and their children" (italics added). Larry Childs has recently identified eighty-four such occurrences of epanalepsis in the Book of Mormon. It was apparently helpful in ancient texts to use resumptive repetition, since those texts did not have the benefit of modern punctuation or paragraphing.

The Childs study also lists and analyzes the use and distribution of epanalepsis among all Book of Mormon authors. Interestingly, some authors use the device more frequently than others. In particular, forty-nine of the eighty-four occurrences of epanalepsis are found in the writings of Mormon, while seven are in the writings of Nephi. The remaining twenty-eight are distributed among twenty-four other authors. Childs concludes: "The study of epanalepsis gives us some insight into the writing style of the Book of Mormon authors." Especially for an author like Mormon, who was engaged in a process of abridging other records, epanalepsis was really the best means available to return the reader's attention to the original train of thought.

Based on research by Larry Childs, reported in Insights, *Summer 1986. Childs's study was published as a F.A.R.M.S. Paper in 1986.*

Chapter 47

ANTITHETICAL PARALLELISM IN THE BOOK OF MORMON

Alma 5:40 "Whatsoever is good cometh from God, and whatsoever is evil cometh from the devil."

The writers of ancient scripture often contrasted one idea in one line or stanza with an opposite or antithetical idea in a parallel line or stanza. Proverbs 13:9 records an example of antithetical parallelism:

The light of the righteous rejoiceth:
but the lamp of the wicked shall be put out.

Notice that the contrasted elements (righteous/wicked) are not simple contradictions but opposite aspects of the same idea. The Book of Mormon contains many fine examples of antithetical parallelisms. Alma, in his great discourse to the saints of Zarahemla, utilized this poetic form. His words are brief yet conclusive:

Whatsoever is *good*
  cometh from *God,*
and whatsoever is *evil*
  cometh from the *devil.*
(Alma 5:40)

Note the italicized antonyms. Two words epitomize the perfect contrast, "good" and "evil," and two beings are also considered opposite extremes. Alma's method of contrast establishes this opposition in the plainest of terms.

A second example of extended antithetical parallelism is found in Alma 9:28:

If they have been *righteous*
they shall reap the *salvation* of their souls,
according to the *power and deliverance*
of *Jesus Christ;*
and if they have been *evil*
they shall reap the *damnation* of their souls,
according to the *power and captivation*
of the *devil.*

In the first strophe the words "righteous," "salvation," "deliverance," and "Jesus Christ" stand in direct contrast to the terms of the second strophe – "evil," "damnation," "captivation," and "devil." Both strophes begin with an "if" statement, immediately followed by the results that come from righteousness or evil. The sides are clearly drawn between good and evil.

Antithetical parallelism not only contrasts two ideas, but also connects them. The meaning of the contrasted items separates them clearly, but the parallelistic format joins them so that the reader must consider them together. One purpose of this poetic form is thus to allow, or even force, the reader to make a mental comparison, and often a choice, between two diametrically opposed but related ideas. Whether consciously or intuitively, the reader sees in antithetical parallelism a unique reciprocity, as well as a strong contrast between the two elements.

Another Book of Mormon verse illustrates the principle again, where Alma speaks to his son Helaman:

Yea, I say unto you, *my son,*
that there could be *nothing so exquisite*
and so *bitter* as were *my pains.*
Yea, and again I say unto you, *my son,*
that on the other hand,
there can be *nothing so exquisite*
and *sweet* as was *my joy.*
(Alma 36:21)

In this verse Alma obviously intends by phrasing the issue in this bold way to push his son to side mentally with and feel an affinity with righteousness rather than with evil. In such a teaching situation, antithetical parallelism has the ability to produce an emotional response in the original audience and also in subsequent readers that leads them to follow the teachings.

Comparison between two terms has always been an accepted tool of rhetoricians to invoke the reader's involvement. As Aristotle wrote, "This kind of style is pleasing, because contraries are easily understood and even more so when placed side by side, and also because antithesis resembles a syllogism; for refutation is a bringing together of contraries."[1]

Recognizing this antithetical parallel structure can help us see more clearly the issues that writers of the Book of Mormon wanted us to focus on. Appreciating the connections and contrasts between the ideas that they felt were most important may lead us to feel as they felt and act as they admonish us to act.

Based on research by Donald W. Parry, September 1990. Further work on this topic was presented by Parry at the Book of Mormon Symposium at Brigham Young University, February 1991, in a paper titled "Teaching in Black and White: Antithetic Structure in the Book of Alma—Its Form and Function."

Note

1. Aristotle, *The Art of Rhetoric,* trans. J. H. Freese (London: Heinemann, 1967), III, 9, 7–10.

Chapter 48

THE LAND OF JERUSALEM: THE PLACE OF JESUS' BIRTH

Alma 7:10 "He shall be born of Mary, at Jerusalem which is the land of our forefathers."

It has been alleged that the Book of Mormon commits a foolish error by predicting that Jesus would be born "at Jerusalem." But just as Rome was *urbs et orbis,* "city and world," so Jerusalem was not simply a city, not even just a city-state. It is and was a symbol of Zion. It typified all that which the exiles in Babylonia had lost (see Psalms 137:5–6), and, in our time, it is the focus of the return of other exiles from their nearly two millennia of dispersion. Every synagogue faces Jerusalem—the Holy City and City of David. In several ways, recent scholarship strongly confirms and elaborates upon the excellent older studies by professors Sperry and Nibley answering the critics on how Jerusalem could be called the place of Jesus' birth.[1]

With the rise of the classical Israelite state, the role of the hereditary tribes declined, and the monarchy imposed administrative districts upon the nation: twelve in the North, and twelve in the South. The delineation of these districts is available in the Bible (see Joshua 15:20–63 [Septuagint]; 1 Kings 4:7–19), and Bethlehem was included in the district of Jerusalem.[2]

In the same way that the "land" or district of Jerusalem was administratively distinguished from the city of Jerusalem, so, according to Kenneth Kitchen, the great city of Hazor (Tell el-Qeda) was distinguished from the state of Hazor. Thus, Abraham had dwelt or "sojourned" in the territory of Gerar, rather than in the city itself (Tell Abu Hureira; Genesis 20:1). The "city and state often have the same name in the Ancient Orient, although distinct entities. This applied to Carchemish in Hittite politics, for example, where city and land (same name) had distinct roles."[3] Indeed, the land of Jerusalem ultimately extended far beyond mere district borders during its phase as a Latin kingdom, covering about 500 to 550 square kilometers.[4]

Thus it is quite apparent that Jerusalem "did double duty as the royal and the district capital."[5] As early as Canaanite times, Jerusalem held royal status, and it was termed *mat URU sa-lim* ("land of Jerusalem") in the Amarna Letters.[6]

Where then was Jesus born? Truly, in Bethlehem of the land of Judaea (see Micah 5:2; Matthew 2:1–6; Luke 2:4)—any child could tell you that in Joseph Smith's time as well as in ours. What no one in modern times would have known for sure (before the 1887 discovery of the Tell El-Amarna Tablets) was that Bethlehem was also part of an area anciently called the *land of Jerusalem.*[7]

Only once in the King James Bible is the term *land of Jerusalem* even remotely recognizable, and then within a parallel phrase: "And the king and his men went to Jerusalem unto the Jebusites, the inhabitants of the land" (2 Samuel 5:6). This verse is obviously insufficient to suggest to Joseph Smith how "lands" were constituted in Old Testament times. Yet the Book of Mormon twice refers to a "land of Jerusalem" in which Jesus was to be born (Alma 7:10; Helaman 16:19). This is consistent with the broader pattern of toponymy that appears in the Book of Mormon (i.e., the lands and cities of Nephi and Zarahemla).

It is apparent now that the Book of Mormon's casual statements about the "land of Jerusalem" are in full agreement with what recent scholarship tells us about the geography of ancient Judaea.

Based on research by Robert F. Smith, May 1984.

Notes

1. Sidney B. Sperry, "Was Jesus Born in the 'Land of Jerusalem,' " in *Answers to Book of Mormon Questions* (Salt Lake City: Bookcraft, 1967), 131–36; Hugh W. Nibley, *An Approach to the Book of Mormon,* in *The Collected Works of Hugh Nibley* (Salt Lake City: Deseret Book and F.A.R.M.S., 1988), 6:102.

2. As discussed by John Bright, *A History of Israel,* 3rd ed. (Westminster: Philadelphia, 1981), 221–22. Anson F. Rainey, "The Biblical Shephelah of Judah," *Bulletin of the American Schools of Oriental Research* 251 (1983): 68, provides a map and discussion of the districts of Judah, including *district 9,* which contained such towns as Zobah, Manahath, Bether, Peor, Etam, Tekoa, Beth-haccerem, Bahurim, Netophah, Kullani, Tatam, Gallim, Bethlehem, and their district capital, Jerusalem.

3. Kenneth A. Kitchen, *Ancient Orient and Old Testament* (London: Tyndale, 1966), 68, and n. 43; *The Bible in Its World: The Bible and Archaeology Today* (Inter-Varsity Press, 1979; Paternoster Press, 1977), 40, 53 n. 9. Asshur was also a capital city and a state.

4. See Dan Barag, "A New Source Concerning the Ultimate Borders of the Latin Kingdom of Jerusalem," *Israel Exploration Journal* 29 (1979): 197–217.

5. Yohanan Aharoni, *The Archaeology of the Land of Israel: From the Prehistoric Beginnings to the End of the First Temple Period,* ed. Miriam Aharoni, trans. A. F. Rainey, (Philadelphia: Westminster, 1982), 259.

6. Nos. 287:25, 46; 290:15.

7. *The Macmillan Bible Atlas,* 2nd ed. (New York: Macmillan, 1977), Map 39.

Chapter 49

THE NEPHITE CALENDAR IN MOSIAH, ALMA, AND HELAMAN

Alma 16:1 "in the eleventh year of the reign of judges over the people of Nephi, on the fifth day of the second month"

At many points in the Book of Mormon, especially in the books of Mosiah, Alma, and Helaman, the record keepers refer to dates in their time-reckoning system ("thus ended the ninth year of the reign of the judges," "it came to pass in the fifty and fourth year," etc.). Translating these references to our calendar has seemed impossible. For example, the Israelite new year began in August, but we have no idea what changes might have taken place from Lehi's day to Mosiah's.

An aspect of the Book of Mormon that has just been noticed may give us a key to solving the problem. With remarkable consistency, the Nephite record reports a pattern of seasonality in Nephite warfare. Since wars in pretechnical societies are usually launched at opportune times of the year, the Nephite pattern of warfare tells us something about the seasons and their calendar.

The beginning and ending of the Nephite year frequently falls around the time of major battles. For example, Alma 44 ends with the defeat of a Lamanite army and the return of Moroni's forces to their houses and their lands: "Thus ended the eighteenth year of the reign of the judges" (Alma 44:24). When all such dates are tabulated, the distinct pattern emerges that most wars were fought in the eleventh through second months of the year. (Actually, we are not certain that there were twelve months in this calendar, since the highest number mentioned is eleven; yet based on Near Eastern and Mesoamerican calendar systems, the likelihood is very high that the Nephites at this time followed a pattern of twelve months probably with thirty days per month.) But virtually no battling took place in months six through ten. Instead, that period was when the mass of part-time soldiers were required to till the ground, "delivering their women and their children from famine and affliction, and providing food for their armies" (Alma 53:7).

When the seasons for cultivation and warring in Mesoamerica before the time of Columbus are studied, an equally sharp division is seen. (The schedule is essentially the same anywhere in tropical America, in fact.) The preparation and cultivation of farmlands and other domestic chores went on from about March through October, which constituted the rainy season. Wars began after the harvest and mainly went on during the hot, dry months, November through February. Of course, camping in the field was sensible at this time, and movement was least hampered by the swollen streams or boggy ground common in the other part of the year.

Putting these two sets of information together, we see that the fighting season referred to in the annals of the wars in the books of Mosiah through Helaman—their months eleven through two—likely coincided approximately with November through February in our calendar. Moreover their new year's day is likely to have fallen near winter solstice (December 21/22), as with many other peoples of the ancient world.

Interestingly, December was a hot season both in Mesoamerica and in the Book of Mormon, as we read in Alma 51:32–37 and 52:1. Recall that Teancum slew Amalickiah on the Nephite/Lamanite new year's eve as he slept deeply from fatigue "caused by the labors and heat of the day" (Alma 51:33). In Joseph Smith's New England, of course, New Year's Eve would have been icy.

If our equation is correct, the Nephite months ran like this:

First month began near our December 22.
Second month began near January 21.
Third month began near February 20.
Fourth month began near March 22.
Fifth month began near April 21.
Sixth month began near May 21.
Seventh month began near June 20.
Eighth month began near July 20.
Ninth month began near August 19.
Tenth month began near September 18.
Eleventh month began near October 18.
Twelfth month began near November 17.

Probably five extra (leap) days completed the year, as in both Egyptian and Mesoamerican calendars. After the birth of Christ, of course, the calendar was changed (see 3 Nephi 2:8); by how much, we cannot tell from the Book of Mormon.

Based on research by John L. Sorenson, June 1990. The extensive tabulation of Sorenson's data is presented in his article, "Seasonality of Warfare in the Book of Mormon and in Mesoamerica," in Stephen Ricks and William Hamblin, eds., Warfare in the Book of Mormon *(Salt Lake City: Deseret Book and F.A.R.M.S., 1990), 445–77, and a useful popular summary appears in his "Seasons of War, Seasons of Peace in the Book of Mormon," in John Sorenson and Melvin Thorne, eds.,* Rediscovering the Book of Mormon *(Salt Lake City: Deseret Book and F.A.R.M.S., 1991), 249–55.*

Chapter 50

THE DESTRUCTION OF AMMONIHAH AND THE LAW OF APOSTATE CITIES

Alma 16:9 "Every living soul of the Ammonihahites was destroyed."

Alma 16:9–11 records the utter destruction of the wicked city of Ammonihah by Lamanite soldiers. Recent research has uncovered several striking affinities between that account and the ancient Israelite law regarding the annihilation of apostate cities. That law is found in Deuteronomy 13:12–16:

> If thou shalt hear say in one of thy cities, . . . Certain men, the children of Belial, are gone out from among you, and have withdrawn the inhabitants of their city, saying, Let us go and serve other gods, which we have not known; then shalt thou enquire, and make search, and ask diligently; and, behold, if it be truth, and the thing certain, that such abomination is wrought among you; thou shalt surely smite the inhabitants of that city with the edge of the sword, destroying it utterly. . . . And thou shalt gather all the spoil of it into the midst of the street thereof, and shalt burn with fire the city, and all the spoil thereof every whit . . . : and it shall be an heap for ever; it shall not be built again.

Alma, who had been the Nephite chief judge, was most likely well aware of this provision, since the law of Moses was contained on the plates of brass, which were in his possession. Accordingly, Alma's concept of justice would have included the idea that an apostate city should be destroyed and anathematized in the specific way set forth in their governing law.

While Alma clearly lacked both the desire and the power to have the city of Ammonihah destroyed by a Nephite military force, and certainly no legal decree was ever issued calling for the extermination of the city, Alma carefully recorded and documented the fact that the inhabitants of Ammonihah had satisfied every element of the crime of being an apostate city. When the justice of God destroyed that city, Alma effectively showed in the record that this fate befell them in accordance with divine law. Consider the following elements:

1. The Deuteronomic law pertains to "certain men [who] are gone out from among you." Alma clearly states that the leaders in Ammonihah were Nephite apostates: "If this people, who have received so many blessings from the hand of the Lord, should transgress contrary to the light and knowledge which they do have, . . . it would be far more tolerable for the Lamanites than for them" (Alma 9:23).

2. The law applies when men have led a city to withdraw from God to serve other gods. Alma explains that certain men in Ammonihah, the followers of Nehor, had undertaken to pervert their people, to turn them away from the statutes, and judgments, and commandments of the Lord (see Alma 8:17).

3. Deuteronomy describes the offenders as "the children of Belial." Likewise, Alma made it a matter of record that "Satan had gotten great hold upon the hearts of the people of the city of Ammonihah" (Alma 8:9).

4. The law required officers to investigate the situation thoroughly, to enquire, search, and ask, to be sure that the offensive condition in fact existed. Alma did this too. After being rejected, Alma was instructed to return to preach in the city, to give them the necessary warning that they would be destroyed if they did not repent (see Alma 8:16). Then, acting as the two required eyewitnesses (see Deuteronomy 17:6), Alma and Amulek stood and witnessed the abominable scene of the burning of the faithful, innocent wives and children of their followers (see Alma

14:9). This was a revolting experience, but it completed the case against the city and sealed its fate (see Alma 14:11).

5. The prescribed mode of execution for an apostate city was by "the sword, destroying it utterly." This is the only place in the law of Moses where slaying by the sword is required. When the day of judgment came upon Ammonihah, the Lamanites did "slay the people and destroy the city" (Alma 16:2), presumably by the sword, their primary weapon of hand-to-hand combat.

6. The law demanded that the city should be destroyed completely by fire, "and it shall be a heap for ever." Alma records, "Every living soul of the Ammonihahites was destroyed, and also their great city, . . . [and] their dead bodies were heaped up upon the face of the earth" (Alma 16:9–11). Alma does not say how Ammonihah was destroyed, but that fire was involved would have been normal.

7. Finally, the law stated that the ruins "shall not be built again." In the case of Ammonihah: "the people did not go in to possess the land of Ammonihah for many years. . . . And their lands remained desolate" (Alma 16:11). These lands were deemed untouchable for just over seven years, a ritual cleansing period (there are eight years, nine months, and five days between Alma 16:1 and Alma 49:1). Apparently, the prohibition against reinhabitation could expire or be revoked. In a similar fashion, an early Christian synod removed a ban that the island of Cyprus remain unoccupied seven years after its inhabitants had been annihilated.[1]

Thus, the destruction of Ammonihah conforms quite thoroughly with the legal provision of Deuteronomy 13, making this a remarkable case of the falling of the vengeful sword of God's justice (see Alma 54:6).

Based on research by John W. Welch, July 1987. Further research on this topic has been published in John W. Welch, "Law and War in the Book of Mormon," in Stephen Ricks and William Hamblin, eds., Warfare in the Book of Mormon *(Salt Lake City: Deseret Book and F.A.R.M.S., 1990), 91–95, and in Stephen D. Ricks, " 'Holy War': The Sacral Ideology of War in the Book of Mormon and in the Ancient Near East," ibid., 110–14.*

Note

1. Constantinus Prophyrogenitus, *De Administrando Imperio* 47, in *Patrologia Graeca* 113:366.

Chapter 51

AMMON AND CUTTING OFF THE ARMS OF ENEMIES

Alma 17:39 "Bearing the arms which had been smitten off . . . of those who sought to slay him; and they were carried in unto the king for a testimony of the things which they had done."

The practice of cutting off the arms or other body parts of enemies, specifically as a testimony of the conquest of victims, is attested in the ancient Near East.[1] On the extreme left of band 4 on the decorated Gates of Shalmaneser III (858–824 B.C.), Assyrian troops are shown cutting off the heads, feet, and hands of vanquished enemies. "In other reliefs, the artists of the Assyrian kings depict the military scribes recording the number of enemy dead in accordance with the number of severed heads, hands and feet which Assyrian soldiers hold up before them."[2] This practice seems related to that of the astounded servants of King Lamoni, who took the arms that had been cut off by Ammon into the king as "a testimony" of what Ammon had done.

There may be several reasons behind this widespread phenomenon in the ancient world, ranging throughout the Near East and Egypt:

First, there was a need to obtain an accurate count of the dead. Military officers tended to exaggerate their conquests for self-aggrandizement and political gain; thus, a precise statistic was necessary to avoid misrepresentation. Similarly, Ammon (or his companions) was scrupulous to present precise evidence, so that no one could be accused of overstating his feat.

Second, there was a need for mercenary soldiers to be paid,

and they were often rewarded based on the number of victims they had killed. Ammon, of course, had no interest in receiving compensation for his loyal service to King Lamoni, but the fact that the evidence was presented to the king, which could have entitled him to payment, heightens all the more the fact that Ammon sought no recognition or reward.

Other reasons for the practice may have included the need to identify the dead; thus, body parts were usually selected that were somehow unique to the victims. Taking an arm may also have had symbolic significance in punishing thieves who had misappropriated property by hand. Such became a common punishment for thieves in the Moslem world, although Jewish jurisprudence came to avoid any bodily mutilation.

Finally, an often-heard threat in the Near East today is that of vowing to cut down any arms raised against a person. Similarly, "as many of their arms as were lifted against" Ammon were smitten off (Alma 17:28).

Based on research by John M. Lundquist and John W. Welch, from the F.A.R.M.S. newsletters, October 1983 and Fall 1986.

Notes

1. Yigael Yadin, *The Art of Warfare in Biblical Lands,* 2 vols. (New York: McGraw Hill, 1963), 2:399.
2. Ibid.

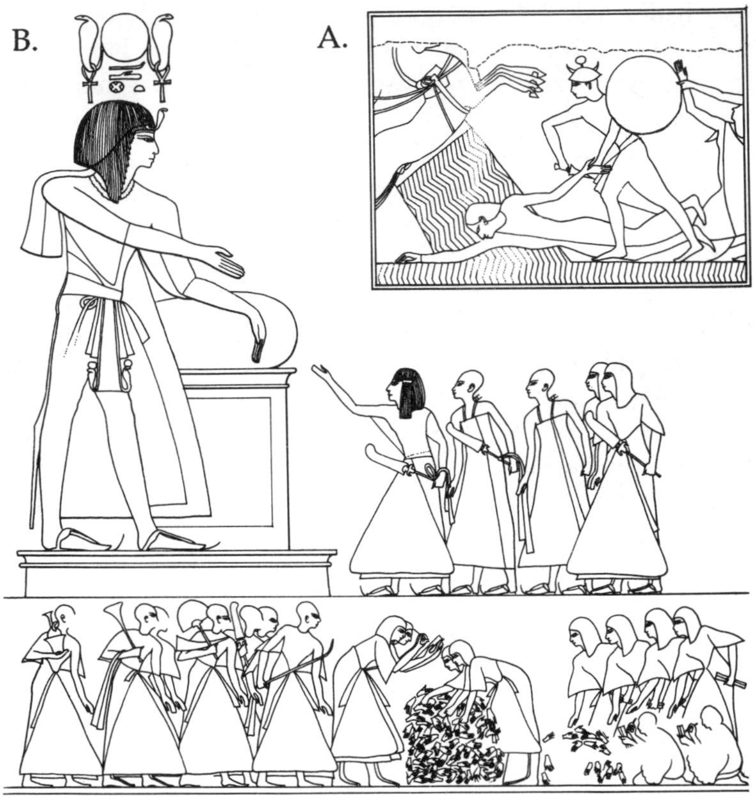

Ancient Near Eastern warriors often cut off the hands or other body parts of their victims and presented them to their commander as a witness of those they had killed in battle. Figure A shows soldiers at the time of Ramses II cutting off the hands of their victims, and Figure B shows hands being piled up at the feet of Ramses III. Line drawings by Michael Lyon.

Chapter 52

DIRECTIONS IN HEBREW, EGYPTIAN, AND NEPHITE LANGUAGE

Alma 22:27 "on the east and on the west"

A great deal of effort has gone into trying to correlate the cities and regions mentioned in the Book of Mormon with the geography of the Americas. The most widely accepted attempt currently is the "limited geography" theory most extensively developed by John Sorenson.[1] Some critics have claimed that Sorenson's theory is incorrect because the lands he ascribes to the Book of Mormon are actually situated along a northwest/southeast axis rather than north/south as described in the Book of Mormon. Sorenson offers an excellent discussion of this issue,[2] to which the following can be added.

How would the Nephites, using the "learning of the Jews and the language of the Egyptians" (1 Nephi 1:2), have written *north, south, east,* and *west?* The Hebrews, like most Semitic peoples, oriented themselves by facing east, toward the rising sun. Thus *east* in Hebrew was simply *front* (*qedem*), with *south* as *right* (*yamîn*), *north* as *left* (*śᵉmôl*), and *west* as *rear* (*achôr*) or "sea" (*yam*).[3]

But the Nephites also knew the "language of the Egyptians" (1 Nephi 1:2; Mosiah 1:4; Mormon 9:32). The Egyptians oriented themselves by facing south, toward the source of the Nile. "One of the terms for 'south' [in Egyptian] is also a term for 'face'; the usual word for 'north' is probably related to a word which means the 'back of the head.' " The word for *east* is the same as for *left,* and *west* is the same word as *right.*[4]

Thus the Hebrew orientation is shifted 90 degrees from the Egyptian. The Hebrew word for *west* (rear) has the same basic meaning as Egyptian *north* (back of the head); Hebrew *east* (front) equals Egyptian *south* (face); Hebrew *north* (left) matches Egyptian *east* (left); with Hebrew *south* (right) being Egyptian *west* (right).

Thus when Nephi or his descendants wrote in "the language of the Egyptians," they would conceptualize the *land westward* in terms of the Hebrew word *back*. But in writing the Hebrew *land backward* in Egyptian characters, they would actually be writing the Egyptian word for *land northward*. So when the Nephites wrote the Egyptian word for *north,* did they have the Hebrew meaning *west* in mind, or the Egyptian meaning *north?*

If Nephi used the Egyptian terms with Hebrew meanings in mind, and if Joseph Smith then translated those terms literally, a remarkable coincidence occurs. In the Hebrew (and modern) concept of directions, *land westward* (Hebrew *rear*) would have been written in Egypto-Nephite characters as *land northward* (Egyptian *behind*), and *land eastward* (Hebrew *front*) would have been written in Egypto-Nephite as *land southward* (Egyptian *front*). In other words, the conceptual geography of the Hebrew universe must be "distorted" in relation to the Egyptian vocabulary in precisely the way that Nephite geography seems "distorted" in relation to Mesoamerica.

Such Nephite behavior would parallel the way the Egyptians dealt with the problem of fitting their conceptual scheme to strange landscapes encountered when they traveled outside Egypt. They did not change their world view to fit the new geographical facts but simply kept the same terminology. This is shown in their handling of the direction of flow of the Euphrates River. As we have seen, "The Egyptian word 'to go north' is also the Egyptian word 'to go downstream,' and the word 'to go south' is also the word 'to go upstream,' against the current [of the Nile]. When the Egyptians met another river, the Euphrates, for example, that flowed south instead of north, they had to express the contrast by calling it 'that circling water which goes downstream in going upstream,' " which could also be translated as "the river which flows 'north' [Egyptian downstream] by flowing 'south' [Mesopotamian downstream]."[5] In other words, they kept their own cosmographic mindset unchanged while they adjusted the "real-world" geography to fit it—which seems to be what the Nephites did.

If this way of translating directions did not bother the Egyptians, it may not have bothered their contemporaries, the Nephites. Thus we can see that cardinal directions were not expressed by ancient civilizations in the same way they are by modern civilizations. We need to consider how the Nephites in fact labeled their geography, rather than simply to presume that *north* must mean the direction north as we now understand it.

Based on research by William J. Hamblin, May 1990. See also the appendix on directions in John L. Sorenson's "The Geography of Book of Mormon Events: A Source Book" (Provo: F.A.R.M.S., 1990).

Notes

1. John L. Sorenson, *An Ancient American Setting for the Book of Mormon* (Salt Lake City: Deseret Book and F.A.R.M.S., 1985).
2. Ibid., 38–42.
3. See Brevard S. Childs, "Orientation," in George Buttrick, ed. *The Interpreter's Dictionary of the Bible* (New York: Abingdon Press, 1962), 3:608.
4. John A. Wilson, in Henri Frankfort, et al., *Before Philosophy: The Intellectual Adventure of Ancient Man* (Baltimore: Penguin Books, 1972), 51.
5. Ibid., 45–46.

Modern Hebrew *Egyptian*

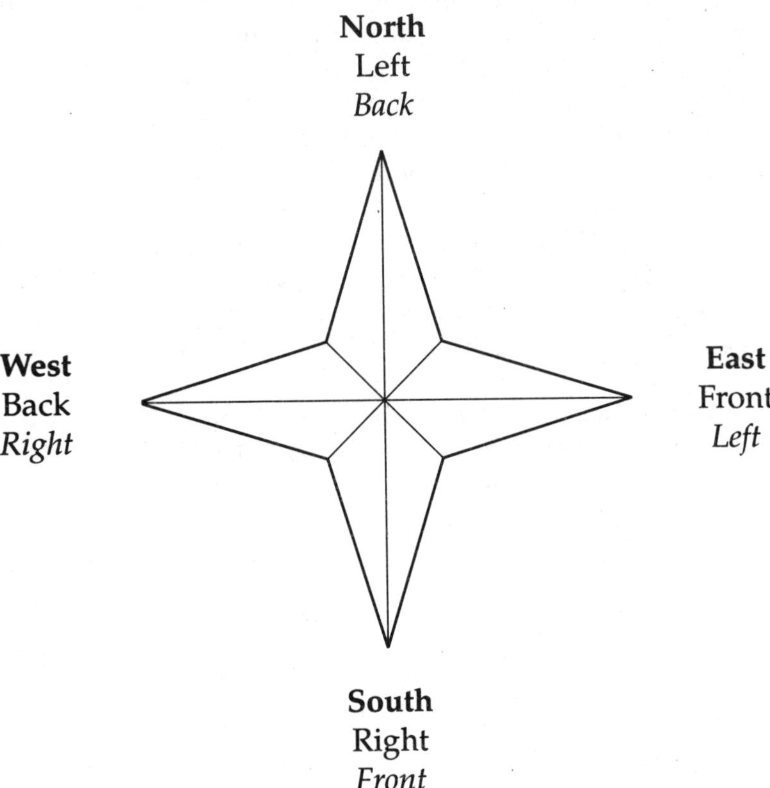

Cardinal directions may be expressed differently from culture to culture.

Chapter 53

"A DAY AND A HALF'S JOURNEY FOR A NEPHITE"

Alma 22:32 "It was only the distance of a day and a half's journey for a Nephite, on the line Bountiful and the land Desolation, from the east to the west sea."

The narrow neck of land is an important geographical feature in the Book of Mormon. For many years people have debated whether the narrow neck was the Isthmus of Panama, the Isthmus of Tehuantepec in southern Mexico, or somewhere else. Some have argued that the neck must have been very narrow, because Alma 22:32 says that the distance across the "narrow neck" of the promised land from the east to the west sea was "a day and a half's journey for a Nephite." How wide could this distance have been? Recently analyzed information suggests that it could have been quite wide indeed.

First, since the Limhi explorers (see Mosiah 8:7–8; 21:25–26) passed through this narrow neck without knowing that they had done so (they thought they were still in or around the land of Zarahemla), this warns us that the narrow neck must be of some substantial width.

Second, we also know that some people can go a long way in a day and a half. For example, a new BYU Media Productions film *Tarahumara: Footrunners Live On* describes a northwest Mexican Indian group who call themselves the Raramuri (footrunners). Some of them have been known to run five hundred miles in six days and to return that distance after a day's rest. Even more, the book *Ultra-Marathoning, the Next Challenge* documents such accomplishments as Edward Weston's *walking* five hundred miles in six days. The record for the greatest distance traveled on foot in twenty-four hours was set in 1973 by Ron Bentley of Great Britain—161 miles.[1] Since the Nephite record says that it was a day and half's journey for *a Nephite,* we might infer that this was a significant feat and that it would have taken longer for someone else.

Moreover, the isthmus itself may have been wider than the "day and half's" distance since we cannot be sure that the measuring point began on the east *at the sea.* Alma says that it was a day and a half's journey from "the east" to the west sea. The journey may have begun some distance inland.

Obviously, we do not yet know how wide the narrow neck was, but these figures show that it could have been a substantial distance. The width of the Isthmus of Tehuantepec, which is now accepted by many Book of Mormon scholars as the Nephite narrow neck of land, is 120 miles—an acceptable distance for the day-and-a-half journey.

Based on research by John L. Sorenson, first appearing in Insights *(February 1985). See the appendix on distances in John L. Sorenson's "The Geography of Book of Mormon Events: A Source Book" (Provo: F.A.R.M.S., 1990).*

Note

1. Tom Osler and Ed Dodd, *Ultra-Marathoning, the Next Challenge* (Mountain View, California: World Publications, 1979), 10, 126.

Chapter 54

EXEMPTION FROM MILITARY DUTY

Alma 27:24 "We will guard them from their enemies with our armies, on condition that they will give us a portion of their substance to assist us that we may maintain our armies."

The only Book of Mormon group given an exemption from military service was the famous people of Ammon. In repenting of their previous shedding of blood, they had sworn an oath that they would never again take up arms (see Alma 24:11–13). After they arrived in Zarahemla, they were granted an extraordinary exemption from active military duty if they would help to sustain the Nephite armies with provisions (see Alma 27:23–24). Surprisingly, the grant of this exceptional privilege was consistent with ancient Israelite law.

Normally one duty of ancient peoples was to take up arms in defense of their tribe or nation: "Among nomads there is no distinction between the army and the people: every able-bodied man can join in a raid and must be prepared to defend the tribe's property and rights against an enemy. . . . This was probably true of Israel also."[1] Saul called "all Israel" to take up arms against the Ammonites and the Amalekites (see 1 Samuel 11:1–11; 15:4). Threats and curses were pronounced upon anyone who would not join in the battle. Once, Saul sent messengers to marshall the troops; he symbolically cut a yoke of oxen into pieces in view of the people and proclaimed, "Whosoever cometh not forth after Saul and after Samuel, so shall it be done unto his oxen" (1 Samuel 11:7). Yaqim-Addu, governor of Sagaratum, executed a criminal in prison and paraded his head among the villages as a warning of what would happen if the men did not assemble quickly for battle.[2]

The same basic duty to serve in the army existed in Nephite law and society. Indeed, Moroni had power to punish any person in the land of Zarahemla who would not "defend [his] country" (Alma 51:15; Alma 46:35). Like Saul and Yaqim-Addu, he symbolically portrayed the brutal fate of those who would not fight (see Alma 46:21–22). Under extreme and desperate circumstances, this duty fell even upon old men, women, and children (see Mosiah 10:9; Alma 54:12).

Why, then, were the able-bodied Ammonites granted exemption? There may be several reasons. Unquestionably, their reason for not fighting was righteous and bona fide. But beyond that, it may have been justified by four specific provisions in the law of Moses, especially as they were interpreted in traditional Jewish law.

1. The absolute duty to go to war applied only in fighting against an *enemy*. Deuteronomy 20:1–2, instructing the Israelite leader to speak to his troops in a holy tongue when they go up to battle against an *enemy*, was interpreted in the Talmud as not applying in a conflict against other Israelites: " 'Against your enemies' but not against your brethren, not Judah against Simeon nor Simeon against Benjamin."[3] (The Talmud was a text later than the departure of Lehi from Jerusalem, but it often reflected older material. It was not translated into English until after the Book of Mormon was in print.) A similar feeling may be reflected in the Ammonite reluctance to "take up arms against their *brethren*" (Alma 24:6, 18; 27:23; italics added).

2. The laws of Deuteronomy afforded humanitarian exemptions for those who had recently married, built a new house, planted a new vineyard, or were "fearful or fainthearted" (Deuteronomy 20:5–9; 24:5). Since everyone going into battle was likely "fearful and fainthearted," the exemption undoubtedly had a narrow meaning in actual practice, otherwise nearly everyone would be exempt. Indeed, as the Talmud explains, this "alludes to one who is afraid *because of the transgressions he had*

committed."[4] If a soldier would cower in the face of enemy battle because of his previous sins (fearing that his sins prevented God from defending him or that he might die a sinner), he was deemed unfit for battle. Certainly the Nephites would have recognized that the profound fears of the Ammonites rendered them unsuitable for military duty under such a rule.

3. The rabbis limited the exemption for the "fearful and fainthearted" to "voluntary" exploits of the king; in a "compulsory war" of national defense, even the fainthearted were obligated to go into battle. A similar distinction may have contributed to the Ammonites' feeling, several years later, that they could no longer claim their exemption in the face of the extreme "compulsory" war that threatened the Nephites' entire existence. Moved by compassion and no longer afraid, they were willing to take up arms (see Alma 53:13). Only Helaman's fear that they might lose their souls if they were to violate their oath stopped them. Instead, they sent their sons into battle (see Alma 53:15–17).

4. The men who remained at home, however, continued to support the war behind the lines. Their exemption was granted only on the condition that they would contribute substance to maintain the army. This arrangement is especially noteworthy, since the Talmud likewise holds that those who are exempted from military service under the law of Moses are "*only* released from actual fighting, *but not from serving in the rear:* 'They must furnish water and food and repair the roads.' "[5]

The exemption granted to the Ammonites was logical, religiously motivated, and consistent with the spirit of ancient Israelite law, which placed a high civic obligation on all citizens to contribute, as appropriate, to the defense of their country, their God, their religion, and their people.

Based on research by John W. Welch, June 1989. This topic is discussed further in John W. Welch, "Law and War in the Book of Mormon," in Stephen Ricks and William Hamblin, eds., Warfare in the Book of Mormon *(Salt Lake City: Deseret Book and F.A.R.M.S., 1990), 62–65 and 85–86.*

Notes

1. Roland de Vaux, *Ancient Israel,* 2 vols. (New York: McGraw Hill, 1965), 1:214.

2. From the royal archive in Mari, II, 48:15–20; cited in Victor H. Matthews, "Legal Aspects of Military Service in Ancient Mesopotamia," *Military Law Review* 94 (1981): 143.

3. Babylonian Talmud, *Sotah* VIII, 1, 42a.

4. Ibid., VIII, 3, 44a; italics added.

5. Ibid., VIII, 2, 43a; italics added.

Chapter 55

SYNAGOGUES IN THE BOOK OF MORMON

Alma 31:12 "The Zoramites had built synagogues, and . . . they did gather themselves together on one day of the week."

Synagogues are mentioned several times in the Book of Mormon. Places of worship were called synagogues during the time of Nephi and Jacob (see 2 Nephi 26:26). Several centuries later, they were still being built by the Nephites "after the manner of the Jews" and were used along with temples and other sanctuaries as places of preaching (Alma 16:13).

Later, unusual forms of synagogue worship developed. The Amalekites and Amulonites built synagogues "after the order of the Nehors" in the city of Jerusalem joining the borders of Mormon (Alma 21:4), where Ammon preached. The Zoramites also built synagogues in Antionum (see Alma 31:12), which contained rameumptoms upon which the elect were allowed to pray.

Several points should be noted and explored here. First is the diversity evident in Book of Mormon synagogues. The institution was not rigid. There were synagogues after the manner of the Jews, after the manner of the Nehors, and in Antionum after a manner that amazed Alma and his companions. Similarly, ancient Israelite communal worship appears to have begun as a flexible practice and was known in several developmental stages.

The earliest hints possibly relevant to the origins and development of the synagogue in Israel are references to "holy convocations" (Leviticus 23:4; 2 Kings 4:23; Isaiah 4:5); according to some scholars these were the antecedents of the later established synagogue. It is noteworthy that these very early convocations were for the purposes of prayer and worship, which also seems to be the dominant function of the early synagogues in the Book of Mormon. Nephi expressly calls his synagogues "houses of worship."

It is a matter of much scholarly debate when and how the synagogue as known to later Judaism actually developed. As the *Interpreter's Dictionary of the Bible* cautions, the specific origins of the synagogue are too faint "to venture a conjecture in this kind of antiquity."[1] But there are certain possibilities. Some historians see the development of the synagogue occurring during the captivity of the Jews in Babylonia during the sixth century B.C. Others point to the reforms of Josiah in 621 B.C. as giving rise to the use of local congregations for worship, prayer, and instructions among the Israelites. It is, of course, possible that both are right: there is no reason to believe that the Jewish synagogue suddenly came from nowhere and appeared in one instant in its fully developed form as known to later Rabbinic Judaism.

The Book of Mormon, of course, lends credence to the idea that synagogues, at least as places of worship, were known to Israel before the departure of Lehi from Jerusalem (although no specific statement makes that claim). While most scholars focus their attention on the development of the synagogue in postexilic Israel, those who discuss the preexilic origins of the synagogue include Leopold Loew, Julian Morgenstern, Louis Finkelstein (long-time Chancellor of the Jewish Theological Seminary of America), Azriel Eisenberg, and others. Jacob Weingreen writes: "It would be natural to suppose that, following upon the enforcement of Josiah's edict, religious services continued to be held outside Jerusalem, but now without sacrifices. . . . These must . . . have constituted the basis of the synagogue service of later times."[2]

Another interesting point deals with the word *synagogue,* which is of Greek origin. It is the term used in the Septuagint to translate several Hebrew words, including *camp, assembly, community,* and *congregation.* The Hebrew roots involved here should be explored to cast light on the underlying practices of ancient Israel. Of course, we do not know what Hebrew or other word the Nephites or Zoramites used in naming their places of worship. Note, however, that the English word *synagogue* is made from two parts: the Greek prefix *syn,* which means together, and the verb *agō,* which means to gather or to bring together. Interestingly, in Alma 31:12 the phrase "gather themselves together" appears in immediate literal conjunction with the term *synagogue*: "the Zoramites had built synagogues, and . . . they did gather themselves together."

Although considerably more work is needed before we fully understand the nature of ancient Israelite places of worship, their sanctuaries, temples, and the names by which they knew them, this history is significant and takes on particular interest to the student of the Book of Mormon.

This Update was based on research by John W. Welch and appeared in the F.A.R.M.S. newsletter, March 1983.

Notes

1. "Synagogue," in George Buttrick, ed., *The Interpreter's Dictionary of the Bible* (New York: Abingdon Press, 1962), 479–80.

2. An extensive treatment of all sides of the history of the synagogue can be found in Joseph Gutmann, *The Synagogue: Studies in Origins, Archaeology, and Architecture* (New York: KTAV, 1975).

Chapter 56

THE SONS OF THE PASSOVER

Alma 35:16 "He caused that his sons should be gathered together, that he might give unto them every one his charge, separately."

In August 1984 for the first time, several stunning similarities between Alma 36–42 and the traditional Israelite observance of Passover were discovered. Finding evidences of Jewish festivals in the Book of Mormon is just a small part of what promises eventually to be a meaningful study.

Passover, of course, commemorates the deliverance of the Israelites from Egypt by the power of God. As part of this celebration, fathers would gather their sons (as in Alma 35:16) in accordance with Exodus 10:2, which told the Jews "to tell in the ears of thy son, and of thy son's son, what things I have wrought in Egypt." Alma would have followed this rule since the Nephites "were strict in observing . . . the law of Moses" at this time (Alma 30:3).

According to traditions at least as early as the time of Christ and probably earlier,[1] after gathering his family the father then instructed his sons and answered their questions. His words were not fixed but were "to fit the knowledge and understanding of the child" and were supposed "to spell out the sequence of sin, suffering, repentance, and redemption."[2] Each of Alma's admonitions to his sons, Helaman (Alma 36–37), Shiblon (Alma 38), and Corianton (Alma 39–42), does this precisely, each in its own way.

Moreover, three Passover questions are found in the Bible. Traditionally, each of these questions was asked in turn by the sons and was answered by the father. In time, each of these questions came to be associated with a different type of son.

First, "What is the *meaning* of the testimonies, and the statutes, and the judgments, which the Lord our God hath commanded you?" (Deuteronomy 6:20). This question was asked at Passover by a *wise son*. Helaman stands as the wise son: In talking to Helaman, Alma mentions "wisdom" at least eight times in Alma 37. Notice also how Alma explains the *meaning* of the laws and testimonies of God as he explains the meaning of the plates of Nephi (preserved for a "wise purpose"), the twenty-four gold plates, and the Liahona in Alma 37. The Jewish father was especially expected to explain the meaning of traditional things to "future generations"[3] and to use "allegorical interpretation."[4] Alma does exactly this. See Alma 37:19 ("future generations") and Alma 37:45 ("is there not a type in this thing?").

Second, "What mean ye by this service?" (Exodus 12:26). This question was asked by a *wicked son*. This son is depicted in the Jewish literature as one guilty of social crimes, who had excluded himself from the community, and believed in false doctrines. According to Jewish practice, he is to be told, in a manner that will "set his teeth on edge," that he will be punished for his own sins, and that, had he been in Egypt, he would not have been redeemed.[5] Such is unmistakably the thrust of Alma's words to Corianton—who had left the ministry (see Alma 39:3), caused social problems (see Alma 39:11), followed false doctrines (see Alma 41:9), and is taught by his father about nothing but redemption and one's personal suffering for sin (see Alma 41:3–4, 7).

Third, "What is this?" (Exodus 13:14), is an ambiguous question. Is it sarcastic or serious? Israelite tradition said that the *uninformed son* who asked this question needed to be taught the law and given preventative instruction to keep him well away from any risk of breaking the law.[6] This, indeed, is what Alma tells Shiblon, as he teaches him to be diligent (see Alma 38:10) and gives him a high code of conduct (see Alma 38:11–14).

Many other Passover themes are detectable in Alma 35–42.

Alma speaks of "crying out" (compare Deuteronomy 26:7; Alma 36:18) for deliverance from "affliction" (compare Deuteronomy 26:6; Alma 36:3, 27; especially the unleavened Passover "bread of affliction") and from bondage in Egypt (Alma 36:28), from the "night of darkness" (compare Alma 41:7; Exodus 12:30), and from bitter suffering (Alma 36:18, 21; related to the Passover "bitter herbs"in Exodus 12:8). The Paschal lamb may parallel some of Alma's references to Christ; and the hardness of Pharaoh's heart (see Exodus 11:10) may parallel Alma's reference to the hardness of his people's hearts (see Alma 35:15). Just as Alma's deliverance was preceded by three days and nights of darkness (see Alma 36:16), so was the first Passover (see Exodus 10:22).

Although still tentative, the proposition is already quite intriguing, if not compelling: Alma's messages to his three sons were spoken in conjunction with a Nephite observance of the feast of the Passover.

Based on research by Gordon C. Thomasson and John W. Welch, August 1984. For further research regarding Israelite festivals in the Book of Mormon, see pages 117–19 and 135–41 in this book.

Notes

1. See Abraham P. Bloch, *The Biblical and Historical Background of the Jewish Holy Days* (New York: KTAV, 1978), 128–33.
2. Ibid., 131–32.
3. Ibid., 153.
4. Ibid., 157.
5. See ibid., 159–63.
6. See ibid., 163–64.

Chapter 57

CONFERENCE ON WARFARE IN THE BOOK OF MORMON

Alma 43:3 "And now I return to an account of the wars between the Nephites and the Lamanites."

On August 21–22, 1987, F.A.R.M.S. sponsored a working conference in Provo. Chaired by Stephen Ricks and William Hamblin, twelve participants, plus a few observers, came from as far away as California, Missouri, and Mississippi. Over a day and a half of concentrated activity, this group project involved formal presentation of written work.

Even though warfare plays an especially prominent role in several sections of the Book of Mormon, what is known about the armies, weapons, strategies, fortifications, captives, rituals, causes, and results of war reported in the scripture has never been comprehensively examined. One task of this conference was to develop an agenda of those topics that merit scrutiny.

The first presentations dealt with military technology and organization. Brent Merrill gave two papers, one on swords and cimeters, and the other on Nephite captains and their role in military organization. He noted that the office of chief captain apparently emerged when Alma split the chief judgeship into three separate offices (see Alma 4:20; 16:5).

William Hamblin examined all descriptions of the bow and arrow in the Book of Mormon, relating them to a wide variety of archaeological and art evidence from the Near East and Mesoamerica. One interesting observation was that the Hebrew idiom for "shooting" an arrow literally also means "throwing"; thus Alma 49:22 refers to arrows "thrown" at the Lamanites.

John Sorenson summarized the dramatic shift that has occurred in thought about warfare in studies on Mesoamerica in recent decades. Where scholars once saw utopian peace prevailing throughout ancient Mesoamerica, now at least a hundred fortified sites have been identified, and the pervasive role of war in Mesoamerican life over at least two thousand years is widely recognized.

Bruce Warren compared a number of war practices and beliefs thought to have prevailed in the Maya civilization to practices and beliefs of the Nephites and Jaredites, especially the reasons for imprisoning or killing kings. Matthew Hilton looked at reasons and motivations for war in the modern world and compared them with concepts of freedom, peace, righteousness, and just war in the Book of Mormon.

Gordon Thomasson suggested that certain rituals were associated with warfare in the Book of Mormon, as may be evidenced by the slaying of Amalickiah (see Alma 51:34–52:2) and Ammoron (see Alma 62:36–39) immediately before royally important new year's days.

Evidence for martial law among the Nephites was presented by John Welch and Robert Eaton. As in Israel, law and war interact in several ways in the Book of Mormon, as in justifying and controlling the use of military force, suspending the normal judicial process (see Alma 51:19), imposing civic and international obligations, and prescribing treatment of prisoners of war.

John Tvedtnes examined tribal and political affiliations within the Book of Mormon and proposed that leaders of Nephite armies were drawn from particular lineage groups or a military caste. This would explain why Moroni at age twenty-five (see Alma 43:17), his son Moronihah at about age eighteen (see Alma 62:39), Mormon at age sixteen (see Mormon 2:2), and others in this line or group were made chief captains while surprisingly young.

Terrence Szink presented several parallels between the ritual behavior of Moroni's soldiers when he raised the banner of liberty and ancient Near Eastern practices. A Hittite soldier's oath offered an intriguing counterpart to the Nephite soldier's covenant in Alma 46:21–22. Finally, Daniel Peterson gave an insightful interpretation of the Gadianton Robbers as a counterculture. He pointed out ways we fail to understand their motives and practices.

Following this Update, which appeared in September 1987, F.A.R.M.S. sponsored a formal conference on warfare in the Book of Mormon in the Spring of 1989, at which time finished versions of these projects and additional papers were presented. They were then published in Stephen Ricks and William Hamblin, eds., Warfare in the Book of Mormon *(Salt Lake City: Deseret Book and F.A.R.M.S., 1990), the first topical Book of Mormon treatise of its kind. This significant and informative historical treatment is discussed further with additional substantive research in two reviews by David B. Honey and Kurt Weiland, in* Review of Books on the Book of Mormon *3 (1991): 118–46.*

Chapter 58

"HOLY WAR" IN THE BOOK OF MORMON AND THE ANCIENT NEAR EAST

Alma 46:22 "We covenant with our God, that we shall be destroyed, even as our brethren in the land northward, if we shall fall into transgression; yea, he may cast us at the feet of our enemies."

In a sense, every conflict in the ancient Near East—as reflected in Egyptian, Babylonian, Assyrian, Hittite, Persian, and Syro-Palestinian texts—was considered to be prosecuted under the divine direction of the gods or of God. War was begun at the command of, or with the approval and aid of, the gods or God. It was generally accompanied by sacrifices, fought by men who were in a state of ritual readiness for conflict, and ended by the victors with thanksgiving and offerings to deity.[1]

Like other nations of the ancient Near East, Israel's ideology of war centered on God. The Lord himself is described as a "warrior" and "the Lord strong and mighty . . . in battle" (Psalm 24:8). "The Lord is a man of war; the Lord is his name" (Exodus 15:3; see also Isaiah 42:14). The wars that Israel fought were "the Lord's battles" (1 Samuel 18:17); indeed, among the lost books of ancient Israel is "the Book of the Wars of the Lord" (Numbers 21:14). The enemies of Israel were the enemies of the Lord (see Judges 5:31; 1 Samuel 30:26), who assists Israel in battle (see Joshua 10:11, 24:12; 1 Samuel 17:45). The Lord was consulted (see Judges 20:18, 28; 1 Samuel 14:37) and sacrifice was offered (see 1 Samuel 7:9; 13:9, 12) before hostilities were initiated. When

Israel went to war, its army was called "the people of the Lord" (Judges 5:11), "the people of God" (Judges 20:2), or "the armies of the living God" (1 Samuel 17:26).

Combatants in the Israelite armies were expected to be ritually clean at the time they went out to battle. Thus, Joshua tells the camp of Israel, "Sanctify yourselves: for tomorrow the Lord will do wonders among you" (Joshua 3:5). In particular, members of "the armies of the living God" were expected to keep away from women before battle (2 Samuel 11:11). Further, "when the host goeth forth against [Israel's] enemies," every member of the camp had to "keep . . . from every wicked thing" (Deuteronomy 23:9; see further 23:10–15).

God insisted on strict observance of his commands when Israel was going to war. The consequences for violations could be devastating. They could suffer defeat in battle that could only be rectified by the punishment of the wrongdoer (see Joshua 7), or they could be wholly rejected by the Lord (see 1 Samuel 15). Just as the Lord would direct the righteous Israelites in their battles against their enemies, he would also punish a straying Israel through war (see Isaiah 5:26–28; Jeremiah 5:15–17; Ezekiel 21:1–32; 23:22–28). Indeed, the language of war is used to depict the judgment of God (see Joel 2:1–11).

The Book of Mormon reflects a similar pattern. The great captain Moroni, in fighting the Lamanites, "knowing of the prophecies of Alma, sent certain men unto him, desiring him that he should inquire of the Lord whither the armies of the Nephites should go to defend themselves against the Lamanites. And it came to pass that the word of the Lord came unto Alma, and Alma informed the messengers of Moroni, that the armies of the Lamanites were marching round about in the wilderness, that they might come over into the land of Manti, that they might commence an attack upon the weaker part of the people. And those messengers went and delivered the message unto Moroni" (Alma 43:23–24; see also 18:5–6, 8; 48:16; compare 1 Kings 22: 1–28).

The story of the Ammonite stripling soldiers is also striking for its religious content: the young men who entered a covenant with God (see Alma 53:17) not only were "exceedingly valiant for courage, and also for strength and activity," but their lives also reflected outstanding purity. "They were men who were true at all times in whatsoever thing they were entrusted. Yea, they were men of truth and soberness, for they had been taught to keep the commandments of God and to walk uprightly before him" (Alma 53:20–21). Their protection in war was attributed directly to their righteousness.

While the Nephites inquired of the Lord before entering battle, sought his aid in battle, and purified themselves ethically (and perhaps also ritually) for combat, on the contrary his departure from the midst of their armies was thought to portend disaster. Mormon 2 through 6 – surely some of the most heartrending chapters in all of scripture – provide ample proof of these things.

Hopeful that God would aid the Nephites in their struggle against the Lamanites, Mormon assumed command over their armies. Soon, however, he realized that his hope was "vain, for their sorrowing was not unto repentance, because of the goodness of God; but it was rather the sorrowing of the damned, because the Lord would not always suffer them to take happiness in sin" (Mormon 2:13). He took an oath to lead them no longer, but he finally "did repent of the oath" (Mormon 5:1) and returned to command the army once again, though with no expectation of victory, since God was no longer with the Nephite people. The final battle at Cumorah validated the principle given already to the ancient Israelites: through war, and by means of the wicked, God will punish his people when they have turned from righteousness (see Mormon 4:5).

Based on research by Stephen D. Ricks, March 1989, and dealt with more extensively in his chapter, " 'Holy War': The Sacral Ideology of War in the Book of Mormon and in the Ancient Near East," in Stephen Ricks and William

Hamblin, eds., Warfare in the Book of Mormon *(Salt Lake City: Deseret Book and F.A.R.M.S., 1990), 103–17.*

Note

1. See Roland de Vaux, *Ancient Israel,* 2 vols. (New York: McGraw-Hill, 1961), 1:258–59; Dino Merli, "Le 'Guerre di sterminio' nell'antichità orientale e biblica," *Bibbia e Oriente* 9 (1967): 57–66.

Chapter 59

SYMBOLIC ACTION AS PROPHETIC CURSE

Alma 46:22 "even as we have cast our garments at thy feet to be trodden under foot"

At one point in his ministry, Isaiah was instructed by the Lord to remove his garment and shoes and walk "naked [like a slave, without an upper garment] and barefoot" among the people. Isaiah's action was to be a sign, for as Isaiah walked like a slave, even so would the Egyptians become slaves to the Assyrians (Isaiah 20:2–4). This prophetic symbolic action by Isaiah represented a prophetic curse that destruction and ruin would come upon the Egyptians.

Ezekiel conducted a symbolic act that had anathematical tones. He cut off the hair of his beard and his head, and divided it into three portions. One third Ezekiel burned, one third he scattered into the wind, and one third he smote with a knife. This was a prophetic curse, demonstrating the three ways in which Israel would perish—by fire, by scattering, and by the sword of war (see Ezekiel 5:1–17).

Such prophetic symbolic curses are well attested in the Bible.[1] Fohrer and Aune take a broad approach to prophetic symbolic actions, listing several examples (see, for instance, Numbers 21:6–9; 1 Kings 22:11; 2 Kings 13:14–19; Isaiah 2:9–10; 3:1–4; 8:1–4; 7:10–17; Jeremiah 19:1–15; 27–28; 28:10–11; 32:6–44; Ezekiel 4:1–3; 4:4–8; 4:9–17). Several F.A.R.M.S. publications have previously noted various types of symbolic actions that are present in the Book of Mormon.[2]

Book of Mormon prophets carried on the Old World tradition of performing symbolic actions that revealed a prophetic curse.

The incident of the title of liberty was much more than a rally behind a standard. Moroni rent his coat, wrote upon it the title of liberty, placed it upon a pole, and "went forth among the people, waving the rent part of his garment in the air, that all might see" (Alma 46:19). After this dramatic act, Moroni likened his rent coat to the garment of Joseph that had been rent by Joseph's brothers and proclaimed, "Let us remember to keep the commandments of God, or our garments shall be rent by our brethren, and we be cast into prison, or be sold, or be slain" (Alma 46:23). A curse is clearly implied. Those who fail to keep the commandments of God would be imprisoned, sold, or slain.

Those who witnessed Moroni's symbolic activity responded in turn with another symbolic action by casting their garments at Moroni's feet and then promising not to fall into transgression, lest God "cast us at the feet of our enemies, even as we have cast our garments at thy feet to be trodden under foot" (Alma 46:22).

A prophetic symbolic action accompanied by a curse is found in the hanging of Zemnarihah on the top of a tree. After his death the Nephites felled the tree and called out in unison, "May the Lord preserve his people in righteousness and in holiness of heart, that they may cause to be felled to the earth all who shall seek to slay them . . . even as this man hath been felled to the earth" (3 Nephi 4:28–29). This act predicted the way the wicked would be slain if they continued their attempts to murder the righteous.

A third example of symbolic action as a prophetic curse is found in the episode of the scalping of Zerahemnah. After Moroni's soldier scalped Zerahemnah, the warmongering leader of the Lamanites, the soldier displayed the scalp on the point of his sword and stated with a loud voice, "Even as this scalp has fallen to the earth . . . so shall ye fall to the earth except ye will deliver up your weapons of war and depart with a covenant of peace" (Alma 44:12–14).

The symbolic actions in these examples were so effective that in each instance the audience reacted immediately and positively. Those who viewed Moroni gathered around the title of liberty; those who witnessed the felling of the tree had a great emotional and spiritual experience (see 3 Nephi 4:30–33); and the followers of Zerahemnah who were present when he was scalped "were struck with fear" and "threw down their weapons of war," promising to live in peace (Alma 44:15).

Based on research by Donald W. Parry, July 1991.

Notes

1. Georg Fohrer, *Die symbolischen Handlungen der Propheten* (Zürich: Zwingli Verlag, 1953), 17–19, and David E. Aune, *Prophecy in Early Christianity and the Ancient Mediterranean World* (Grand Rapids: Eerdmans, 1983), 100–101.

2. Mark Morrise, "Simile Curses in the Ancient Near East, Old Testament, and Book of Mormon" (Provo: F.A.R.M.S., 1982); and Terrence Szink, "An Oath of Allegiance in the Book of Mormon," in *Warfare in the Book of Mormon,* ed. Stephen Ricks and William Hamblin (Salt Lake City: Deseret Book and F.A.R.M.S., 1990), 36–38, present examples of simile curses. John W. Welch discusses parabolic acts performed by prophetic oracles, in "Law and War in the Book of Mormon," in *Warfare in the Book of Mormon,* 62; see also pages 239–41, "Was Helaman 7–8 an Allegorical Sermon?" in this book.

Chapter 60

NEW YEAR'S CELEBRATIONS

Alma 52:1 "on the first morning of the first month"

Covenant renewal and New Year's resolutions have more in common than meet the eye. Recent research has turned up some interesting details about the importance of New Year's celebrations in the Bible and in the Book of Mormon. Here are a few interesting results:

In the ancient Old World, the New Year celebration was viewed as the birthday of the world. It was a day of coronation of divine and earthly kings, a day of victory over chaos, a day of renewal of covenant and the reenactment of the king's enthronement, and a day of temple dedication and record keeping. There is good evidence that King Benjamin's address in Mosiah 1–6 was delivered on just such a great feast day, for it included nearly all the typical ancient New Year's features.[1]

Other Book of Mormon events may show the importance of New Year's Day to those people. Imagine the confusion caused when the Lamanites awoke on New Year's Day to find that King Amalickiah had been murdered on New Year's Eve (see Alma 51:34–52:1). Note too the parallel timing of Teancum's killing of Amalickiah's brother Ammoron in Alma 62:36–39. This was the day when the king should have ceremonially conquered death and been reenthroned! Other significant events occurring around the turning of the year may be found in both the Bible and the Book of Mormon (see 1 Kings 8:2–66; Nehemiah 8:1–18; Alma 28:4–30:2; 44:24–45:1; Helaman 14:2–16:25; 3 Nephi 1:1–19; compare Exodus 40:2; Helaman 9:10).

Consider also the *when* of New Year's Day as well as the

what: We tend to have very short memories culturally. As Orson Pratt pointed out in Salt Lake City in 1872, from the fourteenth century A.D. until 1751, March 25 was New Year's Day for everybody in England and the American Colonies.[2] Before that, under the Julian Calendar, New Year's Day fell on December 25, winter solstice (i.e., the shortest day of the year and the traditional birthdate in the West of Jesus—since about the fourth century A.D.), which was 22/23 of December in the later Gregorian Calendar.[3] Egyptian Christians put January 6 on the winter solstice; thus, this was the Armenian and Eastern Orthodox date for Christmas. Earlier yet, the winter solstice had been the traditional birthday of the Sun-god: Mithra, Re', Sol Invictus, etc.

The British Parliament in 1751 shortened the calendar year by eighty-four days in order to place the beginning of the year on January 1 (a neoclassical Roman revival, similar to the ancient Roman switch from March 1 to January 1, though in this case tied to the astronomical perihelion of the earth). Parliament also shortened the year 1752 by eleven days in order to finally adopt the sixteenth-century Calendar Reform of Pope Gregory XIII—and thus bring the English calendar into proper alignment with the seasons.

As if that did not play enough havoc with modern genealogical research, in 1792 the infant French Republic adopted September 22, the autumnal equinox, as its New Year, but Napoleon ordered a return to January 1 in 1805.[4] In ancient Egypt, the agricultural New Year came at the heliacal rising of the star Sirius—around July 20—which coincided with the rising of the Nile River. The Babylonian and Phoenician New Year was on the first day of the first month, but in the spring in Babylon and in the fall in Phoenicia! In ancient Israel and Judah, the New Year could come with either the beginning or ending of harvest season—near either the vernal or autumnal equinox, i.e., Passover/Unleavened Bread for Israel, and Trumpets/Atonement/Tabernacles for Judah, respectively.[5] This undoubtedly accounts in part for the odd fact that, for Jews, New Year's Day comes on *1 Tishri,* the first day of the *seventh* Jewish month (in the fall)!

The point should begin to be clear: A year need not begin when we today assume it will, and Joseph Smith apparently had no inkling of the significance of the special day upon which he removed the golden plates of the Book of Mormon from the hill near his home. It was the Jewish New Year's Day. It was also the autumnal equinox, September 22, 1827. How appropriate for the renewed appearance of the Book of Mormon, which itself focuses on several important events at the New Year concerning covenant renewal and reenthronement of the king.

Based on research by Robert F. Smith and Stephen D. Ricks, January 1985.

Notes

1. See Hugh W. Nibley, "Old World Ritual in the New World," in *An Approach to the Book of Mormon,* in *The Collected Works of Hugh Nibley* (Salt Lake City: Deseret Book and F.A.R.M.S., 1988), 6:295–310; John Tvedtnes, "King Benjamin and the Feast of Tabernacles," in *By Study and Also by Faith,* 2 vols. (Salt Lake City: Deseret Book and F.A.R.M.S., 1990), 2:197–237; Stephen D. Ricks, "The Treaty/Covenant Pattern in King Benjamin's Address," *Brigham Young University Studies* 24 (Spring 1984): 151–62; and Frank Moore Cross on cosmic and Canaanite temple dedication in Truman G. Madsen, ed., *The Temple in Antiquity* (Provo: Religious Studies Center, 1984), 93.

2. Orson Pratt, "True Christmas and New Year," *Journal of Discourses* 15 (29 December 1872): 261.

3. *Encyclopedia Britannica,* 15th ed. (Chicago), *Macropaedia,* 3:603; *New Catholic Encyclopedia* (New York: McGraw-Hill, 1967–79), 3:656.

4. *Encyclopedia Britannica,* 15th ed., 3:603.

5. Edwin R. Thiele, *A Chronology of the Hebrew Kings* (Grand Rapids: Zondervan, 1977), 14.

Chapter 61

CONCRETE EVIDENCE FOR THE BOOK OF MORMON

Helaman 3:7 "The people who went forth became exceedingly expert in the working of cement."

Helaman 3:7–11 reports that Nephite dissenters moved from the land of Zarahemla into the land northward and began building with cement. "The people . . . who went forth became exceedingly expert in the working of cement; therefore they did build houses of cement," "all manner of their buildings," and many cities "both of wood and of cement." The Book of Mormon dates this significant technological advance to the year 46 B.C.

Recent research shows that cement was in fact extensively used in Mesoamerica beginning largely at this time. One of the most notable uses of cement is in the temple complex at Teotihuacan, north of present-day Mexico City. According to David S. Hyman, the structural use of cement appears suddenly in the archaeological record. Its earliest sample "is a fully developed product." The cement floor slabs at this site "were remarkably high in structural quality." Although exposed to the elements for nearly two thousand years, they still "exceed many present-day building code requirements."[1]

After its discovery, cement was used at many sites in the Valley of Mexico and in the Maya regions of southern Mexico, Guatemala, and Honduras. It was used in the construction of buildings at such sites as Cerro de Texcotzingo, Tula, Palenque, Tikal, Copan, Uxmal, and Chichen Itza. Further, the use of cement "is a Maya habit, *absent* from non-Maya examples of corbelled vaulting from the south-eastern United States to southern South America."[2]

Mesoamerican cement was almost exclusively lime cement. The limestone was purified on a "cylindrical pile of timber, which requires a vast amount of labor to cut and considerable skill to construct in such a way that combustion of the stone and wood is complete and a minimum of impurities remains in the product."[3] The fact that very little carbon is found in this cement "attests to the ability of these ancient peoples."[4]

John Sorenson further noted the expert sophistication in the use of cement at El Tajin, east of Mexico City, after Book of Mormon times. Cement roofs covered areas of seventy-five square meters! "Sometimes the builders filled a room with stones and mud, smoothed the surface on top to receive the concrete, then removed the interior fill when the [slab] on top had dried."[5]

The presence of expert cement technology in prehispanic Mesoamerica is a remarkable archaeological fact, inviting much further research. Cement seems to take on significant roles in Mesoamerican architecture close to the time when the Book of Mormon says this development occurred. It is also a significant factor in locating the Book of Mormon lands of Zarahemla and Desolation, for Zarahemla must be south of areas where cement was used as early as the middle first century B.C. Until samples of cement are found outside of the southwest areas of North America, one may reasonably assume that Book of Mormon lands were not far south of the sites where ancient cement is found.

Based on research by Matthew G. Wells and John W. Welch, May 1991.

Notes

1. David S. Hyman, *A Study of the Calcareous Cements in Prehispanic Mesoamerican Building Construction* (Baltimore: Johns Hopkins University, 1970), ii, sect. 6, p. 7.

2. George Kubler, *The Art and Architecture of Ancient America,* 2nd ed. (Baltimore: Penguin, 1975), 201; italics added.

3. Tatiana Proskouriakoff, *An Album of Maya Architecture* (Norman: University of Oklahoma Press, 1963), xv.

4. Hyman, *A Study of the Calcareous Cements,* sect. 6, p. 5.

5. John Sorenson, "Digging Into the Book of Mormon," *Ensign* 14 (October 1984): 19.

Extensive use of cement begins in Teotihuacan, in the Valley of Mexico, around the time of Christ. This corresponds significantly with the description of cement given in Helaman 3. Photograph courtesy of John W. Welch.

Chapter 62

MESOAMERICANS IN PRE-SPANISH SOUTH AMERICA

Helaman 3:8 "They did multiply and spread, and did go forth from the land southward to the land northward."

Many Latter-day Saints are used to thinking of the entire Western Hemisphere as the place where Book of Mormon events were played out. When they encounter facts in the scripture that demonstrate that only a limited territory constituted that scene (Mosiah 23:3 and 24:25, for example, combine to show that the cities of Nephi and Zarahemla were not very far apart), some are puzzled about how the ancient cultures of South America might connect with the book.

Archaeologists, ethnohistorians, and linguists in recent years have amassed data demonstrating beyond question that for at least four thousand years people, materials, and ideas have moved fluidly between the two American continents. This gives us an avenue for understanding how elements of the localized Book of Mormon civilization could appear over the entire hemisphere. For example, a late Peruvian people like the Incas (prominent in the thirteenth to sixteenth centuries A.D.), while having no direct connection with Book of Mormon events a thousand years earlier, can be safely assumed to incorporate genes and cultural elements from Book of Mormon peoples.

Data that prove this longstanding cultural interaction can be found in many sources. Stephen de Borhegyi has identified scores of cultural parallels between Mesoamerica (central Mexico and Guatemala) and Ecuador.[1] Michael Coe was one of the first to argue persuasively that direct sea-voyaging could explain many of these similarities.[2] Excavator Emilio Estrada concluded, on the strength of voluminous evidence, that "linkages were so continuous that it would be better for Ecuador to be considered an integral part of Meso America in culture."[3] This connection began very early and probably continued until the Spaniards arrived.

Allison C. Paulsen is similarly confident that "from about 1500 B.C. until [at least] about A.D. 600, the inhabitants of the [Santa Elena] Peninsula[, Ecuador,] were involved in a network of maritime trade with certain parts of Mesoamerica."[4] Donald Lathrap went so far, perhaps with overenthusiasm, as to suggest "scheduled and routinized sea trade."[5]

Language comparisons also tell us that whole peoples migrated between the two continents. By the technique known as glottochronology, Evangelina Arana O. demonstrated that Quechua (the tongue of the Incas) and Tarascan (of western Mexico) may have shared a common ancestral language only forty-six centuries ago.[6] A Jaredite-age connection would be indicated if that calculation is reliable. But a more recent connection is suggested by a tradition among the Huave of the Isthmus of Tehuantepec in Mexico that their ancestors had come from Peru, having been driven out by wars.[7]

Marshall Newman has mustered biological data to support the idea that sizable groups of people migrated southward.[8] Important parts of the culture of the Olmec in southern Mexico seem to derive from the Amazon drainage, and cultures on that river's delta in Brazil also show Mesoamerican-like features. Peru, Colombia, Venezuela, Panama, and Costa Rica were all involved in the network of movements linking the Book of Mormon homeland with the southern continent.[9]

Applied to the Book of Mormon, this information suggests to us that Jaredites, Nephites, Lamanites, and "Mulekites," or their descendants, or aspects of their culture, could have filtered out over the entire hemisphere. Just as Book of Mormon peoples spread into the lands northward (see Alma 63:4; Helaman 3:8), we can assume they eventually had direct or indirect connections with the lands to the south as well.

Based on research by John L. Sorenson, November 1986. More recently on the whole topic, see Jorge G. Marcos, ed., Arqueologia de la Costa Ecuatoriana: nuevos enfoques, *Biblioteca Ecuatoriana de Arqueologia 1 (Guayaquil, Ecuador: Escuela Politecnica del Litoral, Centro de Estudios Arqueologicos y Antropologicos, and Corporacion Editora Nacional, 1986).*

Notes

1. Stephen F. de Borhegyi, *Middle American Research Records* 2, nos. 6–7 (New Orleans: Tulane University, 1961).

2. Michael Coe, "Archaeological Linkages with North and South America at La Victoria, Guatemala," *American Anthropologist* 62 (1960): 363–93.

3. Emilio Estrada, "Arquelogio de Manabi Central," *Publ. Museo Victor Emilio Estrada* 7 (1962): 89.

4. Allison C. Paulsen, "Patterns of Maritime Trade between South Coastal Ecuador and Western Mesoamerica, 1500 B.C.–A.D. 600" in Elizabeth P. Benson, ed., *The Sea in the Pre-Columbian World* (Washington: Dumbarton Oaks, 1977), 143.

5. Donald W. Lathrap, *Ancient Ecuador* (Chicago: Field Museum of Natural History, 1975), 61.

6. Evangelina Arana O., "Posible relaciones externas del grupo linguistico Maya," *Anales, Instit. Nac. Antro. y Hist.* (Mexico) 19 (1967): 120.

7. Matthew Wallrath, "Excavations in the Tehuantepec Region, Mexico," *Transactions of the American Philosophical Society,* n.s., 57 (1967): 14.

8. Marshall Newman, "A Trial Formulation Presenting Evidence from Physical Anthropology for Migrations from Mexico to South America," in *Migrations in New World Culture History, University of Arizona Social Science Bulletin* no. 27 (1958).

9. See articles by Irving Rouse, Clifford Evans and Betty Meggers, and Donald Lathrap in *Handbook of Middle American Indians* 4 (1966); and Allison Paulsen, "Patterns of Maritime Trade," in Elizabeth P. Benson, ed., *The Sea in the Pre-Columbian World* (Washington: Dumbarton Oaks Research Library and Collections, Trustees for Harvard University, 1977), 152.

Chapter 63

MESOAMERICANS IN PRE-COLUMBIAN NORTH AMERICA

Helaman 3:8 "They began to cover the face of the whole earth, from the sea south to the sea north."

The F.A.R.M.S. Update for November 1986 presented recent archaeological evidence to show that ancient Mesoamerican peoples interacted extensively with cultures in South America (see preceding chapter), suggesting ways that aspects of Nephite civilization and actual people could have become dispersed widely to the south. Material is pointed out here similarly linking Mesoamerica with North America.

In Joseph Smith's day there was a view that the western hemisphere was populated across the Bering Strait, and that civilization moved from the Northwest through North America and then to Central America. Contrary to that view, the Book of Mormon speaks of migrations going the opposite way, from the land southward to the north, in the first century before Christ (see Alma 63:4; Helaman 3:8). Today, archaeologists, linguists, and historians who have studied the matter are agreed that a long sequence of cultural transmissions and migrations moved northward from southern Mexico.

The data from the southwestern United States is impressive. For example, the Hohokam culture of Arizona shows so many similarities to the cultures of Mexico that all who have investigated the matter have concluded that much of Hohokam culture originated in Mesoamerica. Canal irrigation, a ball game using a specially prepared court and rubber ball, and "temple mounds" are among these shared elements. They date from before the time of Christ to around A.D. 1400.[1] Florence Hawley, a leading scholar in this area, concludes that the attributes of the gods worshipped in these two areas were so similar that "derivation must be assumed" from the south. She and Laurens Hammack describe in detail the ritual and cosmological role of caves, solstice marking, the two-headed snake, lakes, shrines, and kickball games intended to make rain. The parallels also include the deities known in Mexico as Quetzalcoatl, Tlaloc, and Tezcatlipoca.[2] The domesticated barley recently discovered among the Hohokam ruins and elsewhere offers another significant linkage with Mosiah 9:9 and Alma 11:7.[3]

In the Mississippi and Ohio River valleys and in the southeastern states, evidence for cultural and linguistic intrusions from Mexico is also strong. Charles Wicke observes, "Most Southeastern specialists now seem to grant that the concept of the temple mound is Mesoamerican in origin. Indeed, the evidence for this is overwhelming."[4] The pyramid concept arrived in the southern Mississippi River Valley by around the time of Christ. Even earlier, burial mounds had appeared, also likely originating in Mesoamerica, which agrees with the fact that the corn grown by the Hopewell people in the centuries just before Christ was a Guatemalan type.[5] Massive mounds and evidence of solar orientation along with artifacts that recall the Olmecs have also been found at Poverty Point, Louisiana, dating to Jaredite times.[6]

Apparently, from these and many other studies, peoples and cultural elements have spread by migration and trade from Mexico into North America periodically since well before the time of Christ. Although we cannot identify these movements with the Book of Mormon account specifically, we can see that the kind of migrations northward mentioned in the Book of Mormon are substantiated in general. Through avenues such as these, we again can also see how some of the Jaredites, Nephites, Lamanites, or Mulekites, or their descendants, or aspects of their culture, could easily have spread out, here a little and there a little, over the North American continent.

MESOAMERICANS IN PRE-COLUMBIAN NORTH AMERICA

Based on research by John L. Sorenson, February 1987.

Notes

1. See Martha Molitor, "The Hohokam-Toltec Connection," *University of Northern Colorado Museum of Anthropology Occasional Publications* 10 (1981): 32–155; Julian D. Hayden, "Of Hohokam Origins and Other Matters," *American Antiquity* 35 (1970): 87–93.

2. Florence Hawley, Ellis and Laurens Hammack, "The Inner Sanctum of Feather Cave, A Mogollon Sun and Earth Shrine Linking Mexico and the Southwest," *American Antiquity* 33 (1968): 25–44; Carroll L. Riley and Basil C. Hedrick, eds., *Across the Chichimec Sea* (Carbondale: Southern Illinois University Press, 1978).

3. See pp. 130–32 in this book.

4. Charles R. Wicke, "Pyramids and Temple Mounds: Mesoamerican Ceremonial Architecture in Eastern North America," *American Antiquity* 30 (1965): 410; James B. Griffin, "Mesoamerica and the Eastern United States in Prehistoric Times," in Gordon R. Willey and Gordon F. Elkholm, eds., *Archaeological Frontiers and External Connections,* volume 4 of *Handbook of Middle American Indians* (Austin, Texas: University of Texas Press, 1966), 111–31.

5. See Thomas M. Lewis and Madeline Kneberg, *Tribes that Slumber: Indians of the Tennessee Region* (Knoxville: University of Tennessee Press, 1958), 57.

6. See Clarence H. Webb, "The Extent and Content of Poverty Point Culture," *American Antiquity* 33 (1968): 297–321.

Chapter 64

WORDPRINTS AND THE BOOK OF MORMON

Helaman 3:13 "And now there are many records kept of the proceedings of this people, by many of this people."

The Book of Mormon expressly claims that its many texts and records were written by several people. Modern computers have given birth to a new science of analyzing word patterns in documents whose authorship is disputed. By wordprint analysis, it is now possible with a high degree of certainty to tell which suspected authors did *not* write a given work.[1] Wordprinting is based on the somewhat surprising fact that every author that has been studied thus far subconsciously uses sixty-five identifiable patterns, involving words like "and," "the," "of," and "that," at statistically significant different rates from others.

For the last seven years a team of researchers has been at work refining the techniques of this "stylometry." Recently reported work has improved the methods of counting and comparing the wordprints in different texts. The main problems found in earlier approaches seem to have been solved. Distinctive criteria emerged from 325 proof tests run on texts of known authorship (292 tests compared works of different authors; 33 compared blocks of texts written by the same author). In all cases, five-thousand-word blocks of text were used. Among the works studied were texts by Samuel Johnson, Mark Twain, Oliver Cowdery, Solomon Spaulding, and samples of Joseph Smith's holographic and dictated writings (see Figure 1 below).

Also tested were the English translations of several German

texts. These works were written by different German authors, but they were all translated by the same English translator. The wordprint measurement showed that each translated work was not only consistent within itself, but also clearly separable from the others, as well as from the translator's own original English writings. This demonstrates, at least for these cases, that the uniqueness of an original author's wordprint can survive translation.

Among the results of these studies are the following:

1. Texts written by one author typically differed from each other in respect to only one, two, or three of the sixty-five testable wordprints.

2. No two texts written by one author differed from each other in more than six tests.

3. Texts written by different authors usually manifested six, seven, or more differences or rejections. The presence of seven or more rejections was found to yield a very high degree of sensitivity in detecting which samples had been written by different authors.

4. In six tests, writings of Nephi were compared with other writings of Nephi, and writings of Alma were tested against other writings of Alma. Only one to five wordprint differences were ever found in the writings of a single author (see Figure 2 below).

5. In nine tests, writings of Nephi were measured against writings of Alma. In eight of these nine tests, five or more rejections resulted. Four of them produced seven, eight, nine, and ten rejections, respectively (see Figure 3 below). These results tell us that there is a 99.5, 99.9, 99.99, and 99.997% chance that the writings said to be by Nephi were authored by a different person than whoever wrote Alma's pieces (hence Joseph Smith could not have originated both). The combined probability that the same author wrote all these texts is computed by taking one minus each of these four measurements and multiplying them all together. The result is vanishingly small.

6. Thirty-six tests were run, comparing writings of Nephi

and Alma with the words of Joseph Smith, Oliver Cowdery, and Solomon Spaulding (see Table 1 below). In every set matching many texts by Nephi or Alma with texts of these three other writers, at least seven (and often many more) rejections were measured with respect to at least two (and often many more) of the ancient-to-modern comparisons run for all five of these authors. Never were fewer than three rejections found for any given single textual comparison within these sets. In thirty-one tests, six or more rejections appeared. These results yield strong statistical evidence that the wordprints of Joseph Smith, Oliver Cowdery, and Solomon Spaulding are not measurable in the tested sections of the Book of Mormon.

7. New vocabulary introduction rates are relatively level throughout the Book of Mormon, as was also found to be the case in academically translated works.

Wordprinting is an objective measurement. Its significance may well be debated, but its detection of phenomena in a text cannot be argued. The group that developed the measuring techniques for these studies came from varying religious and philosophic backgrounds (agnostic, Jewish, Mormon), yet they achieved consensus regarding the techniques used to measure the wordprint data.

The reports now available provide far more information than can be summarized briefly.[2] At the bottom line, the report concludes that people who pay attention to wordprint studies can no longer speculate that the Book of Mormon consists of writings by Joseph Smith, Solomon Spaulding, or Oliver Cowdery. Such a notion is now statistically indefensible. Moreover, the didactic writings of Nephi and Alma are statistically independent from each other. While further stylometric studies are yet underway, a simple (if not the simplest) explanation of all this data is that the Book of Mormon was indeed written by different original authors and translated by a single translator with a restricted working vocabulary.

Based on research by John L. Hilton, September 1988.

Notes

1. See generally Andrew Q. Morton, *Literary Detection* (New York: Scribner's Sons, 1979).

2. In part, see John L. Hilton, "Some Book of Mormon 'Wordprint' Measurements using 'Wraparound' Block Counting" (Provo: F.A.R.M.S., 1988). See also John L. Hilton, "On Verifying Wordprint Studies: Book of Mormon Authorship," *BYU Studies* 30 (1990): 89–108.

Figure 1. Results of Verification Tests Showing the Contrasting Distributions of Rejections for Within-Author and Between-Author Tests

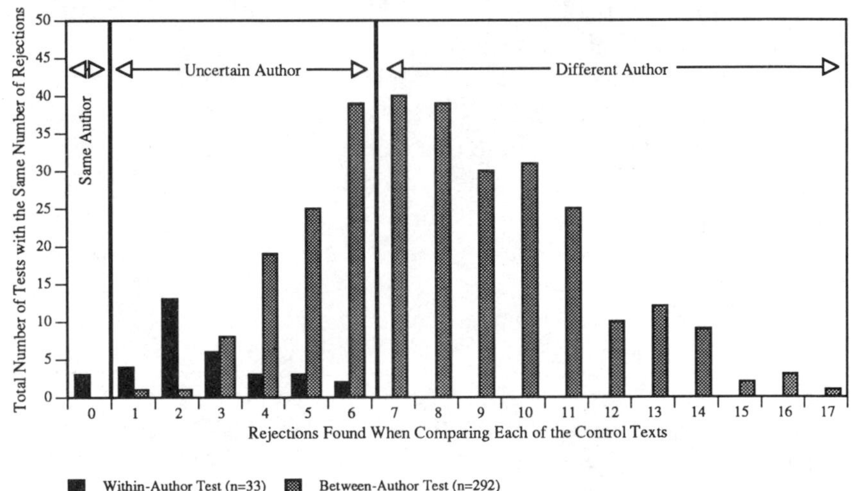

Figure 2. Distribution of Rejections Resulting from the Book of Mormon Within-Author Tests and the Within-Author Control Tests

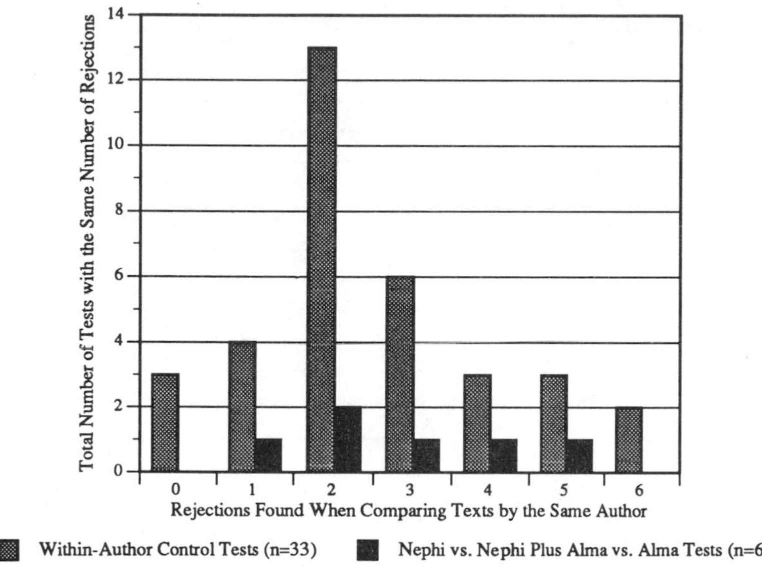

Figure 3. Distribution of Rejections Resulting from the Book of Mormon Between-Author Tests and the Between-Author Control Tests

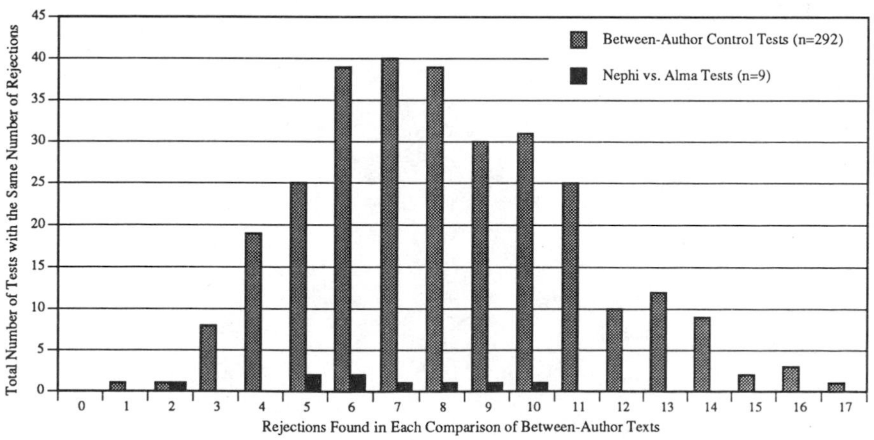

Table 1. Results of Book of Mormon Wordprint Study

	Number of Rejections															
Text vs. Text	0	1	2	3	4	5	6	7	8	9	10	11	12	13	14	15
Nephi vs. Nephi			1		1	1										
Alma vs. Alma		1	1	1												
Smith vs. Smith	1		2													
Cowdery vs. Cowdery		1														
Spaulding vs. Spaulding			1													
Nephi vs. Alma			1			2	2	1	1	1	1					
Smith vs. Nephi					1				2		1	1	1			
Smith vs. Alma				2	1	1		2								
Cowdery vs. Nephi							1	1				2		1	1	
Cowdery vs. Alma								4	1	1						
Spaulding vs. Nephi											1	1	1		1	2
Spaulding vs. Alma							3		2				1			
Conclusion	Same Author	Uncertain Author						Different Author								

Chapter 65

"SECRET COMBINATIONS"

Helaman 3:23 "There was continual peace established in the land, all save it were the secret combinations which Gadianton the robber had established in the more settled parts of the land, which at that time were not known unto those who were at the head of government."

Critics of the Book of Mormon have long argued that, since the book uses the term *secret combination* and since that term was indeed used in New York in the 1820s to refer to a supposed conspiracy among the Freemasons, the Gadianton robbers must simply represent a memory of the Masons (presumably worked into the Book of Mormon by an anti-Masonic Joseph Smith). Such an argument is illogical and flawed in many ways, and it was eventually dropped by Alexander Campbell, its original proponent.[1]

Indeed, use of the term *combination* to mean "conspiracy" or "monopoly" was not unusual at the time of Joseph, as Noah Webster's 1828 American dictionary makes clear. The word also occurs in George Washington's "Proclamation on the Whiskey Rebellion" (1794) and in his "Farewell Address" (1796). It appears numerous times in the Federalist Papers, in Blackstone's *Commentaries on the Laws of England,*[2] and can easily be found elsewhere.

What of the phrase "*secret* combination"? A search of federal and state court opinions available on computer readily yields at least ten occurrences of this phrase, one being in an 1850 decision of the United States Supreme Court. These opinions show that the term *secret combination* was widely used in the second half of the nineteenth century to describe secret agreements, coalitions for exercising undue influence on the legislature, agreements in restraint of trade, secret business transactions, secret societies, and many other such things.

As early as 1548, the laws of Edward VI prohibited merchants and workers from swearing "mutual oaths" in any conspiracy, "society, brotherhood, or company of any craft, mystery, or occupation" to fix prices. The term "combination in restraint of trade" continues today to be used in antitrust regulation as a synonym for "monopoly" and "conspiracy." What better English term, then, could possibly have been used to describe a group who had banded together among the ancient inhabitants of the Americas "that they might get gain"? (see Helaman 6:17).

The laborious task of combing legal and numerous other records from the first half of the nineteenth century—which remain largely unindexed and noncomputerized—is yet to be done. But the widespread use of the phrase *secret combination* in later nineteenth-century litigation, coupled with the highly conservative nature of legal language, gives reason to expect that the phrase will be found in the earlier period as well. For example, in his Proclamation to the Citizens of Nauvoo in 1843, Joseph Smith denounced the thieves and desperadoes on the Mississippi River as a "secret combination for stealing."[3] His usage seems to reflect a general usage without any Masonic overtones.

One other interesting contemporaneous occurrence of a similar phrase has been located. On June 25, 1831, Frederick Robinson, a journalist and Massachusetts legislator, wrote to Rufus Choate attacking the bar association as a "secret brotherhood." This "secret society," he says, is attempting to seize control of the American judicial system and to establish itself as a kind of aristocracy. This, he declares, "is an encroachment on the natural rights of man," and the situation is already far gone. "Most of the offices of government are in your hands," he says to attorney Choate. "You say that the bar is a 'necessary evil,' " Robinson concludes. "I know that it is an evil; that it is necessary I deny. I know of no good resulting to the community from the existence of your *secret* bar *association*. Public good was not the object of your *combination*. It is a conspiracy against the rights and liberties of the people."[4]

Evidently, the terms *combination* and *secret combination* were not special code words in Joseph Smith's day referring solely to the Masons. They were normal words for conspiracies of all kinds in Joseph's day. More extensive searching in period writings will undoubtedly locate a range of meanings for the phrase *secret combination*.

Based on research by David R. Benard, John W. Welch, and Daniel C. Peterson, October 1989. For further recent studies about the Gadianton Robbers, placing them outside the realms of early nineteenth-century America, see Daniel C. Peterson, "The Gadianton Robbers as Guerilla Warriors" and "Notes on 'Gadianton Masonry,' " and Bruce W. Warren, "Secret Combinations, Warfare, and Captive Sacrifice in Mesoamerica and the Book of Mormon," in Stephen Ricks and William Hamblin, eds., Warfare in the Book of Mormon *(Salt Lake City: Deseret Book and F.A.R.M.S., 1990), 146–229.*

Notes

1. Richard L. Bushman, *Joseph Smith and the Beginnings of Mormonism* (Urbana: University of Illinois, 1984), 131.

2. William Blackstone, *Commentaries on the Laws of England* (Oxford: Clarendon Press, 1765–69), 4:159.

3. Joseph Fielding Smith, ed. and comp., *Teachings of the Prophet Joseph Smith* (Salt Lake City: Deseret Book, 1979), 285.

4. Cited in Mortimer J. Adler, ed., *The Annals of America,* 21 vols. (Chicago: Encyclopedia Britannica, 1968–1974), 5:441–47.

Chapter 66

CHIASMUS IN HELAMAN 6:7–13

Helaman 6:10 "Now the land south was called Lehi, and the land north was called Mulek, which was after the son of Zedekiah; for the Lord did bring Mulek into the land north, and Lehi into the land south."

In 1967, John W. Welch first encountered the study of chiasmus in the New Testament. This led within a few weeks to his landmark discovery of chiasmus in the Book of Mormon, followed by the publication of several well-known articles and a book on this subject.[1] Today, the study of inverted parallel structures in the Book of Mormon still continues. Most recently, another fine example of chiasmus was discerned in Helaman 6:7–13, the annual report for the sixty-fourth year of the Reign of the Judges, whose main features can be displayed as follows:

A "And behold, there was *peace* in all the land" (6:7).
  B [Freedom of travel and trade in *both lands* is discussed (6:7–8).]
    C "And it came to pass that they became exceedingly *rich,* both the Lamanites and the Nephites;
      D and they did have an exceeding *plenty* of *gold,* and of *silver,* and of *all manner* of *precious metals, both* in the *land* south and in the *land* north" (6:9).

E "Now the land *south*
was called *Lehi,* and
the land *north*
was called *Mulek,*
which was after the son of Zedek*iah;*
for the *Lord*[2]
did bring *Mulek*
into the land *north,*
and *Lehi*
into the land *south*" (6:10).

D "And behold, there was *all manner* of *gold*
in *both* these *lands,* and of *silver,* and of
precious ore of *every kind;*

C and there were also curious workmen, who did
work all kinds of ore and did refine it; and thus
they did become *rich*" (6:11).

B [Economic prosperity in *both lands* is discussed
(6:12–13).]

A "And thus the sixty and fourth year did pass away in
peace" (6:13).

This composition is remarkable in several ways. First, the report itself is beautifully executed. Words, phrases, and ideas that appear in the first half are repeated with precision and balance in the second half. This entry exhibits both fine quality and admirable length.

Second, since the chiasm encompasses the entire report for the year, this unifying structure strongly suggests that the account was written as a single literary unit that Mormon copied verbatim from the Large Plates of Nephi into his abridgment. Apparently the contemporary historian used chiasmus to record an extraordinary year in the annals of his people. The report documents a great change that occurred during the sixty-fourth year involving prosperity, free travel, and peace between both the Nephites and Lamanites. Significant trade and peace treaties must have been entered into in order for this kind of peace and prosperity to occur, since before this time, restriction on travel was the norm in Nephite society, as is evidenced by Mosiah 7:1; 8:7; 28:1; Alma 23:2; 50:25; and Helaman 4:12. Official decrees of this type may be related to the *misharum* edicts of the Near East that typically proclaimed freedom for slaves and granted "equity" for the land. In addition to marking an unprecedented turning point in Nephite history, using chiasmus would insure against additions to or deletions from the text, since any alteration would be strikingly apparent.

Third, and most remarkable, the center of this chiasm involves two individual words. At the very apex, the words "Zedekiah" and "Lord" stand parallel to each other, which is intriguing since the Hebrew word for "Lord" constitutes the theophoric suffix *-yah* at the end of the name "Zedekiah."

Finally, it may be that other reports from antiquity were written in chiastic form. The Mesoamerican *Chilam Balam of Chumayel,* like Helaman 6, not only focuses chiastically on the migration of the people into the land they now occupy, but also similarly feature, at the center, a word-play on the land's name, as J. E. S. Thompson has noted.[3]

This text deserves to take its place among the finest examples of chiasmus in the Book of Mormon and beyond. Through understanding this masterful composition, we can better appreciate the precision and richness of Old World stylistic influences in the Nephite historical records.

Based on research by John W. Welch, May 1987.

Notes

1. For example, John W. Welch, ed., *Chiasmus in Antiquity* (Hildesheim: Gerstenberg, 1981); and "Chiasmus in the Book of Mormon," *BYU Studies* 10 (Autumn 1969): 69–84. A full bibliography of publications about chiasmus is available from F.A.R.M.S.

2. In Hebrew, the theophoric suffix is *yah* = iah.

3. Personal correspondence to John L. Sorenson, June 13, 1970, referring to pp. 4–6 of Ralph Roys's translation (see paperback edition, University of Oklahoma Press, 1973).

Chapter 67

CHIASMUS IN MESOAMERICAN TEXTS

Helaman 6:7–13

The growing literature on chiasmus deals generally with its use in the Near East and Mediterranean areas.[1] Some students of the Book of Mormon have wondered if the same form might appear in the New World, but until now the labor required to demonstrate it had not been done.

Allen J. Christenson has completed a substantial paper in this regard, investigating thirty-seven native Mayan texts. After reading the manuscript, renowned expert Munro Edmonson said, "It is rare to encounter this kind of dedication and clarity in academic work." He phrased his congratulatory comment in the form of "an enthusiastic chiasmus"—a balanced four-paragraph letter.

While large numbers of hieroglyphic codices were destroyed by the Spanish invaders, some Indians quickly learned Spanish characters and used them to record part of what had been in those books. The most famous of these is the *Popol Vuh.* Christenson displays over fifty significant chiasms in sixteen of these records. Most are from highland Guatemala, but some are from the Yucatan. Those containing chiasms generally meet the following criteria: the original (1) was composed prior to 1575; (2) was written in Mayan and the original text is available; (3) was authored by a member of the ruling lineage; (4) contains internal evidence of having been based on a pre-Columbian codex; (5) includes significant references to pre-Spanish mythology and religion; and (6) is free of notable Christian or European influence.

Two-, three-, and four-line chiasms are numerous in these texts, but longer, complex examples are also evident. For instance, the initial section of the *Popol Vuh,* dealing with the creation of the world, is arranged as a chiasm. Each phase of creation is given in detail from primordial darkness to the formation of the mountains. For example:

Oh Heart of Heaven,
and once it had been created,
the earth,
the mountains and valleys,
the paths of the waters were divided
and they proceeded to twist along
among the hills.
So the rivers then became more divided
as the great mountains were appearing.
And thus was the creation of the earth
when it was created by him
who is the Heart of Heaven.

The final portion of the section then recapitulates the main events in reverse order.[2] The *Annals of the Cakchiquels,* meanwhile, involves a seven-element chiasm incorporating two subordinate chiasms inside it.[3]

Many early colonial native texts did not use chiasmus. Those that did all contain passages of dialogue, an indicator of dependence on a pre-Columbian codex. Interestingly, none of the highland Maya documents composed after 1580 included chiastic passages. Christenson argues that this is evidence that chiasmus had a distinct history as a learned poetic form among these people before the Conquest.

Many implications of Christenson's work remain to be explored. The late Sir Eric Thompson once said, "There are close parallels in Maya transcriptions of the colonial period, and, I am convinced, in the hieroglyphic texts themselves, to the [two-line parallel] verses of the Psalms, and the poetry of Job," but when chiasmus proper was drawn to his attention in 1970, he could point only to brief hints of it in the native texts.[4] The work by

Christenson focuses new attention on Mesoamerican poetic form with the possibility of further breakthroughs.

Based on research by Allen J. Christenson, January 1988. Following the publication of this Update, part of Christenson's work appeared as "The Use of Chiasmus by the Ancient Quiche-Maya," Latin American Literatures Journal *4, no. 2 (Fall 1988): 125–50. His full research was published as "The Use of Chiasmus in Ancient Mesoamerica" (Provo: F.A.R.M.S., 1988); and a short report appeared in "Chiasmus in Mayan Texts,"* Ensign *18 (October 1988): 28–31.*

Notes

1. For example, John W. Welch, ed., *Chiasmus in Antiquity* (Hildesheim: Gerstenberg, 1981).

2. See Munro Edmonson, *The Book of Counsel: The Popol Vuh, Tulane Univ., Middle Amer. Research Inst. Publ.* 35 (New Orleans: Tulane University, 1971), 9–13.

3. The text is in Daniel G. Brinton, *The Annals of the Cakchiquels* (Philadelphia: Brinton's Library of Aboriginal American Literature, 1885), 75–77.

4. See Eric Thompson, *Maya Hieroglyphic Writing: An Introduction,* (Norman: University of Oklahoma Press, 1960), 2:61–62, and personal communication to John L. Sorenson.

Chapter 68

NEPHI'S GARDEN AND CHIEF MARKET

Helaman 7:10 "which was by the highway which led to the chief market, which was in the city of Zarahemla"

Helaman 7:10 clearly states that Nephi had a "garden" and that it was near the highway that led to the "chief market" in the city of Zarahemla. Such ideas have seemed incompatible with what was known about ancient American life. Recent discoveries about Mesoamerican urban settlements, however, have now made these features seem highly reasonable.

The text says that Nephi "was upon a tower, which was in the garden of Nephi, which was by the highway which led to the chief market, which was in the city of Zarahemla." The "tower" might easily refer to pyramidal mounds, some built and used by families and lineage leaders for religious ceremonies, and which were referred to by the Spanish conquerors as "towers."[1] Highways too are now well known in Mesoamerica during Book of Mormon times.[2] But what evidence is there of gardens and chief markets in ancient Mesoamerican cities?

Gardens. For decades the prevailing view was that cities with high-density populations did not exist at all in Mesoamerica. In the last twenty years, however, intensive work at places like Teotihuacan and Monte Alban have demonstrated unquestionably that cities in the modern sense were indeed known during the Book of Mormon times.[3]

Indeed, in at least some of those cities, garden areas were cultivated immediately adjacent to single habitation complexes. At the archaeological site of El Tajín near the coast of the Gulf of Mexico east of Mexico City are the remains of a city that occupied at least five square kilometers at its maximum period, probably between A.D. 600–900. At that time, the houses of its middle-class people were surrounded by gardens and fruit trees.[4] Likewise, the famous city of Tula, north of the capital of Mexico, was even larger, up to fourteen square kilometers around A.D. 1000–1100, and gardened houselots were common there too.[5]

Chief Markets. No one knowledgeable of pre-Columbian Mexico has had any doubt that markets were found in all sizeable settlements. Cortez and his fellows were amazed by the market in Tlatelolco in the Valley of Mexico, by its diversity of goods, and by the complexity of its organization. Yet until recently, only little attention has been given to the fact that a number of these cities had *multiple markets*.

The evidence, however, seems quite clear. Blanton and Kowalewski, for example, have noted that Monte Alban had both a chief market and subsidiary ones.[6] For Teotihuacan, Rene Millon identifies one location as "the principal marketplace" and suggests that other markets existed for special products, such as kitchen wares.[7] George Cowgill, the other leading expert on Teotihuacan, concurs.[8] The Krotsers point out the same phenomenon at El Tajín.[9] Meanwhile Edward Calnek's reexamination of documentary evidence on the organization of the Aztec capital, Tenochititlan, has established that each major sector of the city had its own market, in addition to the giant central one.[10] Apparently Zarahemla was no different.

These things once seemed problematic in the book of Helaman's casual description of Nephi's neighborhood. They turn out instead to have substance beyond what was known only a few years ago.

Based on research by John L. Sorenson, April 1985.

Notes

1. Albert Idell, ed., *The Bernal Diaz Chronicles* (Garden City, New York: Doubleday, 1956), 151, 173–74.

2. John L. Sorenson, "Digging into the Book of Mormon: Our Changing

Understanding of Ancient America and Its Scripture, Part 2," *Ensign* 14 (October 1984): 18–19.

3. See Rene Millon, "Teotihuacan: City, State, and Civiliation," and Richard Blanton and Stephen A. Kowalewski, "Monte Alban and After in the Valley of Oaxaca," in *Handbook of Middle American Indians, Supplement* (Austin: University of Texas Press, 1981), 1:208 and 94–116, respectively.

4. See Paula H. and G. R. Krotser, "The Life Style of El Tajín," *American Antiquity* 38 (April 1973): 199, 204.

5. See Richard Diehl, "Tula," in Robert C. West, ed., *Natural Environment and Early Cultures*, vol. 1 of *Handbook of Middle American Indians* (Austin: University of Texas Press, 1964), 1:277–95.

6. See Richard Blanton and Stephen Kowaleski, "Monte Alban and After in the Valley of Oaxaca," 106.

7. Rene Millon, "Teotihuacan: City, State, and Civilization," 225, 229.

8. See George Cowgill, "Rulership and the Ciudadela," in Richard M. Leventhal and Alan L. Kolata, eds., *Civilization in the Ancient Americas* (Albuquerque: University of New Mexico Press, 1983), 342.

9. Paula H. and G. R. Krotser, "The Life Style of El Tajín," 199–205.

10. See Edward Calnek's "The Internal Structure of Cities in America: The Case of Tenochtitlan," *The International Congress of Americanists* 40 (1972): 41–60.

Chapter 69

WAS HELAMAN 7–8 AN ALLEGORICAL FUNERAL SERMON?

Helaman 7:15 "Because of my mourning and lamentation ye have gathered yourselves together."

It was not uncommon for early Israelite prophets to use example, when Jeremiah wanted to impress the people of Jerusalem with his prophecy that they would be yoked into bondage by the Babylonians, he draped himself with thongs and a yoke and thus went forth proclaiming his message of doom (see Jeremiah 27:2–11). Other similar symbolic or parabolic acts performed as prophetic oracles are found in Jeremiah 13:1–11 (hiding a waistcloth), Jeremiah 19:1–13 (smashing a bottle), 1 Kings 11:29–39 (tearing a garment into twelve pieces), 2 Kings 13:15–19 (shooting an arrow), and Isaiah 20:2–6 (walking naked).

Is it possible that Nephi's sermon in Helaman 7–8 was similarly staged as a prophetic allegory in the form of some kind of a funeral sermon?

Nephi, the son of Helaman II, had just returned from a disappointing mission to the land northward. At his ancestral home in the city of Zarahelma, he was further dismayed at the "awful wickedness" of the people there (Helaman 7:4). Nephi's first stated reaction was to remember his deceased ancestors who had lived in the days of Lehi (see 7:7–8). Next he positioned himself conspicuously on top of a tower in his garden near a main highway. There his behavior somehow attracted a large crowd (see 7:10–12). He then delivered a powerful message on repentence (see 7:13–29) and the impending coming of Christ (see 8:11–24). His status as a true prophet was finally confirmed by his correctly prophesying the assassination of a wicked chief judge (see 8:25–28).

Several clues indicate that Nephi may have attracted attention to his message by carrying on as if someone had just died.

1. Nephi was in "great mourning" (7:11) and "lamentation" (7:15). Mourning generally means more than just feeling sorry or crying privately. One can imagine Nephi dressed in traditional Nephite mourning attire (whatever that might have been), gesticulating on top of his tower perhaps in motions of bereavement. Onlookers would have wondered immediately who in the important aristocratic household of the great Alma's descendants had just died.

2. He continued with this conduct for a fair amount of time—at least long enough for people to go tell many others in town who then turned out in multitudes (see 7:11). If during this time Nephi was conducting a recognizable mock mourning or funeral ceremony, this would have been quite a curiosity.

3. Whatever he did, it was something of a public spectacle that worked the crowd into a state of awe, for Nephi told them they indeed had "great need to marvel" (7:15).

4. The tower would probably have been a pyramid or similar structure. Typically, such mounds were used for burials, as well as for prayer. If Nephi's tower was the family burial site, his reference to the righteousness of his ancestors in his allegorical funeral for the Nephite nation would have been all the more poignant.

5. If Nephi was mourning and lamenting, the crowd would have wondered, of course, who had died. It would have struck them personally, therefore, when Nephi began decrying *their* iniquities (see 7:13–14). Moreover, since he speaks later of "murder" (7:21; 8:26), it is possible that he spoke the word "murder" as he poured out his soul to God while the crowd was gathering.

6. Nephi surprised the crowd when he asked them, "Why will *ye* die?" (7:17). Unless they repent, he told them, God will

turn them into "meat for dogs and wild beasts" (7:19), and their souls will be hurled to everlasting misery (see 7:16). Nephi predicted slaughter and utter destruction at the hands of enemies (see 7:22, 24) and prophesied that the people would be "destroyed from off the face of the earth" (7:28).

7. Nephi then cited examples of people who had been delivered from death (see 8:11–19) and spoke of other destroyed peoples. Thus, the themes of death and deliverance from death characterize Nephi's words throughout this speech.

8. Nephi concluded by being specific. For one person in particular, Nephi's funeral may have been more than mere allegory. Nephi announced prophetically the death of the chief judge in Zarahemla (see 8:27). His death not only would have validated Nephi's words in general, but also would have presented a corpse, symbolically representing all the people of Zarahemla and potently completing the allegorical message of this apparent funeral sermon.

We cannot be certain that this is what Nephi did, but this interpretation adds a rich and interesting possibility of symbolic meaning to this text.

Based on research by John W. Welch, May 1986.

Chapter 70

THE CASE OF AN UNOBSERVED MURDER

Helaman 9:38 "And he was brought to prove that he himself was the very murderer."

The trial of Seantum in Helaman 7–8 raises some interesting points of Nephite and Israelite law. The story is familiar, how Nephi spoke from his garden tower (see Helaman 7:10), was threatened with a lawsuit for reviling against the government, but in the end revealed that the chief judge was "murdered, and he [lay] in his blood; and he [had] been murdered by his brother, who [sought] to sit in the judgment-seat" (Helaman 8:27). Five men ran and found things to be as Nephi had said.

A public proclamation was then sent out by heralds announcing the murder and calling a day of fasting, mourning, and burial (see Helaman 9:10). The day after the death of a political leader was traditionally a day of fasting, mourning, and burial (see 1 Samuel 31:13; 2 Samuel 1:12).

Following the burial, five suspects (the men who had been sent to investigate) were brought to the judges. They could not be convicted, however, on circumstantial evidence, for such was ruled out under Israelite law, which required every fact to be substantiated by the testimony of two eyewitnesses (see Deuteronomy 19:15). This presented a serious problem in this particular case, however, for no one had witnessed the killing of the chief judge. Seantum had killed his brother "by a garb of secrecy" (Helaman 9:6).

Cases of unwitnessed murders presented special problems under the law of Moses. While the two-witness rule would seem to stand insurmountably in the way of ever obtaining a conviction in such cases, such slayings could not simply be ignored. If a person was found slain in the land and the murderer could not be found, solemn rituals, oaths of innocence, and special purification of all the men in the village had to be performed (see Deuteronomy 21:1–9). Things turned out differently in Seantum's case, however, for he was soon exposed in a way that opened the door to an exceptional rule of evidence that justified his conviction.

Nephi first revealed to the people that Seantum was the murderer, that they would find blood on the skirts of his cloak, and that he would say certain things to them when they told him, "We know that thou are guilty" (Helaman 9:34). Indeed, Seantum was soon detected and immediately confessed his guilt (see Helaman 9:37–38).

Seantum's self-incriminating admission would normally not be admissible in a Jewish court of law. Under the Talmud, no man could be put to death on his own testimony: "No man may call himself a wrongdoer," especially in a capital case.[1] But from earlier times came four episodes that gave rise to an exception to this rule against self-incriminating confessions under certain circumstances. Those precedents, each of which involved convictions or punishments based on confessions, were the executions of (1) Aachan (see Joshua 7), of (2) the man who admitted that he had killed Saul (see 2 Samuel 1:10–16), and of (3) the two assassins of Ishbosheth, the son of Saul (see 2 Samuel 4:8–12), as well as (4) the voluntary confession of Micah, the son who stole from his mother (see Judges 17:1–4).

The ancients reconciled these four cases with their rigid two-witness rule by explaining that they involved confessions *before* trial or were proceedings before kings or rulers instead of judges.[2] An exception was especially granted when the confession was "corroborated by an ordeal as well as by the production of the *corpus delicti*,"[3] as in the case of Aachan, who was detected by the casting of lots and whose confession was corroborated by the finding of the illegal goods under his tent floor.

Thus, one can with reasonable confidence conclude that in the biblical period the normal two-witness rule could be overridden in the special case of a self-incriminating confession, if the confession occurred outside of court, or if God's will was evidenced in the matter by ordeal, lots, or otherwise in the detection of the offender, and if corroborating physical evidence of the crime could be produced.

Seantum's self-incriminating confession satisfies all three of these requirements precisely, and thus his conviction was ensured. His confession was spontaneous and before trial. The evidence of God's will was supplied through Nephi's prophecy. Tangible evidence was present in the blood found on Seantum's cloak. These factors, under biblical law, would override the normal Jewish concerns about the use of self-incriminating confessions to obtain a conviction.

Given the complicated and important ancient legal issues presented by the case of Seantum, it is little wonder that the text makes special note of the fact that Seantum himself was legitimately "brought to prove that he himself was the very murderer" (Helaman 9:38). No further evidence was legally needed to convict him under these circumstances.

Based on research by John W. Welch, February 1990.

Notes

1. TB, *Sanhedrin* 9b.

2. See Menachem Elon, *The Principles of Jewish Law* (Jerusalem: Keter, 1975), 614.

3. Ze'ev Falk, *Hebrew Law in Biblical Times* (Jerusalem: Wahrmann, 1964), 71.

Chapter 71

MORMON'S AGENDA

Helaman 12:3 "Thus we see that except the Lord doth chasten his people with many afflictions, . . . they will not remember him."

Again and again Mormon reminds us that he is drastically selecting and condensing as he constructs the Book of Mormon. We can learn much about the man by examining his choices of what to include and what to leave out.

His editing may be responsible for some of the puzzling features in the scripture, such as its emphasis on warfare (Mormon was a military man) and its omission of details about the law of Moses (he was a Christian, perhaps little interested in the ancient ways after they were fulfilled by Christ's atonement and ministry).

But the choices Mormon made are perhaps most revealing when his editing shows him to be a real human being trying to draw uplifting lessons from mean and ugly events. This is manifest in two approaches: (1) a spiritual interpretation of political events and (2) drastic simplification that highlights the distinction between the obedient and disobedient.

For an example of the first point, consider the single thing Mormon chooses to tell us out of Alma's exhortation (which probably lasted for hours) to the people of Limhi in Zarahemla after their arrival there. He features Alma's statement that they "should remember that it was the Lord" that delivered them (Mosiah 25:16). When we read the account of Limhi's escape in Mosiah 22, we see that freedom came through a cunning scheme by which the people of Limhi got the Lamanite guards drunk. Yet Mormon provides a spiritual interpretation of this escape to emphasize that, despite what may seem to be men's own cleverness, planning, and apparent luck, God is really the one making things happen. Mormon's frequent "and thus we see" comments reveal this view.

Another part of Mormon's editorial approach is simplification. The people whose history he is presenting actually existed as diverse groups: the people of Zarahemla, Nephi's own descendents, the people of Ammon, Ishmaelites, Zoramites, Zeniffites, Amulonites, and so forth. Yet Mormon boils these down to just two "sides," the Nephites and the Lamanites. Why does he simplify this way? Because otherwise we might fail to draw the lesson from his record that he considers vital. His aim is not to sketch Nephite society but to turn his readers' hearts to God. That requires selection and arrangement of facts out of the hundreds or thousands of possibilities he could have presented in his record.

Another example of this simplification for a purpose is the report in Alma 16 of the surprise Lamanite attack that destroyed Ammonihah. Mormon emphasizes the hand of God behind this political-historical event. His editorial commentary teaches us that "their great city [was destroyed], which they said God could not destroy. . . . But behold, in one day it was left desolate" (Alma 16:9–10). Actually, as Alma 23–24 makes clear, the Lamanite attack on Ammonihah was triggered by events that started years before. The great Nephite missionaries, the sons of Mosiah, converted thousands of the Lamanites (the Anti-Nephi-Lehies) to the gospel. This angered other Lamanites, and they were stirred up further by Nephite dissenters. Finally in Alma 25:1–2 we learn that those frustrated Lamanites were the ones who launched the attack that struck Ammonihah without warning. The historical events leading to the destruction of Ammonihah had been very complex.

In all these matters Mormon is not ignorant of the complexity—he knew it far better than we now can know it, for his historical resources were vastly greater than ours are. He is just taking an editor's prerogative in putting things into a perspective, choosing material with a prophetic eye to the future as well as with an editor's command of his subject matter. We would do well to recognize the subtlety with which he has produced his volume to match the announced intent on its Title Page.

Based on research by Grant Hardy, July 1990, presented at greater length in "Mormon as Editor," in John Soreson and Melvin Thorne, eds., Rediscovering the Book of Mormon *(Salt Lake City: Deseret Book and F.A.R.M.S., 1990), 15–28.*

Chapter 72

THIEVES AND ROBBERS

3 Nephi 3:12 "Lachoneus, the governor, was a just man, and could not be frightened by the demands and the threatenings of a robber."

Although there is only little difference between a thief and a robber in most modern minds, there were considerable differences between the two under ancient Near Eastern law. A thief (*ganab*) was usually a local person who stole from his neighbor. He was dealt with judicially. He was tried and punished civilly, most often by a court composed of his fellow townspeople. A robber, on the other hand, was treated as an outsider, as a brigand or highwayman. He was dealt with militarily, and he could be executed summarily.

The legal distinctions between theft and robbery, especially under the laws of ancient Israel, have been analyzed thoroughly by Bernard S. Jackson, Professor of Law at the University of Kent-Canterbury and editor of the *Jewish Law Annual*. He shows, for example, how robbers usually acted in organized groups rivaling local governments and attacking towns and how they swore oaths and extorted ransom, a menace worse than outright war. Thieves, however, were a much less serious threat to society.[1]

Recently studies have shown in detail how the ancient legal and linguistic distinctions are also observable in the Book of Mormon.[2] This explains how Laban could call the sons of Lehi "robbers" and threaten to execute them on the spot without a trial, for that is how a military officer like Laban no doubt would have dealt with a robber. It also explains why the Lamanites are always said to "rob" from the Nephites but never from their own brethren—that would be "theft," not "robbery." It also explains the rise and fearful menace of the Gadianton society, who are always called "robbers" in the Book of Mormon, never "thieves."

Other significant details also emerge. It is probably no coincidence that the Hebrew word for "band" or "bandits" is *gedud,* and the most famous Book of Mormon robbers were known as Gadianton's "band." Like *gedud,* the name Gadianton was spelled with two "d"s, *Gaddianton,* in the Original Manuscript of the Book of Mormon.

The importance of this ancient legal tradition in the Book of Mormon is further enhanced by the fact that Anglo-American common law would have provided Joseph Smith with quite a different understanding of the legal definitions of the terms *theft* and *robbery,* inconsistent in many ways with usages found in the Book of Mormon.

Moreover, if Joseph Smith had relied on the language of his King James Bible for legal definitions of these terms, he would have stumbled into error, for that translation renders "thief" and "robber" indiscriminately. For example, the same phrase is translated inconsistently as "den of robbers" and "den of thieves" in Jeremiah 7:11 and Matthew 21:13. The same word (*lestai*) is translated sometimes as "thieves" (Matthew 27:38), other times as "robber" (John 18:40). But there was an ancient distinction between thieves and robbers that no translator should neglect, and over which Joseph Smith did not blunder.

Based on research by John W. Welch and Kelly Ward, reported in Insights, *July 1985.*

Notes

1. Bernard S. Jackson, *Theft in Early Jewish Law* (Oxford: Oxford University Press, 1972).

2. John W. Welch, "Theft and Robbery in the Book of Mormon and in Ancient Near Eastern Law" (Provo: F.A.R.M.S., 1985).

Chapter 73

THE EXECUTION OF ZEMNARIHAH

3 Nephi 4:28 "Their leader, Zemnarihah, was taken and hanged upon a tree, yea, even upon the top thereof."

Third Nephi 4:28–33 recounts in considerable detail the execution of Zemnarihah, the captured leader of the defeated Gadianton robbers. It has recently been suggested that this public execution followed ancient ceremony and law. The text reads:

> Their leader, Zemnarihah, was taken and hanged upon a tree, yea, even upon the top thereof until he was dead. And when they had hanged him until he was dead they did fell the tree to the earth, and did cry with a loud voice, saying: May the Lord preserve his people in righteousness and in holiness of heart, that they may cause to be felled to the earth all who shall seek to slay them because of the power and secret combinations, even as this man hath been felled to the earth (3 Nephi 4:28–29).

After the Nephites had chopped down the tree on which Zemnarihah had been hanged, they all cried out "with one voice" for God to protect them. Then they sang out "all as one" in praise of God (3 Nephi 4:30–33). Is there some kind of ritual involved here? Several evidences point to an ancient background for this execution. Consider these few items.

First, notice that the tree on which Zemnarihah was hung was felled. Was this ever done in antiquity? Apparently it was. For one thing, Israelite practice required that the tree upon which the culprit was hung be buried with the body. Hence the tree had to have been chopped down. Since the rabbis understood that this burial should take place immediately, the Talmud recommends hanging the culprit on a precut tree or post so that, in the words of Maimonides, "no felling is needed."[1]

Second, consider why the tree was chopped down and buried. As Maimonides explains: "In order that it should not serve as a sad reminder, people saying: 'This is the tree on which so-and-so was hanged.' "[2] In this way, the tree became associated with the person being executed; it came to symbolize the culprit and the desire to forget him or her. By way of comparison, the Nephites identified the tree with Zemnarihah and all those like him, that his infamy might not be forgotten, when they cried out: "May [the Lord] cause to be felled to the earth all who shall seek to slay them, . . . even as this man hath been felled to the earth."

Third, the text suggests that the Nephites understood Deuteronomy 21:22 as allowing execution by hanging—a reading that the rabbis saw as possible. While they generally viewed hanging as a means only of exposing the dead body after it had been stoned, they were aware of a Jewish penalty of "hanging until death occurs." For example, there were rare Jewish instances of hanging: Seventy women were "hung" in Ashkelon. Eight hundred Pharisees were crucified by Alexander Jannaeus the High Priest,[3] but the rabbis rejected that means of execution, since this was "as the government does"[4] and the rabbis at that time wanted to keep as much distance as possible between Jewish and Roman practices.

Fourth, observe that the ancient idea of fashioning a punishment that fits the crime was carried out here. For example, if a thief broke into a house, he was to be put to death and "hung in front of the place where he broke in."[5] Ancient punishments were often related symbolically to the offense. Likewise, the punishment for a false accuser was to make him suffer whatever would have happened to the person he had falsely accused (see Deuteronomy 19:19). In Zemnarihah's case, he was hung in front of the very nation he had tried to destroy, and he was felled to the earth just as he had tried to bring that nation down.

Finally, the people all chanted loudly, proclaiming the wickedness of Zemnarihah, which may be reminiscent of the ancient practice of heralding a notorious execution. Deuteronomy 19:20 says that "those which remain shall hear, and fear, and shall henceforth commit no more any such evil among you." How was this to be accomplished? Rabbi Jehudah explained: "I say that he is executed immediately and messengers are sent out to notify the people."[6] Indeed, public matters, such as the execution of a rebelling judge (see 3 Nephi 6:22–28), had to be heralded.[7] An even clearer example of heralding in the Book of Mormon is found in Alma 30:57, where the results in Korihor's case were heralded abroad. In both these cases, the apparent requirement of publishing the wickedness of the culprit was satisfied, so that all who remained would "hear and fear," and the evil would be removed from among God's people.

Based on research by John W. Welch, November 1984.

Notes

1. Maimonides, *Sanhedrin,* XV, 9; see also Babylonian Talmud, *Sanhedrin,* VI, 6.
2. Maimonides, *Sanhedrin,* XV, 9.
3. Josephus, *War* I, 97.
4. TB, *Sanhedrin* VI.5–6.
5. Code of Hammurabi, section 21.
6. TB, *Sanhedrin* X.6.
7. Ibid.

Chapter 74

THE SERMON AT THE TEMPLE

3 Nephi 11:1 "There were a great multitude gathered together, of the people of Nephi, round about the temple which was in the land Bountiful."

No sermon is more famous than Jesus' Sermon on the Mount in Matthew 5–7. These unforgettably simple words are prime movers of the Christian world. Yet no sermon is more challenging to the scholars, for "New Testament scholarship up to the present has offered no satisfactory explanation of this vitally important text."[1] The Book of Mormon here makes a unique and marvelous contribution.

One of the main problems facing the scholars is their lack of context in which to view the Sermon on the Mount. To whom was Jesus speaking? How did he intend his words to be understood—as ultimate ideals or as practical ethics? Hundreds of interpretive essays have been written, failing to settle such issues. Third Nephi 11–18, however, offers clues to connect the Sermon on the Mount with the context of making covenants at the temple.

The first clue is that Jesus spoke to the Nephites at their temple (see 3 Nephi 11:1). For this reason, this speech may well be termed the Sermon at the Temple. Indeed, the term "sermon on *the mount*" recalls the fact that the temple in Israel was equated with the "the mountain of the Lord" (see Isaiah 2:3).

Second, the Sermon at the Temple was delivered to the Nephites in a covenant-making context. Priesthood ordinations and baptismal instructions came at the beginning of the discourse (see 3 Nephi 11:18–28); the administration of the sacrament came at the end (see, e.g., 18:1–11); and the theme of covenant was strong throughout (see, e.g. 16:11). According to this interpretation, the Lord's promises ("they shall be filled," "they shall see God," etc.) and the stated obligations ("deny yourself," "lay up for yourselves treasures in heaven," etc.) can be understood covenantally.

Third, Jesus gave the stipulations found in the Sermon at the Temple by way of commandment. He called his words in the Sermon at the Temple "commandments" (12:20), and he invited the people to indicate, by partaking of the sacrament, their willingness to keep these very commandments that he had given them (see 18:10).

Fourth, the stated purpose of the Sermon at the Temple is to show the disciple how to be exalted at the final judgment. Jesus said, "Whoso remembereth these sayings of mine and doeth them, him will I raise up at the last day" (15:1). The Sermon contains, therefore, not just broad moral platitudes, but a concise presentation of conditions that must be satisfied in order to be admitted into God's presence (see 14:21–23).

Looking at the Sermon at the Temple in a covenant-making context dramatically enhances its meaning. For example, the prerequisite that no person should come unto Christ having any ill feelings toward a brother (see 12:23–24) then has new meaning. The instruction that people should swear their oaths simply by saying "yes" or "no" (12:37) makes eminent sense as covenantal promises are being made. The reciting of a group prayer ("when *ye* pray" in 13:7–9) appears to call for a collective petition to the Lord. And the obligation of secrecy, that one "give not that which is holy unto the dogs," with its accompanying threat that violators will be trampled and torn (14:6), fits a covenant-making context exactly, even though it has been one of the most puzzling parts of the Sermon on the Mount for many scholars.

Furthermore, the laws and commandments required here by Jesus could hardly be a more succinct preparation for the making of temple covenants. He gave the Nephites laws regarding obedience and sacrifice of a broken heart and a contrite spirit (see 12:19), evil or angry speaking of a brother (see 12:22), chastity and strict attitudes toward divorce (see 12:28), love (see 12:39–45), giving to the poor, and serving God, not Mammon (see 13:3, 19–24).

Christ figured centrally in the Nephites' covenantal experience at the temple. They touched the marks of the wounds on his body with their hands (see 11:14). They solemnly promised to remember his body, which he had shown them (see 18:7). Ultimately they were promised that if they would make a threefold petition (see 14:7), they would have a way opened unto them (see 14:7, 14), and there they would be recognized by the Lord and allowed to enter (see 14:21–23).

Interestingly, a few New Testament scholars have begun hinting that the Sermon on the Mount had cultic or ritual significance in the earliest Christian community. Betz, for example, sees the Sermon on the Mount as revealing the principles that "will be applied at the last judgment,"[2] and thinks that the Sermon on the Mount reminded the earliest Church members of "the most important things the initiate comes to 'know' *through initiation,*" containing things that "originally belonged in the context of *liturgical initiation.*"[3] Indeed, the word "perfect" (*teleios,* Matthew 5:48) has long been associated with becoming initiated into the great religious mysteries.[4]

Obviously, we have only begun to scratch the surface of the Sermon at the Temple. It is a remarkable text, wonderfully suited to the Nephites. It is a rich text, capable of multiple meanings at whatever level the hearer is ready to receive. More than we may have ever imagined, the Sermon at the Temple may prove instrumental in showing us how the Book of Mormon indeed contains the fulness of the gospel (see D&C 20:9) and restores, among other things, the plain and precious covenants (see 1 Nephi 13:26) that were lost as the gospel went forth into Gentile Christianity.

Based on research by John W. Welch, March 1988. For extensive information on this interpretation of Jesus' sermon, see the book-length study on this topic by John W. Welch, The Sermon at the Temple and the Sermon on the Mount *(Salt Lake City: Deseret Book and F.A.R.M.S., 1990).*

Notes

1. Hans Dieter Betz, *Essays on the Sermon on the Mount,* trans. L. L. Welborn (Philadelphia: Fortress, 1985), ix.

2. Ibid., 5.

3. Ibid., 28; italics added.

4. Henricus Stephanus, *Thesaurus Graecae Linguae* (Graz: Akademische Druck-und Verlaganstalt, 1954), 8:1961 and 8:1974.

Chapter 75

THE GOSPEL AS TAUGHT BY NEPHITE PROPHETS

3 Nephi 11:35 "Verily, verily, I say unto you, that this is my doctrine."

The Book of Mormon uses the terms *gospel* and *doctrine* to refer to the way by which individuals come to Christ. Three Book of Mormon passages in particular—2 Nephi 31:2–32:6; 3 Nephi 11:23–39; 3 Nephi 27:13–21—define the gospel of Jesus Christ, each in a distinctive six-point formula. This formula states that if people will (1) believe in Christ, (2) repent of their sins, and (3) submit to baptism in water as a witness of their willingness to take his name upon themselves and keep his commandments, he will (4) pour out his Spirit upon them and cleanse them of their sins. All who receive this baptism of fire and of the Holy Ghost and (5) endure to the end in faith, hope, and charity will be found guiltless at the last day and (6) enter God's kingdom.

Recent research has detected the remarkable clarity and consistency of numerous Book of Mormon passages that operate with this same definition in mind, indicating that it was both a norm and a paradigm for Book of Mormon writers. This gospel formula, taught by the Book of Mormon, provides a standard language for teaching the message of salvation and the means by which people can come to Christ.

The first comprehensive Book of Mormon statement about the gospel occurs in 2 Nephi 31:2–32:6. It appears to be an amplification of the vision first reported in 1 Nephi 10:4–6 and 11:27–33, in which Lehi and Nephi saw Christ's baptism and heard his voice saying, "Follow thou me" and "Do the things which ye have seen me do" (2 Nephi 31:10, 12):

> Wherefore . . . I must speak concerning the doctrine of Christ. . . . I know that if ye shall [1] follow the Son, with full purpose of heart, acting no hypocrisy and no deception before God, but with real intent, [2] repenting of your sins, witnessing unto the Father that ye are willing to take upon you the name of Christ [3] by baptism . . . then shall ye receive [4] the Holy Ghost; yea, then cometh the baptism of fire and of the Holy Ghost. . . . And I heard a voice from the Father saying: . . . He that [5] endureth to the end, the same [6] shall be saved (2 Nephi 31:2–16).

Second, in the report of Christ's visit to the Nephites, especially in 3 Nephi 11:23–39, there are also multiple repetitions of the six points of his doctrine. This is the most authoritative definition, because Christ himself delivers it publicly.

During his visit to the disciples a few days later, Christ gave a third defining presentation of the gospel, recorded in 3 Nephi 27:13–21, in which the six basic elements are again elaborated. The Savior indicates that, just as individuals are to take upon themselves Christ's name, the church will be his if it is called in his name and "if it so be that they are built upon my gospel" (3 Nephi 27:5–13). The one significant difference in this presentation is that it begins by invoking the larger context of the plan of salvation (see 3 Nephi 27:14–16).

These three passages provide the basic definition of the "doctrine" or "gospel" of Jesus Christ as the Nephites understood it. However, they represent only a small portion of the total Book of Mormon statements of the gospel. The same pattern of points of doctrine appears throughout the entire Book of Mormon, informing major sermons and providing an implicit interpretive framework for reports of historical events and discussions or ordinances (e.g., 2 Nephi 9; Mosiah 27; Moroni 3, 7, 8).

Many Book of Mormon statements defining the concept of "gospel" are elliptical, taking the form of merismus,[1] a classical rhetorical device in which an entire topic or statement is represented by some of its parts.[2] The gospel formula composed of ordered elements lends itself well to this rhetorical device. A typical Book of Mormon merism, mentioning only two of the parts, states that believing in Jesus and enduring to the end is life eternal (see 2 Nephi 33:4).

The other LDS scriptures contain similar statements of the gospel of Jesus Christ, many of which also include merisms (see D&C 10:63–70; 11:9–24; 19:29–32; 20:37; 33:10–13; 39:6; 68:25; Moses 5:14–15, 58; 6:50–53). Drawing on this perspective, Latter-day Saints can see the same definition behind more succinct New Testament passages (see Matthew 3:11; 24:13–14; Acts 2:38; 19:4–6; Romans 1:16; Ephesians 2:8).

Based on research by Noel B. Reynolds, September 1991. For an extended treatment of this topic, see Noel B. Reynolds, "The Gospel of Jesus Christ as Taught by the Nephite Prophets," BYU Studies *31 (1991): 31–50.*

Notes

1. See pages 80–82 in this book. Paul Y. Hoskisson first drew attention to this phenomenon and its possible significance for this study.

2. See H. Liddell and R. Scott, *A Greek-English Lexicon,* s.v. "*meris*" (Oxford, Oxford University Press, 1968); Alexander M. Honeyman, "Merismus in Biblical Hebrew," *Journal of Biblical Hebrew* 71 (1952): 15.

Chapter 76

GETTING THINGS STRAI[GH]T

3 Nephi 14:13 "Enter ye in at the strait gate."

In Matthew 7:13 and 3 Nephi 14:13 we read, "Enter ye in at the *strait* gate." It is interesting to consider the meaning of the word "strait" in these texts, and to note the differences between the English words *strait* and *straight.*

In contemporary English, *straight,* of course, usually means "not crooked," but the word *strait* is not often used. The main meaning of this somewhat archaic word is "narrow," as in the Straits of Gibraltar. Thus the "strait gate" (Greek, *stenēs pulēs*) is a narrow gate. This meaning is evident in Jesus' Sermon on the Mount and Sermon at the Temple, since he clearly contrasts the narrow gate and the tribulation-filled path (Greek, *tethlimmenē*) with their opposites, the broad gate and large and spacious (*euruchōros*) way. The meaning of *strai[gh]t,* however, is not always so evident in other passages in the Book of Mormon. Spellings have varied from one edition to the next, and sometimes people have wondered which is correct. Research indicates that both spellings and a range of meanings in several cases may be possible.

Going back to the 1829 manuscripts of the Book of Mormon, one finds that the word *strait* appears over twenty times in the Printer's Manuscript (1 Nephi 8:20; 10:8; 16:23; 21:20; 2 Nephi 4:33; 9:41; 31:18–19; 33:9; Jacob 6:11; Alma 7:9, 19; 37:12, 44; 50:8; 56:37; Helaman 3:29; 3 Nephi 14:13–14; 27:33), but the spelling "straight" was never used there. When Joseph Smith said the word *strai[gh]t,* Oliver Cowdery apparently always preferred to spell it "s–t–r–a–i–t."

The only known instance when Oliver Cowdery spelled the word s–t–r–a–i–g–h–t on the Original Manuscript was in Alma 50:8 ("the land of Nephi did run in a strai[gh]t course from the east sea to the west"), but even there he changed it to s–t–r–a–i–t when he copied it over for the printer. Likewise, when Nephi made an arrow out of a straight stick in 1 Nephi 16:23, Oliver wrote "s–t–r–a–i–t." Oliver's spelling is understandable, since the dictionaries of the early nineteenth century, such as Webster's 1828 *American Dictionary of the English Language,* show both spellings as being somewhat interchangeable.

This creates a slight challenge, however, for readers of the Book of Mormon. Sometimes, one must consider the word *strai[gh]t* in context to think what it might mean. For example, the text speaks of a "strai[gh]t and narrow path" (1 Nephi 8:20; 2 Nephi 31:18–19; Helaman 3:29). There are several possible meanings here:

1. This expression may contain an emphatic redundancy, that is, a "narrow [strait] and narrow path." Hebrew writers did not shun such repetitions.

2. It might mean "straight," that is, not crooked. This meaning is attested elsewhere in scriptures affirming that God does not walk in crooked paths (see Alma 7:20).

3. It may also mean "difficult or stressful." The path of righteousness is not an easy one (see 2 Nephi 31:19–20), but it is full of tribulation (see Matthew 7:13; compare Acts 14:22, where the same Greek word meaning tribulation appears; compare also "straitening" in 1 Nephi 17:41).

4. Or it may mean "tight," being "pressed together, crowded" (for a similar notion, see 1 Nephi 8:21).

5. Or again, it might also mean "upright" or "righteous," that is, morally straight. Several scriptures admonish us in this sense to walk "uprightly" before the Lord (see, e.g., 1 Nephi 16:3; Psalms 15:2).

6. Other possible meanings include "close, in the sense of intimate," "strict, rigorous, or disciplined" (compare "strict" in

2 Nephi 4:32); "distressed or perplexed," or even "pressed to poverty."

All these were meanings of the words *straight* and *strait* in Joseph Smith's day. Although one cannot know which of these meanings may have been known to the Prophet, they all have potential applications expecially to the meaning of the "strai[gh]t and narrow path" that Lehi saw.

In addition, the English words *straight* and *strait* are used in the King James Version of the Old Testament as translations for several Hebrew words. Understanding something of their range of meaning in Hebrew may also shed light on the thoughts that writers like Isaiah, Lehi, and Nephi may have intended to convey. For example, Isaiah says, "Make straight [*yashar*] in the desert a highway for our God" (Isaiah 40:3). Together with its primary meaning of "straight," another meaning of the Hebrew word *yashar* is "level, smooth" (Zechariah 4:7; 1 Kings 20:23; Psalms 26:12). Moreover, the ancient Greek translations of this passage use the word *euthus,* meaning straight, whether horizontally or vertically; and both ideas are present in Isaiah 40:4, describing the Lord's highway as straight (*yashar*) and plain (*biq*^{c}*ah*).

Thus, if Lehi used the same terminology as Isaiah, in addition to the meanings mentioned above, Lehi's "straight and narrow path" may also be thought of as a "*smooth* [or level] and narrow path." This Hebrew meaning is especially consistent with Nephi's plea to the Lord: "Make my path straight before me! Wilt thou not place a stumbling block in my way" (2 Nephi 4:33). Nephi's straight path is a "plain road," a smooth and "clear" path in the low valley (2 Nephi 4:32), which is "straight" because it is smooth, unobstructed with stumbling blocks.

These meanings open to our spiritual understanding a number of possible insights. By considering the possible meanings on several occasions when the word "strai[gh]t" appears in the Book of Mormon, we may discern more specifically the many ways the text may apply to us today.

Based on research by John W. Welch and Daniel McKinlay, January 1989.

Chapter 77

PROPHECY AMONG THE MAYA

4 Nephi 1:34 "They were led by many priests and false prophets."

A variety of forms of prophecy existed among the Maya Indians and other people of Mesoamerica at the time of the Spanish Conquest and long before. Several aspects of Maya prophecy are noteworthy and suggest possible connections with the Book of Mormon peoples in that area.

First, prophecy among the Maya was a well-established cultural institution termed *bobatil*. Much of their prophecy used calendar units such as the 260–day *tzol kin* ("year"), or the four yearbearers and the 52–year Calendar Round (*kin tun y abil*). Among the Yucatec Maya the *katun* (a 7200–day unit, or twenty 360–day years or *tuns*) was also used. Their prophecies were written down in books (*huunob*). All these features were normal in Post-Classic Maya life (after about A.D. 800), and thus Munro Edmonson cautiously concludes: "It would be surprising if they had not had books of historical prophecy" in the Classic era (A.D. 200–800).[1]

Second, Maya prophecy foretold specific events. The early Catholic Bishop of Yucatan, Diego de Landa, described Maya prophecies for the day, for the year, for the *katun,* and for the coming of the Spaniards. The prophets were called *chilans,* and each served as priest, registrar, prophet, and examiner of officials alongside a political lord. One of the most famous was named Ah Cambal, who lived in the area around Mani in the province dominated by the Tutul Xiu lineage. Shortly before the coming of the Spaniards, he prophesied that his people would soon be subjugated by a white, bearded race coming from the east who would preach to them one God and the power of a tree, called *uahom che,* represented by a cross and meaning "a tree erected with great virtue against the evil spirit." As a result the Tutul Xiu group (and certain other Yucatecans) welcomed the Spaniards. What the *chilan* had in mind was apparently the return of Quetzalcoatl and his white-robed priests.[2]

Third, the Maya view saw history in cycles. Their calendar featured Short Count cycles of 13 *katuns*. About every 256 of our years, these 13 repeated themselves. Each cycle was named for its concluding day. A historical "record of the *katuns*" kept track of events and served as a basis for prophecy. The basic pattern of good or ill fate that characterized each *katun* was expected to appear again when the named *katun* returned. Thus, for example, the Itza of Tayasal living in the lowland forest of Guatemala in 1618 resisted Christianization because "the time [had] not yet arrived" for a change in their ways. Finally, in 1696, Father Avendano, who had familiarized himself with the *katun* prophecies, persuaded them that the time to become Christians was near. When in the following year (1697) a Spanish army finally conquered them with ease, the event was only 136 days short of the prophesied time when the rulership was to change.

Fourth, the Maya governed their lives by their prophetic outlook. Dennis Puleston maintains that changes in Maya civilization were "triggered by an internal mechanism" consisting of Maya assumptions about the power of prophetic time. When change was to come, it would *inevitably* come.[3] Strong faith in the inevitability of prophecy may have led leaders and commoners alike to act in ways that helped to bring about the expected results. Yet more than belief was involved: actual climatic changes correlate significantly with Maya prophecies about the weather.[4]

Earlier traces of this pattern of prophecy might be visible at a number of points in the Book of Mormon. Prophets likewise regularly lived among the Nephites; they wrote books; they prophesied of specific times and events; their records especially note recurring times of good and evil; they served in juxtaposition to political lords and judges; and their followers gauged their lives prophetically. Thus, the prophecies of Nephi (see 1 Nephi 12:11–15; 2 Nephi 26:9–10), Alma (see Alma 45:10–14), and Samuel the Lamanite (see Helaman 13:5, 9) about when the Nephites would be destroyed may be an even *baktun* (400 years = 20 twenty-year *katuns*), the main cycle of the Long Count.[5]

Furthermore, the Maya cycle of thirteen *katuns* may correlate with certain other events in Nephite history. One cycle of thirteen *katuns* before the known Maya evil hiatus beginning in A.D. 534 would be close to the time in 4 Nephi 1:41–42 when "the wicked part of the people began again to build up the secret oaths and combinations of Gadianton." One cycle of thirteen *katuns* earlier begins in A.D. 22, which is just prior to the collapse of the Nephite central government (see 3 Nephi 7:1–2; 8:1–4), followed by the great destruction accompanying the crucifixion.

Further research may identify other possible relationships between events and tendencies in Nephite cultural history and prophecy among the ancient Mesoamericans.

Based on research by John L. Sorenson, July 1986.

Notes

1. See Munro Edmonson, "Some Postclassic Questions about the Classic Maya," *Estudios de Cultura Maya* 12 (1979): 157–78.

2. Alfred E. Tozzer, ed., *Landa's Relacion de las Cosas de Yucatan,* Paper 18 (Cambridge, Massachusetts: Harvard University Peabody Museum of American Archaeology and Ethnology, 1941), 26–27, 42–43.

3. See Dennis Puleston, "An Epistemological Pathology and the Collapse, or Why the Maya Kept the Short Count," in Norman Hammond and Gordon Willey, eds., *Maya Archaeology and Ethnohistory* (Austin: University of Texas Press, 1979), 63–71.

4. See William H. Folan and Burma H. Hyde, "Climatic Forecasting and Recording among the Ancient and Historic Maya," in William Folan, ed., *Contributions to the Archaeology and Ethnohistory of Greater Mesoamerica* (Carbondale: Southern Illinois University Press, 1985), 15–48.

5. See John L. Sorenson, *An Ancient American Setting for the Book of Mormon* (Salt Lake City: Deseret Book and F.A.R.M.S., 1985), 270–76.

Chapter 78

THE SURVIVOR AND THE WILL TO BEAR WITNESS

Mormon 3:16 "I did stand as an idle witness."

A striking new study has been initiated comparing a subtle, recurring pattern in the Book of Mormon with a particular type of human behavior recently identified in the writings of the "survivors" of Hitler's and Stalin's death camps. A link between these testimonies might at first seem unlikely, but upon reflection, however, it is clear that Mormon and Moroni, Lehi and Nephi, Alma and Amulek (Alma 14:10–11), Ether (Ether 15:34) and Coriantumr (Omni 1:21), and others in the Book of Mormon were also witnesses of atrocious deaths and genocide. Did these ancient annihilations and modern holocausts generate similar human reactions from their final survivors?

Preliminary results indicate that they did, and that a specific pattern of witness and a unique literary genre emerge from these extreme conditions. The best account of this "literature of survival" is by Terrence Des Pres.[1] He says that survival is a "specific kind of experience. It has a definite structure."[2]

What is that structure? Of the many possible ways in which humans might react to the man-made horrors of genocide—bitterness, anger, indignation, or despair, for example—the dominant response of the few who survived the European concentration camps has been an irrepressible desire "to bear witness." The world of death camps and *gulags* produces a consistent reaction, a will to survive not for oneself, but rather to bear witness to the world in a particular kind of testament or indictment against man's inhumanity to his fellows. "Survival is an act involving choice [even when death might seem easier]; . . . bearing witness is a typical response to extremity."[3] The "utmost concern" of such survivors was to hide up a record "preserved for future generations."[4] One survivor speaks of his duty to witness as a "mission," a "sacred task," and a "burning within me, screaming: 'Record!' "[5]

Survivors often covenant together to make sure that at least one should make it through to warn the world: "In extremity men and women make a special promise among themselves, always implicit and often openly declared. Whoever comes through will take with him the burden of speaking for the others."[6]

Des Pres's research yields an elaborate profile of the survivor's behavior. That profile has much in common with the human conduct of several people in the Book of Mormon, like Mormon and Moroni. For example, there is the will "to remember and record"[7] that overcomes one's fears of the surrounding savagery (see Mormon 2:15; 4:11–21). There is the survivor viewing his task as a sacred duty, born out of the realization that no one will be left.

As the call came to Mormon fairly early to retell the Nephite saga, so the will to bear witness normally has arisen early in other survivors "during the initial stage of adjustment to extremity."[8] The task is frequently carried out in secret,[9] often by depositing the record in a hidden archive (see Mormon 4:23; 8:3–5). The witness speaks simply as a sorrowful eyewitness to the whole world.[10] He is a necessary connection between the past and the future, speaking as it were "out of the dust" on behalf of those who have died (see 2 Nephi 26:15–18; 27:6; Mormon 3:16–18; 5:8–10; 6:17–22; 7:1–10; 8:26).[11] The survivors, according to Des Pres, perceive that "good and evil are only clear in retrospect." Thus their mission is to display the "objective conditions of evil."[12]

Obviously, there are several differences among the personalities, conditions, and divine callings of each survivor witness in the Book of Mormon, as well as between them and the survivors of modern holocausts. But there are also many distinctive and unexpected similarities. By understanding through human eyes the inspired responses of Book of Mormon prophets to the unimaginably extreme situations they faced, modern readers can appreciate another dimension of their effective, penetrating testimonies. Thus the message of the survivor is especially important to students of the Book of Mormon. The true-to-life, urgent testimony of the survivors in that record provides us several unexpectedly powerful examples of the "will to bear witness."

Based on research by Gordon C. Thomasson, April 1984. Other insightful similarities and examples are cited in the study on this topic that appeared shortly after this Update: Lisa Bolin Hawkins and Gordon C. Thomasson, "I Only Am Escaped Alone to Tell Thee: Survivor Witnesses in the Book of Mormon" (Provo: F.A.R.M.S., 1984).

Notes

1. Terrence Des Pres, "Survivors and the Will to Bear Witness," *Social Research* 40 (1973): 668–90; *The Survivor: An Anatomy of Life in the Death Camps* (New York: Pocket Books, 1977).
2. Des Pres, "Survivors and the Will to Bear Witness," 669.
3. Ibid., 672–73.
4. Ibid., 670.
5. Ibid.
6. Ibid., 678; compare Mormon 8:3.
7. Ibid., 668–69.
8. Ibid., 679.
9. See ibid., 670.
10. See ibid., 671.
11. See ibid., 676.
12. Ibid., 687–89; compare Helaman 12:3, Mormon 8:36–41.

Chapter 79

MORMON AND MORONI AS AUTHORS AND ABRIDGERS

Mormon 5:9 "Therefore I write a small abridgment."

The Book of Mormon is a composite work, compiled from several archaic records that were abridged ultimately by Mormon or his son Moroni. Generally speaking, Mormon edited the materials from Mosiah to 4 Nephi, which he took from the Large Plates of Nephi, and Moroni abridged the record of Ether, which itself was a condensation of the history and records of the Jaredites.

In addition to abridging the records of others, Mormon and Moroni each wrote books and other parts of the Book of Mormon as original authors. For example, Mormon wrote Helaman 12, Mormon 1–7, Moroni 7–9, and the Words of Mormon. Moroni wrote Mormon 8–9, Ether 12, and Moroni 1–6 and 10.

Recent research by Dr. Roger R. Keller has taken a closer look at the works of Mormon and Moroni to analyze these writers as authors and abridgers, comparing their techniques and identifying unique and distinctive characteristics in the editorial styles of each. Keller has created a series of computer data bases, dividing the texts of the Book of Mormon by author, so far as that can reasonably be determined. He has then run computer separations on these files to determine vocabulary frequencies and distributions. His initial findings indicate the following:

1. When Mormon is acting as an abridger, he interacts extensively with the underlying documents he is abridging. It is usually possible (although not always) to distinguish Mormon's own words and comments from the words that he draws from

the materials he is condensing. As one reads along in many sections of the Book of Mormon abridged by Mormon, one often senses that a subtle shift has taken place as a smooth, almost imperceptible transition has occurred from the underlying historical narrative to Mormon's commentary on that narrative. By carefully backtracking, one can discern, however, where the transition was made.

Moroni, on the other hand, interacts far less extensively with the text he is abridging. Moroni is usually careful about marking the beginning and ending of the comments that he has inserted into the abridged record. For example, his comments in Ether 3:17–20, 4:1–6:1, 8:18–26, and 12:6–13:1 are readily distinguishable from the abridged portions in the book of Ether. His frequent use of the phrase "I, Moroni" in Ether 1:1, 3:17, 5:1, 6:1, 8:20, 8:26, 9:1, 12:6, 12:29, 12:38, and 13:1 makes it easy to tell what Moroni has written and what he has abridged. Indeed, the seams in the underlying record are often visible in the abridged works of Moroni.[1] This seems to indicate that Moroni was less aggressive than Mormon as an abridger, perhaps because the fugitive Moroni's task was limited to completing the record of his father. Thus he may have felt less liberty than Mormon in molding, shaping, and interacting with the texts he was editing.

2. A thorough statistical examination of vocabulary gives considerable evidence that the original writings of Mormon and Moroni are distinguishable from each other. For example, the widely spaced sections of Mormon's own writings manifest an affinity for certain words, such as *baptism, hope, love,* and *wickedness*. On the other hand, the various, scattered writings of Moroni have another set of prevalent words in common, including *blood, destruction, suffer, faith, miracles,* and *power*. Furthermore, the vocabulary of the record of Ether separates noticeably from all other portions of the Book of Mormon, Keller finds.

Another significant difference is found in the use of the well-known but characteristic expression "and thus we see that. . . ." Mormon used it over twenty times to insert moral conclusions in the sections he wrote or abridged (i.e., Alma 12:21; 24:19;

28:13; 30:60; 46:8; 50:19; Helaman 3:28; 6:34–36; 12:3). Moroni used the phrase only once (see Ether 14:25).

3. Furthermore, if one examines the words that are of importance to Mormon or to Moroni when they are writing as authors, and then examines the relative frequency of these words in the abridged portions of their records, some interesting observations can be made. Words prevalent in the writings of Mormon himself are usually of less importance in the edited texts. However, should a word important to Mormon appear in the underlying materials, this tends to increase Mormon's usage of that word as he comments on the matter, especially in the books of Mosiah and Alma. The situation appears to be quite different with Moroni; he seems to be uninfluenced in this way by the material he is editing.

Further research will be required to fully analyze and digest the large amount of raw data and useful charts generated by Keller in this regard. Other interesting comparisons can also be drawn to the rules or outlines (*hypogrammois*) that are mentioned in the Abridger's preface of 2 Maccabees[2] to be followed in making an abridgment. Already, however, one can begin to appreciate the individual differences between Mormon and Moroni, both as authors and as abridgers.

Based on research by Roger R. Keller, April 1988.

Notes

1. See also John W. Welch, "Preliminary Comments on the Sources behind the Book of Ether" (Provo: F.A.R.M.S., 1986).

2. Abridger's preface in 2 Maccabees 2:19–32, esp. 28; noted by Gordon C. Thomasson.

Chapter 80

NUMBER 24

Mormon 6:11 "all my people save it were twenty and four of us"

Consider the significance of the number twenty-four in ancient Israel and in the Book of Mormon. Certain numbers were clearly meaningful in antiquity: seven was the number of spiritual perfection (as in the seven seals in the book of Revelation); twelve was a governmental number (as with the twelve tribes, twelve apostles). The number twenty-four, being a multiple of twelve, was associated with heavenly government, especially priestly judgment and temple service.[1]

At Qumran, judicial disputes were brought before a court called "the council of the community."[2] This deliberative body was composed of two panels of twelve, twelve priests and twelve laymen, for a quorum of twenty-four judges. These judges "give light by the judgment of the Urim and Thummim."[3]

In the New Testament apocalypse, the book of Revelation, twenty-four elders judge the world. These twenty-four elders are mentioned twelve times in the book (Revelation 4:4, 10; 5:5, 6, 8, 11, 14; 7:11, 13; 11:16; 14:3; 19:4).

In Rabbinic Judaism, local courts having jurisdiction over most capital cases consisted of twenty-four (or twenty-three) judges. These "small sanhedrins" were composed of two panels, one for the defense and the other for the prosecution (the odd number twenty-three prevented a tie vote and was a minimum quorum requirement). If one of the judges had to leave the trial, "it had to be ascertained if twenty-three . . . would be left, in which case he might go out; if not, he might not depart."[4]

How far back can such duodecimal courts be found? The

following evidence exists: Moses established courts in each of the twelve tribes (see Deuteronomy 16:18). Jehoshaphat appointed "Levites, priests and elders" as judges (2 Chronicles 19:8); related literature from Qumran assumes there were twelve in each group.[5] The apocalyptic idea of God being surrounded by a body of elders when he judges the world is at least as old as Isaiah 24:23. Twenty-four courses of priests continuously operated Davidic tabernacle and Solomonic temple services (see 1 Chronicles 24:3–18), and when David appointed his prophetic cantors, he established twenty-four orders, each with twelve members (see 1 Chronicles 25:1–31). Thus, although we have no direct evidence of duodecimal courts in preexilic Israel, the indirect evidence along with the postexilic sources give that number presumptive significance in Lehi's day and before.

Turning to the Book of Mormon, we see that twenty-four has remarkably similar significance:

1. Apparently there were twenty-four judges on King Noah's court, since Noah and his priests kidnapped twenty-four Lamanite daughters (see Mosiah 20:5). Alma's dismissal would have left twenty-three priests on the court, in addition to Noah.

2. There were twenty-four survivors of the final destruction of the Nephites who witnessed the judgment of God upon this people (see Mormon 6:11, 15, 22). There were other survivors (see Mormon 6:15), but the twenty-four apparently stood as a body of special witnesses. This number may have been coincidental, but nevertheless it was significant enough to be specifically mentioned.

3. Particular mention is made of the number of the gold plates of Ether, probably because their number was twenty-four (see Mosiah 8:9; Alma 37:21; Ether 1:2). These plates were seen as a record of the "judgment of God" upon those people (Alma 37:30). Their contents were brought "to light" by the use of two seer stones (Mosiah 28:13–16; Alma 37:21–25).

4. God's heavenly court, which passed judgment upon Jerusalem (see 1 Nephi 1:13), consisted of twelve members (see 1 Nephi 1:10).

5. Like the twelve apostles, the twelve Nephite disciples (for a total of twenty-four) will act as judges in the final judgment of the world (see 3 Nephi 27:27).

6. Perhaps it is not coincidence that Mormon, the "idle witness" (Mormon 3:16), was given charge of the legal records at age twenty-four (see Mormon 1:3), and that Helaman I and II were about that age when they were given the records too.

7. We can also note that the Jaredite king Orihah, whose single recorded virtue was that he "did execute judgment upon the land in righteousness all his days" (Ether 7:1), had twenty-three sons (see Ether 7:2).

8. The text of the governmental oath of the Nephite chief judge to "judge righteously" happens to be reported only in the account of the twenty-fourth year of the reign of Judges (Alma 50:39–40).

Prophets, judges, witnesses, God's tribunal, God's judgment, the Urim and Thummim, and heavenly righteous government are all elements of what Baumgarten calls "duodecimal symbolism."[6] These elements appear with remarkable consistency associated with the number twenty-four in the texts of the Book of Mormon.

Based on research by John W. Welch, December 1985. This topic was selected because this report was the twenty-fourth F.A.R.M.S. monthly Update.

Notes

1. Ethelbert W. Bullinger, *Number in Scripture: Its Supernatural Design and Spiritual Influence* (London: Eyre and Spottiswoode, 1894; reprinted Grand Rapids, Michigan: Kregel, 1967), 264.

2. 1QS 8:1.

3. Pesher on Isaiah 54:11–12, tr. Joseph Baumgarten, "The Duodecimal Courts of Qumran, Revelation, and the Sanhedrin," *Journal of Biblical Literature* 95 (1976): 59–78, quote on p. 63.

4. Babylonian Talmud *Sanhedrin* 37a (the Mishnah lists decisions that require confirmation by the Urim and Thummim, *Shebuoth* 2:2).

5. 1QM 2:1–3; Temple Scroll.

6. Baumgarten, "The Duodecimal Courts," 65.

Chapter 81

THE "GOLDEN" PLATES

Mormon 9:33 "if our plates had been sufficiently large"

What did Joseph Smith notice when he first closely examined the plates of the Book of Mormon? How heavy were the plates? How difficult would it have been for Joseph to have carried the plates while doing that broken-field running through the forest near his home several days after receiving the plates and hiding them in a birch log?[1]

Joseph evidently managed to knock down and elude several pursuers despite the weight of the plates (which he might have carried like a football in that "farmer's smock" in which he wrapped them that day[2]). It is not simply a matter of Joseph being "large" and "stout," since Emma Smith later described having moved the plates around in a linen cloth while cleaning house. Better still, what would any one of us be able to say about them after having "hefted" and examined the plates for ourselves, just as the Eight Witnesses did in 1829?

A surprising amount of consistent information can be gleaned from eyewitnesses: Joseph himself gave us the length, width, and thickness of the whole set of plates as 6″ x 8″ x 6″ in his famous Wentworth Letter.[3] On separate occasions, David Whitmer gave larger dimensions of 7″ x 8″, and 6″ x 9″, and 8″ x 10″;[4] Martin Harris claimed a smaller set at 7″ x 8″ x 4″.[5] Following Joseph's dimensions would amount to .1666 cubic foot (.005 cubic meter), and such a volume of solid, pure twenty-four karat gold at 1204.7 pounds per cubic foot would weigh 200.8 pounds (90.4 kilograms).

As shown many years ago by metallurgist/blacksmith Reed

H. Putnam, hammered plates of pure twenty-four karat gold would probably not weigh more than about 50 percent of the solid dimensions, i.e., 100.4 pounds (45.2 kilograms). However, Putnam also pointed out that, if the plates were made of the more practical Central American tumbaga alloy of eight karat gold with copper, they would weigh around 53.4 pounds (24 kilograms).[6]

Unknown to Putnam, William Smith, a brother of the Prophet who had handled and hefted the plates in a pillowcase, claimed on several occasions that the set of plates weighed about sixty pounds,[7] as did Willard Chase,[8] while Martin Harris said that they weighed forty to fifty pounds.[9] William Smith added that the plates were "a mixture of gold and copper."[10]

Moreover, if the plates were made of the tumbaga alloy, other details fit into place. Take the color of the plates: The plates are consistently described as "gold" and "golden." When tumbaga (which is red) is treated with any simple acid (citric acid will do), the copper in the alloy is removed from its surface leaving a brilliant .0006 inch, twenty-three karat gilt coating. Indeed, this process was used in ancient America.[11] Plus, this surface covering is much easier to engrave.

Likewise, pure gold would be too soft to make useful plates. But tumbaga is remarkably tough and resilient, even in sheets as thin as .02 inch. Joseph Smith, Martin Harris, and David Whitmer all suggested that the plates were "not quite as thick as common tin."[12] Whitmer added on another occasion that each plate was as thick as parchment,[13] while Emma described them as like thick paper.[14] Tin in the early nineteenth century may have been around .02 inch or less, and parchment even thinner. Thus, each Book of Mormon plate could have been between .015–.02 inch thick.

If each plate (allowing for air space and irregularities) occupied from .03–.05 inch, the six-inch thick collection would have contained between 120 and 200 plates. If each was engraved front and back, there were 240 to 400 surfaces. Removing the portion that was sealed still leaves at least 80 and perhaps as many as 266 surfaces upon which our present Book of Mormon was contained. The text could fit on this many plates, particularly since there is some evidence that the characters on the plates were written on both sides and were quite fine or small.[15]

Thus, reasonable sense can be made of the physical description of the plates and of their possible metallurgical composition.

Based on research by Robert F. Smith, October 1984.

Notes

1. See B. H. Roberts, *Comprehensive History of the Church,* 6 vols. (Salt Lake City: Deseret News Press, 1930), 1:86.

2. Ibid., 90–91.

3. B. H. Roberts, ed., *History of the Church,* 4:537; compare *Evening and Morning Star,* 1:8, 58b.

4. See "An Old Mormon's Closing Hours," *Chicago Tribune* (Jan. 24, 1888), p. 8, col. 4; "The Book of Mormon," *Chicago Tribune* (Dec. 17, 1885), p. 3, col. 5; *Kansas City Journal* (June 5, 1881), p. 1.

5. See *Iowa State Register* (Des Moines), August 16, 1870; reprinted in Milton V. Backman, Jr., *Eyewitness Accounts of the Restoration* (Salt Lake City: Deseret Book, 1986), 226.

6. See Reed Putnam, "Were the Plates of Mormon of Tumbaga?" presented in 1954 and 1964 to the Society for Early Historic Archaeology, printed by the *Improvement Era* 69 (September 1966): 788–89, 828–31, available as a F.A.R.M.S. Reprint.

7. See *Saints' Herald* 31 (4 October 1884): 644; *William Smith on Mormonism* (Lamoni, Iowa: Herald Steam Book, 1883), 12.

8. See Eber D. Howe, *Mormonism Unvailed* (Painesville, privately published by the author, 1834), 245–46.

9. See *Tiffany's Monthly* 5, no. 2 (1859): 165–66.

10. "Sermon in the Saints' Chapel," *Saints' Herald* 31 (1884): 644.

11. See Heather Lechtman, "Pre-Columbian Surface Metallurgy," *Scientific American* 250 (June 1984): 56–63; and Constance H. Irwin, *Fair Gods and Stone Faces* (New York: St. Martin's, 1963), 298, who refers to it as *mise en couleur*.

12. *Times and Seasons* 3 (March 1, 1842): 707; *Chicago Times* (Jan. 24, 1888), p. 8, col. 1.

13. See *Kansas City Journal* (June 5, 1881), p. 1.

14. See "Last Testimony of Sister Emma," *Saints' Herald* 26 (Oct. 1, 1879): 289–90.

15. See Memorandum of Theodore Turley, statements of John Whitmer, April 4, 1839, cited in Richard L. Anderson, *Investigating the Book of Mormon Witnesses* (Salt Lake City: Deseret Book, 1981), 131.

The Hill Cumorah in New York, 1920. Courtesy LDS Church Historical Department.

Chapter 82

HEBREW AND UTO-AZTECAN: POSSIBLE LINGUISTIC CONNECTIONS

Mormon 9:32–33 "We have written this record according to our knowledge, in the characters which are called among us the reformed Egyptian, being handed down and altered by us, according to our manner of speech. . . . The Hebrew hath been altered by us also."

A few years ago Brian Stubbs, then a doctoral candidate in linguistics at the University of Utah, received a grant from F.A.R.M.S. to study the question of whether elements of Hebrew language could be detected among native tongues of the Uto-Aztecan family of western North America. Preliminary evidence had suggested to him that this unorthodox proposition had a basis in fact.

Stubbs first completed a paper ordering, summarizing, and extending his findings, and he presented some of the material at Brigham Young University. Then he prepared a lengthier piece for further publication.[1]

Stubbs deals with Hebrew, Arabic, Aramaic, Akkadian (Babylonian), and Ugaritic, all of the Semitic family from the Near East. In the New World, he examines the Uto-Aztecan tongues, which range from Northern Paiute and Shoshoni in the Great Basin, through Hopi and Papago in Arizona and Tarahumara and Yaqui of northern Mexico, to Nahuatl, the language of the Aztecs of central and southern Mexico.

The data examined include sound correspondences, vocabulary, semantic patterns, fossilized verb forms, and other morphology. For example, Hebrew *yasav* ("he sat or dwelt") is notably similar to Hopi *yesiva* ("to sit"), and Hebrew *kanap* ("wing") recalls Proto-Uto-Aztecan *?anap* ("wing"; the ? sign indicated a glottal stop). However, the author, a well-trained linguist, does not fall into the trap that so often snares amateurs, of simply listing words "that sound the same," selected from dictionaries of languages, without firm criteria. He brings forward arrays of data showing systematic, consistent shifts in sounds, just as linguists have demonstrated for other diverging tongues. Thus Hebrew */r/* when not at the beginning of a word regularly appears to be replaced by */y/* or */i/* in Uto-Aztecan. Hebrew */g/* is equivalent to Hopi */ng/*, as in *pgl* ("be thick") and *pongala* ("thick"), both patterns being manifested in a number of words.

An interesting ethnobotanical parallel is noted by Stubbs in the fact that two words that in the Near East each mean "truffle" (the edible underground rootlike fungus) have provocative equivalents in Uto-Aztecan with the meaning edible tubers. Arabic *kam?* ("truffle") recalls Nahuatl *kamo?* ("sweet potato"), while *tirmania,* another Mideast word meaning truffle, perhaps long ago borrowed from Greek, compares to Hopi *timna* or *timön* ("potato"). The author wisely calls for further investigation on this. Other cultural hints are scattered throughout the linguistic comparisons.

The present paper presents 203 equivalences between Semitic and Uto-Aztecan. Material still being analyzed contains over two hundred additional Hebrew roots with apparent reflexes in this North American language family. The similarities do not, however, demonstrate that Uto-Aztecan languages are descendants of Hebrew alone, although the number and nature of the relationships already brought out are sufficient to suggest that Hebrew was one of the ancestor languages. (Incidentally, the patterns of sound changes indicate that specifically Hebrew and not other Semitic tongues provides the closest comparisons.) But much non-Semitic morphology and vocabulary is also evident in Uto-Aztecan.

Stubbs, therefore, suggests the possibility that the linguistic process known as "creolization" may have been involved. That term is used to describe the formation of an essentially new "mixed" language from two or more active ones, a process of increasingly active concern in linguistic research nowadays. This description matches quite well the description given by Moroni of the changes that had taken place in Nephite language over the years—that the traditional language was handed down but altered according to the manner of their contemporary spoken language (see Mormon 9:32–34).

Initial assessments of this work by two recognized linguists have been highly positive. Stubbs seems to have demonstrated once again the increasingly evident lesson that while events in the past were complex, meticulous research methods and patient labor may yet give us significant glimpses of what actually took place.

Based on research by Brian Stubbs, December 1987.

Note

1. See Brian Stubbs, "Elements of Hebrew in Uto-Aztecan: A Summary of the Data" (Provo: F.A.R.M.S., 1988).

Chapter 83

WORDS AND PHRASES

Ether 12:25 "Thou hast also made our words powerful and great."

The words and phrases of the Book of Mormon are "powerful and great" (Ether 12:25). Treasures await the pondering mind that contemplates virtually every word, idiom, figure of speech, or semantic value in the texts of this remarkable record.

Several studies are underway to examine distinctive words and phrases in the Book of Mormon. To aid these studies of language in the Book of Mormon, extensive lists of vocabulary, formulaic phrases, and idioms have recently been compiled. The computerized scripture program is also a powerful research tool. Judging by the results so far, many valuable insights wait to be uncovered by careful scrutiny of Book of Mormon expressions.

Some of these studies have focused on particular words. For example, as discussed previously, it has been shown that a fundamental difference existed in ancient law between a "thief" and a "robber."[1] Knowing this distinction brings to light a similar Book of Mormon usage, which appears to differentiate between these two words in precisely the same ways as did the ancients.

Other studies are scrutinizing phrase distributions among individual Book of Mormon authors. It is noteworthy, for instance, that the phrases *Lord God Omnipotent* or *Lord Omnipotent* appear six times in the Book of Mormon, and all six of them are in King Benjamin's speech. Apparently this name for God, spoken four times by the angel in Mosiah 3, and once by the people and once by Benjamin in Mosiah 5, was distinctive to Benjamin's speech and perhaps was not generally used by other Nephites outside of Benjamin's text.

And again, as David Fox has pointed out, the phrase *the Holy One of Israel* never appears in the Book of Mormon except in the Small Plates of Nephi and in passages quoted from Isaiah. This name for God appears some thirty times in the Old Testament, and almost all of those occurrences are in Isaiah or in texts that originated around the time of Lehi. Perhaps this name reflects attitudes about God that were particularly relevant and current around Lehi's time.

Many phrases may shed light on the prevailing ideas or particular experiences of Book of Mormon personalities. The word *island* and the phrase *isles of the sea* appear exclusively in the books of 1 Nephi and 2 Nephi. Why should the important prophecies of Isaiah about the Lord remembering "those who are upon the isles of the sea" (2 Nephi 10:21; Isaiah 11:11; 49:1; 51:5) be so prominent here but unmentioned later? Perhaps at first the Nephites figured they were upon an island of the sea, and it took a few years for the Nephites to explore their new land far enough to realize that they were upon a much larger land mass than an island.

It is also remarkable that the phrase *great and abominable church* likewise appears only in the early Nephite writings—twelve times. Nephi uses the phrase eleven times, and his brother Jacob uses it once in 2 Nephi 6:12. This phrase appears to have remained so distinctively associated with Nephi's vision that it did not enter into any widely used Nephite theological discourse.

Wade Brown has pointed out a number of phrases that are unique to Zenos. Roger Keller is working on the characteristics of the autographic writings of Mormon and Moroni. Paul Hoskisson and Deloy Pack have recently examined words and phrases relating to the *heart*.

Many of these expressions open windows onto ancient Near Eastern concepts. The phrase found in 2 Nephi 1:14 describing the grave as the land "from whence no traveler can return" has been claimed by some to have come from Hamlet. In fact, the phrase is common to many ancient Near Eastern texts.[2] The idea of "the second death" likewise is at home in Egyptian texts and iconography depicting the divine judgment of Osiris (see illustration below).[3]

Relevant impressions may be gleaned from the New World as well. For several years, researchers have been aware that the phrase *and it came to pass* is a good translation of a common Hebrew element.[4] Bruce Warren also reports the confirmation by Mayan experts that an element translated "and it came to pass" functioned in at least four ways in Mayan texts: (1) As a posterior *date* indicator in a text that meant "to count forward to the next date," and (2) as an anterior date indicator that signified "to count backward to the given date." Additionally it could function (3) as a posterior or (4) anterior *event* indicator, meaning "counting forward or backward to a certain event."[5] Warren finds instances of all four functions of *and it came to pass* in the Book of Mormon, as well as *combined* date and event indications in both posterior and anterior expressions. For example, "And it came to pass that the people began . . . " is a posterior event indicator (3 Nephi 2:3), whereas "And it *had* come to pass . . . " is an anterior event indicator (3 Nephi 1:20).

Words and phrases may tell a great deal about such things as the meaning, history, peculiarity, and artistry of the Book of Mormon. Remarkable patterns of word distributions and phrase densities may indeed yield valuable results, although it is too early to tell what such findings may or may not ultimately mean. An enormous amount of research and reflection remains to be done before scholars can speak definitively about such matters.

Based on research by John Welch, David Fox, Roger Keller, Paul Hoskisson, Deloy Pack, Robert Smith, and Bruce Warren, April 1987.

Notes

1. See Bernard S. Jackson, *Theft in Early Jewish Law* (Oxford: Clarendon, 1972), 1–19, 53–58; John W. Welch, "Theft and Robbery in the Book of Mormon and in Ancient Near Eastern Law" (Provo: F.A.R.M.S., 1989); also discussed in this book on pages 248–49.

2. See Robert F. Smith, "Shakespeare and the Book of Mormon" (Provo: F.A.R.M.S., 1980).

3. See Othmar Keel, *The Symbolism of the Biblical World,* trans. Timothy Hallet (New York: Crossroads, 1985), 73.

4. Discussed by Robert F. Smith, " 'It Came to Pass' in the Bible and the Book of Mormon" (Provo: F.A.R.M.S., 1980).

5. Linda Schele, *Maya Glyphs: The Verbs* (Austin: University of Texas Press, 1982), 22; John Eric Sidney Thompson, *Maya Hieroglyphic Writing Introduction* (Washington, D.C.: Carnegie Institute of Washington, 1950; reprinted with the same pagination, Norman: University of Oklahoma Press, 1971), 162–64.

Alma spoke of the "second death," a concept also found in ancient Egyptian religion, as this judgment scene depicts. If one's heart is too hard and heavy, it is devoured by the Chaos Monster in a second death. From the papyrus of Khonsu-mes B (Vienna). Line drawing by Michael Lyon.

Chapter 84

OUR NEPHITE SACRAMENT PRAYERS

Moroni 4:1 "The manner of their elders and priests administering the flesh and blood of Christ unto the church; and they administered it according to the commandments of Christ."

Latter-day Saints most commonly turn to D&C 20:76–79 to find the texts of the sacrament prayers regularly used on Sundays. In fact, however, the words for these prayers were first found in this dispensation in the Book of Mormon, in Moroni 4:3–5:2, and the words in those texts can be traced further to the words of Jesus Christ himself in 3 Nephi 18.

It is enriching to know something of the Nephite backgrounds behind the words and covenants in these prayers. The history can be picked up at an early stage in King Benjamin's speech (especially in Mosiah 5), discerned in the very words of Jesus in 3 Nephi 18, and observed in resultant prayers recorded in Moroni 4–5.

A detailed relationship exists between Mosiah 5, 3 Nephi 18, and Moroni 4–5, and all three texts should be viewed together in minute detail. For example, at the conclusion of Benjamin's speech, his people entered into a covenant, saying "we are willing . . . to be obedient to [God's] commandments in all things that he shall command us," after which they agreed to "take upon [themselves] the name of Christ" and obligated themselves to "remember to retain the name written always in [their] hearts" (Mosiah 5:5–12). These three specific promises are still the essential elements of the sacramental prayers as they eventually appeared in Moroni 4–5 and as they are used today.

The sacrament prayers are most closely related to Jesus' actual words in 3 Nephi 18. In that narrative, he said, "This shall ye do in remembrance of my body, which I have shown unto you. And it shall be a testimony unto the Father that ye do always remember me. And if ye do always remember me ye shall have my Spirit to be with you." On the wine, he said, "This doth witness unto the Father that ye are willing to do that which I have commanded you. . . . Ye shall do it in remembrance of my blood, which I have shed for you, that ye may witness unto the Father that ye do always remember me. And if ye do always remember me ye shall have my Spirit to be with you" (3 Nephi 18:3–11). A close, orderly, and definite relationship exists between the texts of 3 Nephi 18 and Moroni 4–5.

Several interesting points can be observed in these texts.

1. The words in Moroni 4–5 present the very words of Jesus, but now written in the third person plural "they," whereas Jesus had used the second person plural "you." The prayers in Moroni likewise refer to Jesus as "thy Son" and speak of "his Spirit," whereas Jesus in 3 Nephi naturally referred to himself as "me" or "my Spirit." Anyone hearing the prayers in Moroni 4–5 today can thus vividly visualize the personal events at the Nephite temple in Bountiful as the main origin of these words and of the form of the present sacrament prayers.

2. The persistence of certain precise covenantal terms throughout these three texts from Benjamin to Moroni, separated over many years and pages of Nephite history, speaks highly of the cultural sensitivity and logical orderliness of this inspired textual and historical development. Benjamin's words were influential among the Nephites down to the time of Christ (see Helaman 5:9; 14:12 and Mosiah 3:8). Thus it is impressively consistent that Benjamin's three main covenantal phrases should reappear in Moroni 4 in ways that show continuity with the older covenantal pattern as well as sensitivity to the newer revelation at the time of Christ's appearance. The phrase "take upon them the name of Christ," for example, appears in Mosiah 5,

but not in 3 Nephi 18. It seems that Nephite texts and traditions have combined and coalesced beautifully into the final sacrament prayers in Moroni 4–5.

3. Through this, we can see one way that Nephite law and ritual changed with the coming of Christ. Through the ministry of Jesus "all things became new" (3 Nephi 12:47; 15:2). Benjamin's earlier covenant language was not jettisoned, but was transformed in and by Jesus' appearance. This transformation is visible, for example, in the way God is now addressed as Father, in the different way the covenant of obedience is stated without reference to a king, in the new symbolism of the cup, which is no longer a cup of wrath as in Mosiah 5:5, and in the present nature of the spiritual blessings promised.

4. To the Nephites, the sacrament possibly also seemed related to several ancient Israelite antecedents. For example, their bread was eaten in remembrance of the body that Jesus had "shown unto" them (3 Nephi 18:7), thus recording a further dimension beyond the "giving" and "breaking" symbolism in the New Testament. Since the shewbread of the Israelite temple was known as *lechem happanim,* the "bread of the face [or presence] of [God]," the Nephites may have connected the bread of the body "shewn unto" them (1st ed., Book of Mormon) and the shewbread of their temple. The shewbread and the manna kept in a gold bowl in the ancient Israelite temple have been recognized as early Jewish antecedents to the Christian sacrament.[1]

Further comparisons with Jewish blessings, the feeding of the multitude, and the earliest Christian liturgies are additionally informative. For example, the instruction in 3 Nephi 18:5 that the bread and wine should be given "unto all those who shall believe and be baptized in my name" is not found in the New Testament, but it appears in the very early Christian *Didache,* discovered this century: "But let none eat or drink of your Eucharist, except those who have been baptized into the Lord's name."[2]

5. It is also interesting that similar events preceded both the covenant in Mosiah 5 and the sacrament in 3 Nephi 18. The

people in 3 Nephi were first told great prophecies of things to come (see 3 Nephi 16:1–20), and their souls were "filled." "So great was the joy of the multitude that they were overcome" (3 Nephi 17:17–18); they fell down and Jesus instructed them to "arise" (3 Nephi 17:19). He blessed them because of their faith, and after a great spiritual manifestation (see 3 Nephi 17:24), the people bore record that what they had seen and heard was true (see 3 Nephi 17:25). Each of these aspects in the experience at the temple in Bountiful has a specific corollary in the Nephite covenant practice of Mosiah 5:1–4.

Thus, the texts of the sacrament prayers in Moroni 4–5 have a rich and meaningful historical background in the world of Nephite covenant making. They reflect many ancient symbols and the mighty influence of the words of King Benjamin, as well as the deep spiritual power of the inspired words and ministrations of Jesus in 3 Nephi 18 among the Nephites.

Based on research by John W. Welch, June 1986. A detailed discussion of this material was published soon afterward in John W. Welch, "The Nephite Sacrament Prayers: From King Benjamin's Speech to Moroni 4–5" (Provo: F.A.R.M.S., 1986).

Notes

1. See Hippolytus, *Daniel* 4, 35; Origen, *Leviticus* 13, 3; A. Adam, "Ein vergessener Aspekt des frühchristlichen Herrenmahles," *Theologische Literaturzeitung* 88 (1963): 9–20; Hugh W. Nibley, *Since Cumorah*, in *The Collected Works of Hugh Nibley* (Salt Lake City: Deseret Book and F.A.R.M.S., 1988), 7:176, 202.

2. Didache 9:5; in Kirsopp Lake, trans., *Apostolic Fathers* (New York: Loeb Classical Library, 1930), 1:323.

Chapter 85

CLIMACTIC FORMS IN THE BOOK OF MORMON

Moroni 8:25–26 "And the first fruits of repentance is baptism; and baptism cometh by faith unto the fulfilling the commandments; and the fulfilling the commandments bringeth remission of sins; and the remission of sins bringeth meekness, and lowliness of heart; and because of meekness and lowliness of heart cometh the visitation of the Holy Ghost, which Comforter filleth with hope and perfect love, which love endureth by diligence unto prayer, until the end shall come, when all the saints shall dwell with God."

Studies thus far have identified more than twenty different types of parallelistic and poetic structures in the Book of Mormon. Examples include anabasis, catabasis, synonymous, antithetical, and synthetic parallelism; simple, extended, alternate forms, and chiasmus.[1] Another parallelistic type of exceptional quality in its beauty, style, and structural significance is a figure identified as *climax*.

Climactic composition occurs when, in successive clauses or sentences, the same word or words are found at the end of one expression and at the beginning of the next. It is a form of staircase parallelism, demonstrating to the reader a gradual ascent through the recurrence of several identical words. This duplication of words creates a continuation of thought from one sentence to the next, which adds power through repetition to the discourse, while at the same time connecting the lines into an inseparable body.

Biblical climactic forms have been identified by E. W. Bullinger.[2] An example of climax is recorded in the book of Joel:

Tell ye
your children of it, and let
your children tell
their children, and
their children another generation.
That which the palmerworm hath left hath
the locust eaten; and that which
the locust hath left hath
the cankerworm eaten; and that which
the cankerworm hath left hath the caterpiller eaten.
(Joel 1:3–4)

Other biblical examples of climax could be cited. Of special interest to students of the Mormon scriptures, however, are climactic forms attested within the Book of Mormon. Like its Old World counterpart, the New World scripture contains a varied and beautiful selection of climactic forms. Many of the prophets and inspired writers chose to employ this method of expression to expound the doctrines and principles of the gospel. Following is a climactic passage composed by Mormon:

And the first fruits of repentance is
baptism; and
baptism cometh by faith unto
the fulfilling the commandments; and
the fulfilling the commandments bringeth
remission of sins; and the
remission of sins bringeth
meekness, and lowliness of heart; and because of
meekness and lowliness of heart cometh the visitation of
the Holy Ghost, which
Comforter filleth with hope and perfect
love, which
love endureth by diligence unto prayer, until the
end shall come, when all the saints shall dwell
with God.
(Moroni 8:25–26)

Accompanying climax is the idea of an ascension of expression, from a beginning point to a climactic situation. Through the employment of the figure we call climax, the first principles and ordinances of the gospel are reiterated by Mormon in a powerful teaching manner. Mormon mentions each of the first principles—faith, repentance, baptism, and receiving the Holy Ghost. These, coupled with "meekness," "lowliness of heart," "love," and "prayer," ensure that the faithful are able, in the end, to "dwell with God."

In more than a score of instances, the climactic pattern emerges from the pages of the Book of Mormon. Other examples of climax include 1 Nephi 15:13–20, 33–35; 2 Nephi 1:13; Mosiah 2:17–19; Alma 42:17–20; Helaman 5:6–8; Ether 3:15–16; Mormon 9:11–13; Moroni 9:11–13. Due to the care taken by Joseph Smith, who was true to his trust as translator of the Book of Mormon, each of these passages are found to be structurally intact. Each plays its role in detailing the doctrines and teachings of Jesus Christ.

Based on research by Donald W. Parry, August 1989.

Notes

1. See Donald W. Parry, "Poetic Parallelisms of the Book of Mormon," in three parts (Provo: F.A.R.M.S., 1988); Angela Crowell, "Hebrew Poetry in the Book of Mormon," F.A.R.M.S. Reprint, 1986; John W. Welch, "Chiasmus in the Book of Mormon," F.A.R.M.S. Reprint, 1969.

2. E. W. Bullinger, *Figures of Speech Used in the Bible* (Grand Rapids: Baker Book House, 1987), 256–59.

SCRIPTURE INDEX

Old Testament

Genesis

Exodus

Leviticus

Numbers

Deuteronomy

Joshua

Helaman

SUBJECT INDEX